Italian Cinema

Italian Cinema

Mary P. Wood

BERG
Oxford • New York

English edition
First published in 2005 by
Berg
Editorial offices:
First Floor, Angel Court, 81 St Clements Street, Oxford OX4 1AW, UK
175 Fifth Avenue, New York, NY 10010, USA

Berg is the imprint of Oxford International Publishers Ltd.

Library of Congress Cataloging-in-Publication data

Wood, Mary P.
     Italian cinema / Mary P. Wood.—English ed.
       p. cm.
     Filmography: p.
     Includes bibliographical references and index.
     ISBN 1–84520–162–0 (pbk.)—ISBN 1–84520–161–2 (cloth)
   1. Motion pictures—Italy—History.   I. Title.

     PN1993.5.I88W66 2005
     791.43'0945—dc22

                                        2005007952

British Library Cataloguing-in-Publication data

A catalogue record for this book is available from the British Library.

ISBN-13   978 1 84520 161 6 (Cloth)
               978 1 84520 162 3 (Paper)

ISBN-10   1 84520 161 2 (Cloth)
               1 84520 162 0 (Paper)

Typeset by JS Typesetting Ltd, Porthcawl, Mid Glamorgan
Printed in the United Kingdom by Biddles Ltd, King's Lynn.

www.bergpublishers.com

Contents

Illustrations

Figures 2.2, 4.2, 4.3, 5.1, 7.2, 7.3 and 8.3 are reproduced courtesy of
the British Film Institute. While every effort has been made to trace the
owners of copyright material, in some cases this has proved impossible
and we take this opportunity to offer our apologies to any copyright
holders whose rights we may have unwittingly infringed.

Acknowledgements

Italian cinema has been my passion for many years, and the research for this book has relied on the support of many institutions, friends, family members and colleagues. I have used every opportunity to teach Italian cinema and my role as course director of the Film and Media Studies programme of the Faculty of Continuing Education at Birkbeck College, University of London, has meant that I have been able to award myself courses in this area at regular intervals. Past co-teachers, Robert Murphy, Lesley Caldwell and Karen Smith, and my students have provided valuable opportunities for discussion and feedback. Colleagues in other institutions have given me opportunities to work through ideas for lectures – Laura Lepschy at University College London, Richard Dyer at the University of Warwick, Susan Hayward and her MA programme in European cinema at the University of Exeter, Pauline Small at Queen Mary University of London, the University of Oxford Department for External Studies, the Institute of Historical Research University of London, Hilary Smith and her colleagues at the British Film Institute and National Film Theatre, the Italian Consulate, and Mario Fortunato and Giovanna Gruber of the Italian Cultural Institute in London.

The financial support of the Birkbeck College Research Fund was invaluable, enabling me to interview producers and film industry professionals in Rome, and several grants from the Faculty of

Continuing Education Research Fund covered travel and other expenses to libraries in Italy, and for attendance at conferences at which I delivered papers to further this research. Similarly a British Academy small conference travel grant in 2004 helped me to develop research on Italian *film noir*. Several interviews were conducted during the research, and I am deeply appreciative of Francesco Rosi for his courtesy, and to the following for giving up their time to talk to me; Elda Ferri of Jean Vigo International, Conchita Airoldi of Urania Film, Maurizio Tedesco of Sorpasso Film, Dr Roberto Stabile and Dr Massimo Civilotti of ANICA. Letizia Messina of Intra Films and Signora Ivana Di Girolami of RAI Trade were helpful in making available copies of films in which I was interested.

I am grateful for the help of the staff at the British Film Institute library and viewing service, the library of the Italian Cultural Institute in London, the Centro Sperimentale di Cinematografia and Cineteca Nazionale in Rome, and to Dr Umberta Brazzini of the Cineteca Regionale Toscana in Florence.

My friends and colleagues, Emma Sandon and Lesley Caldwell, provided valuable feedback and enjoyable discussions on Italian cinema. Writing this book placed an additional workload on Emma, and on Penny Lazenby and the team, Sarah Edwards, Helen Atkinson, Chris Mottershead and Sara Steinke, and the project would not have been completed without their support. Thanks are also due to my student, Silvia Felce, for assistance with translating letters.

Dr Alison Jones and her team at the Royal Free Hospital Hampstead have kept me going, and my friends at the Branch Hill Allotments have kept my feet on the ground. Above all, I am grateful for the long-standing friendship and hospitality of Francesca Bossi; the love and support of my sister, Hilary Burden, and my husband, Donald Wood, both of whom have seen more Italian films than they might otherwise have done.

Parts of 'Bertolucci' in Y. Tasker (ed.), *Fifty Contemporary Film-makers*, London: Routledge, 2002, appear in Chapter 5. Earlier versions and parts of Chapter 6 appeared as 'Clandestini': the 'Other' hiding in the Italian Body Politic' in G. Rings and R. Morgan-Tamosunas (eds), *European Cinema: Inside Out. Images of the Self and the Other in Postcolonial European Film*, by kind permission of Universitätsverlag Winter, Heidelberg. Some sections of Chapter 7 were originally published in Phil Powrie, Ann Davies and Bruce Babington (eds), *The Trouble with Men: Masculinities in European and Hollywood Cinema*, Wallflower Press, 2004. Part of earlier versions of Chapter 8 appeared in 'Revealing the Hidden City: The Cinematic Conspiracy Thriller of the 1970s', *The Italianist*, 23, 2003, and thanks are due to the editors of the *Journal of the Institute of Romance Studies* for permission to reproduce material that was orginally published in my article, 'Representations of Rome in Italian Cinema: Space and Power', vol. 8, 2000.

We are grateful to the following for permission to reproduce the pictures which appear in this book: Figure 1.1, Alberto Friedemann, *Le case di vetro. Stabilimenti cinematografici e teatri di posa a Torino* (Associazione F.E.R.T, Turin, 2003) reproduced by kind permission of the author. Figure 2.1, Lumière & Co. Figure 2.2, photograph by Franco Vitale, courtesy Opera Film. Figures 2.2, 4.5, 5.3, 6.1, Cristaldifilm. Figures 2.3, 5.2, 8.1, Alberto Grimaldi Productions S.A. Figures 4.6, 7.2, 7.3, Titanus S.p.a. Figure 8.3 Cesare Accetta for the film *L'amore molesto*, distributed by Lucky Red.

The publishers and the author have made their best endeavours to contact all copyright holders of images used in this book. If any oversights have occurred, the publishers welcome the corrections, which will be included in any future editions of the work.

1

What is Italian Cinema?

Outside Italy in the 2000s we see relatively few Italian films in cinemas, or on the small screen delivered by terrestrial or satellite television. Those distributed in other media forms, on videocassette or DVD tend to be art film classics, or films that have already had a limited theatrical release abroad. The commercial, industrial and cultural spaces occupied by Italian film production have always been, and are still, profoundly political in that those involved in making films must negotiate and interact with many institutions and institutional practices in order for their films to be made and distributed as widely as possible. The structures of the film and media industries have changed in relative importance over the years and one of the aims of this chapter is to indicate how some of these changes have influenced the product – film as we know it. Tracing some aspects of the historical development of film in Italy, linking it to artistic, cultural, social, technical and commercial forces in Italian, European and global media will enable a picture to emerge of cultural power relationships within Italy, and the place of Italy in global media power relationships.

Although the majority of Italian cinema production does not travel outside Italy, it is equally true, paradoxically, that the Italian film industry has always had international links. At the beginning of the twentieth century early silent cinema was developed by entrepreneurs influenced by Lumière films and the skills of itinerant

French technicians. Between 1961 and 1976, when Italy was producing about 200 films a year, only roughly 2 per cent were exported
and these were by no means always the most popular Italian films
of each season, yet Italy has always been active in promoting co-
production agreements between one or more countries. Popular
cinema is the bottom of the iceberg, of which we see only the top.

Those studies of Italian cinema that have concentrated on
individual directors and their work, or on defining genres such as
comedy, horror, the western, give only partial accounts of the nature
of Italian cinema, ignoring the interesting work that directors and
producers, and others, have to do in their professional capacity
to enable films to be made. Whatever their industry niche, Italian
film directors and producers have to engage with the structures of
their own country and, especially recently, of the European Union
and the globalized economy. This chapter will briefly consider how
Italian cinema developed some standard forms in the period up
until 1944. The career of the director Francesco Rosi will be used to
demonstrate the development of precisely the sort of international
'quality' production that succeeds outside Italy. His presence in the
Italian film industry from 1945 onwards provides a tool to chart
a way through the complexities of Italian cinema after the Second
World War, and prompts interesting contrasts with contemporary
film-makers who have had difficulties in achieving a national, let
alone an international profile.

Early Cinema

With its centuries of urban culture, visual, literary and theatrical
traditions, Italy enthusiastically embraced film-making at the end
of the nineteenth century. Film-makers were able to take advantage of the abundance of natural light, beautiful scenery, of trained
classical, *commedia dell'arte* and regional actors, and craft traditions
of painting and sculpture. As with all technological innovations
(and the more recent development of video, and the social and
economic consequences of its use, provides an interesting parallel),
Italian cinema between 1895 and 1910 took some time to settle
into standard practices and to establish communication with its
audiences.

Producers in the early years came from a variety of backgrounds,
risking their own capital to make short films of between 10 and
18 minutes, but the new medium rapidly attracted investment from
consortia, banks and private persons (Brunetta 1993a: 26–7). Production companies proliferated in all the major Italian cities but, by
1910, large and flourishing companies in Milan (Luca Comerio, S.
A. Baratti), Turin (Ambrosio, Itala, Aquila), Rome (Cines, Pineschi
brothers, Alberini Santoni) and Naples (Troncone Brothers & Co.,

Manifatture cinematografiche riunite) had established distinctive identities. Although, as Giuliana Bruno has pointed out, Italian silent cinema is generally represented in Anglo-Saxon scholarship as consisting mainly of large-scale epics, in fact, as one might expect in the entrepreneurial climate of the late nineteenth and early twentieth centuries, production was much more differentiated and flourished in many geographical centres (Brunetta 1993a: 47). In her study of the film-maker, Elvira Notari, and her company, Dora Films, of Naples, Bruno reconstructs the company's diverse output in the silent period, from short films *dal vero* (documentaries shot from real life on location), films of real events, hand colouring of film stock, narrative stagings of Neapolitan songs, and popular melodramas (Bruno 1993: 80–100). Here we can observe characteristics typical of Italian cinema of this period, and which would consolidate as business practices and genres in the future. First, the importance of regionalism in Italian culture, proudly drawing on regional accents and dialects, theatrical stories and traditions, local sights and actors. This is still a force in Italian life; it is never forgotten that the great comic, Totò, was a Neapolitan, or that actor/director, Roberto Benigni is a Tuscan. Films like Mario Martone's *L'amore molesto* (1998) or Giuseppe Tornatore's *Cinema Paradiso* (1989) use local character actors to populate the minor roles and convey an overall impression of authenticity of location. Second, Italian cinema has, from the very beginning, been fascinated with actuality and, as we will see, attempted to make sense of forces behind events. Third, the colouring and tinting of film reflected cinema's search for the new and sensational, but also drew on earlier artistic symbolism and traditions. Visual organization and exploitation of the spectacular and picturesque nature of the Italian setting is a constant defining element of Italian cinema. Lastly, the melodrama, in which stories of dramatic events are staged with maximum attention to the emotional charge, is a flexible theatrical form, permeating all genres and capable of being used for serious intent.

Figure 1.1
Itala Films' studio number three.

It is clear from Maria Adriana Prolo's list of genres used by the Pathé company in 1911 that production companies not only knew their national markets and tailored dramas to them but that the short length of early films had resulted in some strain in identifying new stories (Prolo 1951: 47). Early film companies used actors from local and/or dialect theatre, but only a few, such as Mary Cléo Tarlarini at Ambrosio, Letizia and Lydia Quaranta at Itala in Turin, managed to make their names familiar to the public by dint of appearing in a great number of films. Vittorio Martinelli's description of the physical characteristics of the actresses working for Turinese studios is an indication of the range of roles available in short- and medium-length films, embodying different class positions and female types, the brave heroine, the sister, the tomboy, the rebel (Martinelli 1998: 342–53). The glamour of the big studio stars of the mid-1910s to the 1920s, the *dive*, has obscured the fact that, although significant, they were exceptional. The sheer range of female roles is an indication that the traditional stereotype of female calmness and acceptance of social and religious conventions was being superseded by more modern representations of active and adventurous women, and narratives in which women flouted patriarchal conventions by rejecting husbands and choosing their lovers. Monica Dall'Asta (1998: 354–60) has linked the flowering of active, female protagonists to the influence of American 'serial queens' and the importance of women in the workforce during the period of rapid industrialization of northern Italy in the 1910s and 1920s. Other European countries, particularly France, shared Italy's interest in female adventurers and spies, reflecting the potential for new narratives that the colonial conflicts and, in the Italian context, war with the Ottoman empire, generated. However, it is the Italian *diva*, the grand star whose fatal and languid beauty and ability to convey strong emotions who is best remembered as typifying Italian silent cinema.

The development of a star system in which the production company used the name and star persona of an actor as part of a film's publicity went hand-in-hand with other commercial developments, such as standardization of film stock (sprocket holes, number of frames per minute), the increase in length to feature films of several reels, the evolution of the distribution and exhibition sectors, and the growth of publicity opportunities, film critics and film journals of all sorts, and vigourous marketing abroad (Bernardini 1982: 83). In the years before 1910, entrepreneurs bought short films to show as part of varied programmes of entertainments at fairs, circuses, music halls and beer halls. Hundreds of copies were often made of the most popular films. However, in order to reach a 'quality' audience who would pay higher ticket prices, both the film itself and the venue had to deliver a pleasurable and entertaining experience. There was an immediate effect on the mode of viewing, on the social composition of the audience, and on the type of performance and audience reaction to it. Distributors with exclusive rights to a few films could make their fortunes by the intensive exploitation of a few successful titles projected in large theatres. A greater level of professionalism was required of actors playing the main roles in feature films. The recognizably modern system grew up whereby the talents of named, individual actors, the creativity of the director, the cost and complexity of the production, formed the subject of the publicity campaign. Films then premièred in a prestigious location, followed by release in different zones of Italy and abroad, following the distributor's acquisition of the rights to exploit the film for a given length of time in particular cinemas or areas (Bernardini 1982: 82–3). Claudio Camerini (1986: 61) gives 1910 as a key date for the growth of a star system with the importing of films from Scandinavia in which the names of the stars, Asta Nielsen and Henny Porten, dominated film posters, and the prominence given to the names of actors from the Comédie Française in publicity for Pathé's *Film d'art* productions. As a result, Italian actors started to develop their skills and star persona through association with a particular company's films, and, during the golden age of Italian *divismo* (1914–19), production companies used the figures of the biggest stars, the *dive* in order to differentiate themselves in a competitive market. The front rank of Francesca Bertini, Lyda Borelli, Leda Gys commanded huge salaries, convinced of their eternal appeal to 'their' public, without realizing the depth of the crisis in the film industry.

The international appeal of the historical epic films with big stars can be gauged by a letter quoted by Gian Piero Brunetta (1993a: 50–1) from Baron Alberto Fassini, director of the Cines company of

Figure 1.2
A spiky relationship – Francesca Bertini and Gustavo Serena in *Assunta Spina* (Gustavo Serena, 1915).

Rome, to George Kleine in the United States in which he alerts him to future epic productions:

> I wish to inform you that it is my intention to make, twice a year, a feature length film which will necessitate great cost and which will serve as a publicity vehicle for our entire production. Considering these exceptional costs, I am asking if you would be able to give us better conditions for the acquisition of the negatives than at present. Next week we will begin production on one of these films, entitled *Quo vadis?* To this end I have hired twenty lions which will remain in our studios for about 4 weeks. In order to convey to you the wonder of this film, I shall limit myself to telling you that the negative cost will be 80,000 lire and that its length will be around 1,500–2,000 metres.

Italian epics drew predominantly on Italian or Roman history, reworking historical material which was part of the cultural heritage of the European middle class. However, it is clear from the above that it was the spectacular elements of these films that contributed to their wide appeal.

The First World War and the Collapse of the Italian Film Industry

Just as the heyday of the Italian classical epic film was announced, the seeds of the crisis of the film industry were sown. By targeting the 'quality' audience, producers, distributors and exhibitors landed themselves with high costs in making the films and maintaining luxurious cinemas, while alienating the mass audience for whom the ticket prices were too high. Films like *Quo vadis?* (Enrico Guazzoni, 1913) and *Cabiria* (Giovanni Pastrone, 1914) were huge financial and critical successes worldwide so that around fifty production companies operated in Italy producing too many films to be absorbed in Italy alone (Brunetta 1993a: 53–5). As a result, at the very beginning of the First World War, before Italy had entered the conflict, many studios started to close as foreign markets became unavailable or, as Brunetta (1993a: 56) surmises, because panic, or lack of capital, or the lack of sound commercial organization, or even because key people were called up, exposing the lack of planning and foresight in the industry.

Italian producers and film-makers also experimented with the technology. Giovanni Pastrone, the director of *Cabiria*, patented many modifications to camera equipment, experimenting particularly with the dolly (Rondolino 1993: 118). However, Italian entrepreneurs were left floundering by the coming of sound cinema, which gave the commercial advantage to the stronger, American film industry and severely limited the potential market for Italian films. After the First World War Italian film production dropped 'from 200 films in 1920 to fewer than a dozen works in 1927', although large-scale epics and films featuring Bartolomeo Pagano as the giant Maciste continued to be made, public taste responded to the more egalitarian American dramas of the 1920s (Bondanella 2001: 215). Lack of attention to public taste and lack of professional organization had toppled the Italian film industry from the commanding position held prior to 1919 and had been unable to withstand the more competitive expansionist drive of American capitalism.

Cinema under Fascism, 1933–43

The crisis caused by new sound technology was not only commercial but also at the level of content and ideology. Gianni Rondolino (1993: 126–7) remarks that, even before the establishment of 'the talkies', Italian films with their historical subjects and languid divas were looking old-fashioned in comparison with those from America. The causes of the crisis were many and complex and he suggests that the high professional standards that had evolved with the large-scale, international productions in fact led to a lack of freshness and of subject renewal in the industry. Italy underwent enormous changes in the 1920s and the crisis of the film industry was part of a more general set of tensions arising from the country's move towards modernity. Rapid industrialization changed class structures, creating a new middle class and an urban working class. New jobs and working arrangements also brought new patterns of leisure and increased consumption on the capitalist model. Benito Mussolini's March on Rome in 1922 and the establishment of the fascist State was also part of the modernizing process. Mussolini's aim was that all parts of the State should work together to modernize Italy, on the model of a large corporation with a strong director at its head. The expansion of film production, and especially of cinema audiences, formed part of this modernization of Italy in that, although the fascist State never fully controlled commercial film production, it did put in place powerful institutions. This institutional infrastructure laid the foundations both for post-1945 neorealist cinema, and the expansion of popular cinema by providing opportunities for training, and for building a cinema-going public adept at 'reading' cinematic narratives. Directors such as Alessandro Blasetti and Roberto Rossellini started their careers in this period, as did the actor, Vittorio De Sica, and the screenwriter Cesare Zavattini.

After-work activities were targeted by the State by the setting up of the Opera Nazionale Dopolavoro (OND), which supervised groups interested in organizing leisure activities, resulting in '767 cinemas under its supervision' by 1938 (Hay 1987: 15). Cinema-going was essentially an urban experience in the 1920s and 1930s for the very good reason that many rural areas lacked electricity so that the activities of the OND included travelling projection facilities. The Istituto LUCE (L'unione cinematografica educativa) was set up in 1924 to produce and distribute documentaries and newsreels, and a youth organization, the Gioventù universitaria fascista (GUF) set up to promote the study of film. The war on illiteracy and the expansion of a middle-class audience led to an increase in newspaper circulation, and the rise of specialized film magazines. Mussolini's enthusiasm led to the setting up not only of the film school, the Centro Sperimentale di Cinematografia (CSC), in 1935 but also the Cinecittà studios in Rome. The magazine *Film* was distributed to the troops and the training of film personnel developed fast in order to meet the need for wartime newsreels and documentaries.

Fascist measures to promote cinema were essentially pragmatic. Ernesto G. Laura (2000: 63) has shown how Mussolini always in-tended the Istituto Luce to be self-supporting, aiming to achieve this by obliging every cinema in Italy to show Luce documentaries. However, the sheer numbers of technical staff involved in supporting the camera operators who recorded events all over the country meant that a political and cultural policy had to be formulated by government in order to justify financial support. Luce films developed from newsreels recording events deemed important by the Council of Ministers, to more overtly propagandistic and ideologically fascist films such as *Camicia nera* (*Black Shirt*, Giovacchino Forzano, 1933). The impact of these institutions on the population is impossible to judge, although a variety of testimonies indicate that young people in particular used the GUF groups to develop their passion for film and to widen their cultural horizons (Rosi 1970: 53–4). Overall, fascist film institutions represented an attempt to counter the cultural influence of the United States by proclaiming the value of Italian creativity and its ability to engage with a specifically Italian modern reality.

Part of the excitement of film education is the building up of one's film culture and it is clear that those 1930s and 1940s students of the CSC were involved in debates, based on intensive film viewing, about the nature of film, about the purpose of documentary, about realism. The official line was to compare foreign films unfavourably to those of Italy. However, a critical battle developed around the work of Renoir, and the question of realism was hotly debated in the pages of *Cinema*. The supply of non-Axis films in general circulation was not replenished after 1940, although some United States and British films were available in Switzerland and some examples captured in North Africa were viewed by film critics with great interest (Argentieri 1998). The disappearance of American and French competition allowed the Italian film industry space to develop and, in doing so, a new generation of film-makers who had been trained by the CSC and/or in documentaries and newsreels, moved Italian cinema in a markedly more realist direction (Laura 2000: 197–208).

The commercial film industry was also in dire need of modernization. The entrepreneur Stefano Pittaluga attempted to rally the industry against the American threat by establishing L'Unione Cinematografia Italiana (UCI), representing film producers and distributors with the aim of rationalizing the market but it went bankrupt in 1927 (Quaglietti 1980: 14–20; Bondanella 1983: 11–12; Landy 1986: 11–12). Pittaluga's own company, which had absorbed other enterprises, became Cines-Pittaluga, setting in place policies that would be continued after his death in 1931, resulting in the government body, Ente Nazionale Industrie Cinematografiche (ENIC) in 1935. As a result of Pittaluga's initiatives the fascist government also set up the Direzione Generale per la Cinematografia in 1934 with Luigi Freddi at its head. This body was under the Ministero per la Cultura Popolare (Minculpop), as was the fund to finance Italian film production at the Banca Nazionale del Lavoro (Bondanella 1983: 13). Its system of prizes for quality and dubbing tax on foreign films, amongst other initiatives, was later carried over into the post-war era.

Few films of the war genre were made in Italy during the Second World War, perhaps because they were expensive but also because distributors preferred entertainment and melodramatic films. Mino Argentieri's analyses show that references to the war are generally absent, Italy being represented as a peaceful, quiet country (Argentieri 1998: 49–53). Very few films even indicate that Italy is indeed at war, with the exception of Mario Bonnard's *Avanti, c'è posto* (*There's Room at the Front*, 1942) and the allusions to wartime difficulties in obtaining house gas in Bonnard's *Campo de' fiori* (1943). Argentieri reveals the surprising influence of the ideas of the British documentary movement and the theories of Grierson and Flaherty on film-makers like De Robertis and Rossellini, showing how film-makers adapted the idea of dramatized social documentary and the expository mode to the war film.

The fascist era, which ended in 1944 succeeded in its aims of modernizing the film industry, putting in place institutions that slid more-or-less effortlessly into the period of reconstruction, mainly because the Americans preferred existing institutional structures to any that might include communists. Ironically, the fascist dubbing tax was resuscitated in the late 1940s as a means of making money from American film imports, which Italian organizations were unable to stop by other means.

Structures of the Film Industry after the Second World War

Traditionally the film industry was defined in terms of three internal sectors – production, distribution and exhibition. External structures affecting the industry consist of State intervention at the levels of finance or legislation; competition from outside Italy for control of the home market (particularly by the American majors); and the transnational influence of new technological developments. It must now also include European Union directives. The cinema industry does not, of course, operate in a vacuum and it interacts with other cultural industries and other media. From 1945 until the mid-1970s production companies ranged in size from small companies formed to make one film only (making the attribution of rights to the film difficult to establish) to large firms with national and international contacts producing several films a year. Some distributors specialized in a particular region of Italy, such as Fortunato Misiano in Sicily and the south. Others covered the national territory, or had international contacts. The exhibition sector was organized to exploit films from their first run in city centre cinemas, usually part of big cinema chains (the *prima visione*), to suburban cinemas (*seconda visione*), on to small town (*terza visione*), and a variety of church halls, political associations, seaside and seasonal venues.

Mainstream feature films are extremely costly to produce; even small productions involve considerable financial investment and a significant number of creative and service roles. Italian cinema has had to evolve mechanisms for the assessment of successful productions. Since the immediate post-war period these have taken the form of detailed statistical records of the box-office performance of individual films, genres, directors, creative personnel. Statistics attempted to counter large areas of uncertainty and ambiguity deriving from the flourishing black economy of payments made (for example) to stars, which did not appear in any balance sheet.

Italy was divided into twelve zones and details of a film's box-office returns are kept for the main cities in each zone. This has had an impact on film form as it stimulated development of film genres and subgenres, and the careers of those involved in the creative and technical spheres of film production. Moreover, producers make decisions on the basis of projected revenue from national and international markets. From the 1940s to the 1960s these decisions might have resulted in aiming a film at a specific geographic area, such as southern Italy and Sicily. Soft porn films of the 1970s were targetted at suburban *luci rosse* (red light) cinemas, and the Middle East export area. There are also complicated formulae for financing film production and, more recently, for claiming additional State finance (the 'Article 28' finance, and later Article 8) if the product is retrospectively designated as 'quality' on the basis of its cultural or artistic impact, or of the contribution of its creative or technical personnel.[1]

Perrella (1981) suggests that the prolonged relative stability of Italian society and the film industry have generated various standard institutional practices whose aim is to maximize effort and investment. Tailoring products to particular markets is one standard practice; repetition of forms is another. A film is easier to market if it belongs to a standard genre released in a standard way, in particular cinemas at particular times of the year. The danger of very original work is that it is not repeatable; the effort involved in its publicity or shooting does not easily form part of the repertoire of institutional practices. One way of overcoming this disadvantage is to categorize and market the film by director – a 'Fellini film' or 'the latest Rosi'. The director/author is therefore both a legal definition and an institutional necessity used as a criterion of cultural and/or commercial value (Fragola 1984: 3).

To simplify, films were traditionally financed by a package of 'minimum guarantees', presented in the form of bills of exchange presented to a bank, or the Banca Nazionale del Lavoro, at fixed intervals. These guarantees were sought by the producer from distributors and covered the initial production costs. It was up to producers to present an attractive deal. They therefore generally engaged the screenwriters, director and actors and, with script in hand, sought an 'economic package' to present to distributors and/ or a foreign co-producer. It was possible to check the success of previous projects with which director, producer, screenwriter(s), musicians were involved, and how films of a similar genre profile had performed in different geographical areas of Italy, so it was possible to estimate the possible return on a similar film. Study of the film industry between 1945 and 1976 reveals that producers either moved into, and continued to occupy, one market niche, or they came to dominate a particular area of production, within which they attempted to diversify into different genres. The Argento family companies (SEDA, ADC, Opera) specialized in horror films made by Dario Argento, but also produce other directors' low-budget horror films for a niche market. Although Franco Cristaldi was associated primarily with art cinema on 'difficult' subjects, he also produced comedies and less serious films with great success.[2] Screenwriters in this period tended to work right across the industry, but directors rapidly became associated with a particular type of film.

The presence of large numbers of small entrepreneurs to a large extent explains constant complaints at the lack of concerted cultural policies or, when legislation attempts to protect the film industry, the inability of sectors of the industry to obey them. Laws imposing a quota for the obligatory screening of Italian films per year were often ignored by the exhibition sector, which wanted to fill cinemas, usually with well publicized blockbusters. The combination of detailed statistical information and creative administration also accounts for the *filone* phenomenon. A *filone* is a strand of similar films, rather than a genre. Trendspotting successful subjects, names, themes and stars resulted in quickly-made similar films, until public interest was seen to wane. The American practice of huge advance publicity for block-busters could also backfire as films with similar titles were hastily made and released as near to the American *Spartacus* or *Cleopatra* as possible.

After 1976, the year of the explosion of commercial television channels, the practices described above become less transparent and more complex. The film industry polarized and has been dominated by oligarchies, that is, a small but changing group of large, vertically integrated production companies with television interests. We will now explore the evolution of these structures since 1945.

1945–50: the Period of Reconstruction

The early phase of the post-war Italian cinema industry can be characterized to a large extent as organized chaos. With the opening of Cinecittà in 1937, Rome dominated film production during the fascist period, but its studios were damaged by Allied bombing, its equipment was removed by the Germans, and its buildings were used as a refugee camp from 1945 to 1948. Without Cinecittà, production began in other, smaller studios, or in regional centres, the rather ad hoc and disorganized arrangements reminiscent of early silent cinema (Brunetta 1982: 37–45). Despite difficulties, around twenty-five films were produced in 1945, rising to sixty-five and sixty-seven in 1946 and 1947 but these films were unable to conquer more than 13 per cent of their own market (Zanchi 1975: 87). Brunetta (1982: 1–21) provides evidence that the difficulties confronting Italian production derived from American strategies to dominate the Italian distribution sector. Releasing the enormous backlog of their films onto the market under the aegis of the Psychological Warfare Branch (PWB), effectively deprived Italian films of much of a showing. Apart from films identified as more or less neorealist, Italian production sought to counter this deluge by making low-budget genre films, many of them emulating the American style. *Film noir* elements can be identified in many of the successful neorealist films, *Il bandito* (*The Bandit*, Alberto Lattuada, 1946), *In nome della legge* (*In the Name of the Law*, Pietro Germi, 1949), *Senza pietà* (*Without Pity*, Alberto Lattuada, 1948), while melodrama and naked legs did not hurt the success of *Riso amaro* (*Bitter Rice*, 1949).

There were many routes into the film industry but personal contacts were always important. For those with intellectual interests the GUF film groups had been a hotbed of debate and (ironically) of left-wing ideas in the company of other, like-minded people. Small comic magazines and cartoons (Fellini), local theatre and radio (Rosi) also generated important contacts. Neapolitan contacts suggested Rosi's name to Luchino Visconti to work on the film *La terra trema* (1948) as assistant director. The film's seven-month shoot in Sicily increased its cost to Lire 120 million, when the average Italian film in the late 1940s cost around Lire 50 million. Visconti started shooting with money from the Italian communist party, replenished by his own funds when that ran out. Shooting was completed with financing from Universalia, a Catholic production company (Rosi 1996: 25). It made Lire 35 million at the box office but it has to be remembered that, in spite of being classed as one of the most unsuccessful neorealist films, it had a wide international release and is still in circulation on video and DVD. There were many reasons for the film's lack of immediate success, perhaps the main one being its difference, economically, ideologically and aesthetically, from other films of 1948 and 1949. The dialogues recorded were in the Aci Trezza version of Sicilian dialect, incomprehensible outside the immediate area, so that the film was released in a dubbed version in standard Italian supervised by Rosi, and in Visconti's preferred version with his own voice-over commentary. Public and critical reaction to *La terra trema* was very mixed, generally bemoaning the lack of plot, stars, and the slow pace (Anon. 1950: 64).

This example typifies the changing industrial context of the time. Although early neorealist films were popular financially, reflecting the political feeling in the country after the war, when *La terra trema* was released in 1949, it did badly. The late 1940s and 1950s were marked by a rapid return to standard industrial practices and hierarchical working relationships. As production budgets increased in an attempt to compete with American films, so the industry moved towards an American, capitalist model, where the demands of investors were important in defining the product.

The wider political struggle, which resulted in overwhelming Christian Democrat success in the 1948 elections, was also reflected in the Italian film industry. Christian Democrat politicians and appointees to State bodies opposed neorealist films on the grounds that they presented a bad image of Italy abroad. The passing of the Legge Andreotti in 1949 was the culmination of that politician's attempts since 1947 to manipulate and control the film industry. Quaglietti (1980: 52–73) suggests that Andreotti saw that he needed producers on his side if he was to impose controls on the types of films made. Andreotti's dubbing tax, the *leggina* of 1947, swelled the funds available to producers in the form of State loans, but the bureaucratic mechanisms governing access to these funds constituted an additional form of censorship. Not only the screenplay (later amended to the treatment) and budget, but also details of technical and creative personnel had to be submitted to the Sezione Autonoma Cinema of the Banca Nazionale del Lavoro. Similar controls were put in place for the granting of the essential *nulla osta*, licensing the distribution and exhibition of a film.

The impact, in cultural as well as economic terms, of the vast backlog of American films threatened saturation of the market, bringing the industry to crisis point. Quaglietti (1980: 47) maintains that the exhibition sector comprised 6,551 cinemas in 1948 and that this sector therefore needed American films to keep cinemas functioning. That neorealist films were not regarded as an answer to the crisis is shown by industry calls for directors with good story-telling skills and commercial sense (Campassi 1949: 35). Producers wanted films with some guarantee of success; commercial products with stars on the American model (Ferraù 1949: 7). The faces and performances of non-professional actors of neorealist films were inadequate for the emotional melodramas of the later 1940s, and did not fit the dramas of aspiration towards a better life. Actors who made the transition from fascist cinema changed their style of appearance (Carla del Poggio is less *soignée* post-war), were associated with popular genres (Vittorio De Sica, Anna Magnani, Aldo Fabrizi), were needed for middle-class roles (Gino Cervi), or provided some continuity with stereotypes of Italian masculinity regarded as positive (Amedeo Nazzari). Italian films also needed youthful actors who would embody the aspirations of the new political and social situation. Young male actors came from theatre, or sport. The Miss Italia and other beauty contests provided hunting grounds for starlets, launching the careers of Silvana Pampanini, Gina Lollobrigida, Lucia Bosè, Silvana Mangano, Eleonora Rossi Drago and Sophia Loren amongst others, reflecting Andreotti's call for 'less rags, more legs' (Bizzari 1979: 41).

The films of the later 1940s reflect the conflicts and upheavals of the immediate post-war period, neorealist and political films jostling with melodramas of bereavement, generational conflict and revenge, comedies and adventure films.

The Boom Years of the 1950s and 1960s

The extent of Italy's economic recovery can be seen from the in-crease in the number of films per year from ninety-two in 1950 to 190 in 1954 to 160 in 1960 to over 200 films a year during the entire 1960s. Italian associations of producers and distributors (ANICA and AGIS) made many agreements with the Motion Picture Association of America (MPAA) to limit the American domination of the market, the most influential being the blocking of the export of American film revenue earned in Italy. Although some companies resorted to extremely creative strategies to take their money out of the country, significant amounts of American dollars were invested in Italian films. Italian production spanned the entire range of films from successful first run products, to solid, mid-budget examples of genres and *filoni*, to low-budget, ephemeral *filoni*, quickly exploited on the edges of the market. Besides comedies and melodramas, several major *filoni* dominate this period. Around 170 examples

(10 per cent of Italian production) of the sword and sandal peplum epic *filone* were made between 1957 and 1964 (Miccichè 1995: 132–3). The *film sexy* was a constant presence from the late 1950s, and the unexpected success of Sergio Leone's *Per un pugno di dollari* (*For a Fistful of Dollars*, 1964) launched the mega-*filone* of around 300 spaghetti westerns whose numbers trailed off in the early 1970s. Although moderately successful and low-earning films covered a wider genre range, there were still proportionately similar clusters of films in the main categories of comedy and drama. Prizes for quality, predictably enough, tended to be awarded to films in these two categories. In terms of quantity, however, Italian popular cinema represented the hegemonic situation, rather than the small percentage of art films produced each year.

At the beginning of the 1950s the average cost of an Italian film was Lire 100 million, about one sixth of the cost of the average American production. As the number of blockbusters increased, less ambitious films were robbed of income. However, because of the sheer number of films in production, there was enormous breadth of opportunity, at least within the *film medio*, for someone starting out in the industry.

By the time Rosi came to make his first film he had already acquired ten years' experience in the industry at all levels of financial reward. After the experience of *La terra trema* his career profile included popular mainstream films which did well, interspersed with art films which did not. He acted as Assistant Director to Raffaello Matarazzo, one of the most successful and prolific 1950s directors on *Tormento* (*Torment*, 1950) and *I figli di nessuno* (*Nobody's Children*, 1951), starring Amedeo Nazzari and Yvonne Sanson, both florid melodramas with typically convoluted plots, produced by a big studio, Titanus. They came first and second in the national chart, earning over Lire 900 and 700 million respectively, when the average ticket price was Lire 103.7.

In 1951 Rosi also collaborated on the screenplay of Luciano Emmer's popular ensemble comedy, *Parigi è sempre Parigi* (*Paris is Always Paris*), starring Marcello Mastroianni and Lucia Bosè. He was brought in to finish *Camicie rosse* (*Red Shirts*, 1952), a historical drama about Garibaldi, when Goffredo Alessandrini walked out. In 1953 he returned to a collaboration with Ettore Giannini, for whom he acted as Assistant Director on *Carosello Napoletano* (*Neapolitan Roundabout*). The film, produced by Lux, was an extremely successful adaptation for the screen of a theatrical review. With box-office receipts of over Lire 753 million, it came near the top of the financial league for the 1953–4 season. Notable for its panorama of Neapolitan types, characters and customs, it gave a role to Sophia Loren and was the first of the short-lived genre of the musical review. It aroused some interest at the Cannes film festival (Casiraghi 1954: 13). Rosi's output also included two book adaptations by famous authors, *Proibito* (*Forbidden*, Mario Monicelli, 1954) and Moravia's *Racconti romani* (*Roman Tales*, Gianni Franciolini, 1955), a comedy, *Il bigamo* (*The Bigamist*, Luciano Emmer, 1956) and directorial support to Vittorio Gassman on the biopic *Kean, genio e sregolatezza* (*Kean*, 1956).

His credits also included work on scripts or as assistant director on films that won critical praise, *Bellissima* (Luchino Visconti, 1951), *I vinti* (Michelangelo Antonioni, 1952) and *Senso* (Visconti, 1954). From the point of view of constructing a convincing career profile, it is significant that he achieved a balance between consistent box-office successes on recognizable genre products, and work on films which achieved critical recognition and prizes for quality (and little in the way of financial success). This pattern can be seen in the early career of some of his collaborators – the working on a wide range of films, with enough box office and critical successes for one to appear an attractive proposition for a certain type of producer.

Other young directors, Florestano Vancini, Valerio Zurlini, Vittorio de Seta, Ermanno Olmi, prepared themselves for their début in feature films by an apprenticeship in short films. The phase of *neorealismo rosa*, and the proliferation of comedies gave others the opportunity to make their first film.

Art Cinema and Prestige Production

By the end of the 1950s a convergence of economic, social and political factors favoured the emergence of independent film producers willing to take risks on financing more experimental or political films. With the aid of the Marshall Plan, Italian industry picked up, paving the way for the economic miracle of the 1950s and 1960s. There was increased prosperity and greater employment, coupled with expansion of northern industrial centres and immigration from the south. The social upheaval that accompanied the economic boom provided a rich range of new subjects for film-makers and interesting tensions in more traditional narratives. John Foot (2003: 138) claims that '10 million Italians moved from one region to another in a ten-year period; more than 17 million moved house'. Politically there was a more or less smooth movement towards more centre-left forms of government resulting in less censorship; public taste was disposed to be interested in more radical products. Moreover, although the backlog of American films released in Italy after the war had been all but exhausted, the American film industry was going through one of its own crises, which meant less competition for the Italians in their own market. It had, however, come to rely on revenue from European markets and Italian State intervention from the 1960s onwards reflects political attempts to control national cultural space (Guback 1969: 10). One strategy was to build the infrastructure of festivals and prizes for quality that David Bordwell and Steve Neale identify as characteristic of art cinema, and which will be explored in Chapter 5. As many other countries of Europe and Latin America were developing the same strategies, and the exhibition sector recognized the potential audience for art films, art films became more easily exportable, helped by the growth of co-production treaties.

Rosi's first film, *La sfida* (*The Challenge*, 1958) was produced by Franco Cristaldi, who was a determining force in Italian cinema, launching 'new' directors and subjects. It was a Lux/Vides/Cinecittà co-production with Suevia films of Madrid. The presence of Cinecittà in the production arrangements is interesting because the State-run studio facilities provided another level of subsidy to the industry. In the 1960s Cinecittà offered delayed payment facilities, which made it a bank to its own clients (Champenier 1989: 67). The award of a special jury prize (*ex aequo* with Louis Malle's *Les amants*) at the 1958 Venice film festival, and three *nastri d'argento* (silver ribbons, the Italian equivalent of the Oscars) excited a great deal of interest in the film. It came fifteenth in the national box-office listings, a very high placing amidst comedies, mythological and adventure films. Although political in its exploration of how the power of the Neapolitan mafia, the *camorra*, acted between peasant farmers and the Neapolitan fruit and vegetable market, stylistically and narratively the film draws on the American gangster film, *film noir*, and the love story in order to make ideas accessible.

The success of *La sfida* enabled Rosi to make *I magliari* for Vides/Titanus in 1959, starring Renato Salvatori and Alberto Sordi, a big star of Italian comedy. Similar use of popular forms, the investigation, regional comedy and gangster genres, can be seen in Rosi's story of Italian illegal workers in Germany and, again, the film did well and won a 1960 *nastro d'argento* for best photography. The key cinematic event at the beginning of the 1960s was, however, Fellini's *La dolce vita* (1960). *La dolce vita* showed the film industry that it was possible to make money out of controversial subjects, treated in non-standard narrative forms. Rosi's *Salvatore Giuliano* (1961) operated in the same way. Both films provoked scandals, public outcry and, in the latter case, a parliamentary enquiry into allegations of collusion between the police, the carabinieri and the mafia in Sicily.

Salvatore Giuliano was a Lux/Vides/Galatea coproduction. It established Rosi's reputation abroad by winning the Silver Bear at Berlin and, although rejected by Venice, *nastri d'argento* for its direction, music and black-and-white photography, a Golden Goblet for best director, and the San Fedele foreign critics' prize for best film of 1962. *Salvatore Giuliano* was a tremendously important film on several levels. It was a politically committed film that offered a rigorous treatment of the problems of the south and courageously faced up to the material. It was also innovative in form – in a way that neorealist films had not been. In his search for authenticity Rosi shot most of the film in the places where the actions happened and used predominantly non-professional actors, an unusual strategy for a film which made more than Lire 700 million at the box office. With very few exceptions, critical reaction was one of admiration. Like many of his subsequent films, it was discussed not only in the film columns, but also on the cultural pages. *Le mani sulla città* (*Hands Over the City*, 1963) was much less financially successful, but won the 1963 Golden Lion at the XXIV Venice Film Festival, its presence in competition and its prize therefore demanding that it be considered seriously.

After the relative lack of success of *Le mani sulla città*, the opportunity to mount a co-production was a logical step, guaranteeing a broader base of financial investment, access to two or more home markets, with the consequent advantages of eligibility for 'national' exhibition quotas, and prizes, a dual basis for calculating subsidies, and the inclusion of a greater range of stars, artistic and technical personnel without endangering the nationality of the film (Guback 1969: 181). Rosi's bullfighting film, *Il momento della verità* (*The Moment of Truth*, 1964) was an Italo/Spanish co-production in colour, using the story of a matador to explore the exploitation and poverty of rural populations. The most popular genres at the time were costume dramas, dramatic and episodic films. The film was exploited rapidly in first run cinemas, its high earnings reflected its targeting of market needs, and the added attraction of its exotic location.

Rosi's career at this stage also shows that financial pressures were difficult to ignore. His first three films had been successful, his last two less so. In order to continue making the films he wanted he would next have to make a film that made money. But Rosi and his co-writer, Tonino Guerra's project to adapt a Neapolitan fairy story was hijacked by the producer, Carlo Ponti, whose preoccupations resulted from pressures associated with the large injection of money from the American co-production deal. The film had to be made in colour, in scope, using stars. MGM marketed it as a love story, *C'era una volta* (*Cinderella – Italian Style*, 1967) ('Sophia! Omar! Terrific together as the peasant girl and the prince who tames her!'). Small wonder that critics did not really know what to make of it, frantically searching for a message underneath the charming pictures. It was, however, extremely successful financially, coming eighth in the national listings. Interestingly we have in *C'era una volta* an example of the strength of a producer prevailing over that of a director, but the film's success indicated that Rosi could deliver a film which responded to public taste for clear narratives, stars, and visual splendour. However, Rosi and his producer Luciano Perugia had many difficulties in attracting finance for his next project, *Uomini contro* (*Just Another War*, 1969), an adaptation of a prestigious book about an incident in the First World War. They eventually put their own money into the project, plus the guarantee from the distribution company, Euro, and arranged a co-production agreement with Jadran Films of Jugoslavia. Euro films subsequently went bust and Rosi claims never to have made any money out of it.[3]

The film industry at this time was having to beat off the usual challenge from energetically marketed American films, such as wide-screen spectaculars, and from competition from television. Ironically, the Corona Law of 1965, which aimed to spread the rewards of quality more widely among those responsible for production and creative contributions, thus encouraging continued 'quality' productions, presented the industry with yet more dilemmas. The temptation was to go with market imperatives for a quick exploitation of a film as the rewards for a quality film were slower to come (Ferraù 1966: 4); the tax relief subventions to the production team, and the twenty prizes of Lire 40 million each, depended on a film's being designated 'quality', but at some future date. Nonetheless, there were now enough art films in circulation to support the development of alternative art house cinemas, the *cinema d'essai*, where they could be exhibited. Thus the Corona Law was effective in encouraging producers to identify certain directors and creative workers who would be likely to deliver the product necessary to qualify for these attractive financial incentives.

As we have shown, the 1960s were marked by the development of more rigid industrial models for the exploitation of films, one effect of which was to drive into unprofitability, and ultimately out of business, small production companies making cheap, genre products. Co-production deals increased to hedge risks and exploit two or more markets. The art film sector consolidated and, although numerically a very small area of Italian production, was influential on the level of formal experimentation and subject matter. Political or authorial film-making was, however, still a risky business if critical acclaim was not matched by some sort of financial success.

The groups of demonstrators who occupied the State-owned Istituto Luce, and the prestigious film school, the CSC, in 1968, centred their demands around greater artistic freedom and better working conditions. The latter was identified with complete reform of the State's arms of the cinema industry – the producer, l'Istituto Luce; the distributor, Italnoleggio, and the financier, the Banco Nazionale di Lavoro. This was a natural enough ideal in the face of aggressive United States marketing and a native industry relying mainly on formulaic genre products. In common with the situation outside the film industry, the directors of these State concerns were political appointments. Those whose appointments resulted from the centre-left coalition found Christian Democrat appointees firmly in control. The next four years were taken up with the reform of the State cinema apparatus and provision for its more active role in promoting Italian culture and films of quality. The immediate result in the early 1970s was an interesting crop of innovative and political films. At this point, around 1972, some new directors made their début. This impetus was certainly not, however, followed up by the establishment of channels by which political films could easily be made.

Several trends are visible in the period 1967–71. Firstly, directors who started out in low-budget, personal and political cinema, often using avant garde forms, moved into mainstream film production, having to adapt their creative vision accordingly. Elio Petri did this with *A ciascuno il suo* (*We Still Kill the Old Way*, 1967). Petri's cinematography is interesting and the film was a moderate success, but it is significant that he needed a book adaptation to make the jump into big-budget production. More indicative is the case of Bertolucci who experienced a period of despair at the critical and financial failure of *Partner* (1968). He abandoned Godardian strategies as 'a masochistic streak in making films that nobody wanted to watch and that the audience would ultimately reject, in the way it knows best (with their feet)' (Ungari and Ranvaud 1987: 52). *Strategia del ragno* (*The Spider's Stratagem*, 1970), based on a Borges novella, was one of the first films made with RAI television money with a projected theatrical release. A critical success, Bertolucci followed it with *Il conformista* (*The Conformist*, 1970) and *Ultimo Tango a Parigi* (*Last Tango in Paris*, 1972). The huge international success of *Ultimo Tango a Parigi*, like Fellini with *La dolce vita* and Rosi with *Salvatore Giuliano* before him, took Bertolucci into an area of production where he could command large budgets, acclaimed technicians and stars and yet still address serious themes, for an international audience.

Secondly, the financial success of those film-makers who, between 1967–70, remained in the alternative, Godardian, mode of film making generally reflected their limited production investment. The films of Ferreri, the Taviani brothers' *Sovversivi* (*Subversives*, 1967) and *Sotto il segno dello scorpione* (*Under the Sign of the Scorpion*, 1969), Valentino Orsini's *I dannati della terra* (*The Damned of the Earth*, 1969) had some critical consideration, but their distribution and exhibition caused problems. The third trend, typified by Visconti and Fellini at its apex, but with imitators at other levels of production (Bellocchio, Damiani, Petri, Maselli, Bolognini) represented mainstream, quality art films with international appeal. Visconti had used the melodrama (family and historical) and the epic to explore political themes and ideas. Fellini's equally spectacular films depended for their marketing strategy on autobiographical links, and the valorizing of the psychology and creative impulse of the artist as an outsider, licensed to comment on society. Antonioni and Pasolini also moved into international, often foreign language, co-productions.

Rosi's *Il caso Mattei* (*The Mattei Affair*, 1972) and *Lucky Luciano* (1973) were produced by Franco Cristaldi and distributed by Cinema International Corporation. *Cadaveri eccellenti* (*Illustrious Corpses*, 1976) was produced by Alberto Grimaldi, an Italian/French co-production, distributed by United Artists. All three were big budget products that did well financially. The success of films like Elio Petri's *Indagine su un cittadino al di sopra di ogni sospetto* (*Investigation of a Citizen Above Suspicion*, 1970), Mauro Bolognini's *Metello* (1970), Giuliano Montaldo's *Sacco e Vanzetti* (1971) and Pasolini's *Il Decamerone* (1971) meant that financiers could see an identifiable market for political or art films. In fact, from 1970 onwards, the trade press continued to monitor the fate of 'difficult films', coming to the surprised conclusion that they could succeed even without stars, provided that they had an interesting subject and a good script. It was noticed that a large number of them were mainstream productions with considerable budgets and that some of them had been picked up by United States distributors. There existed a successful, artistically and thematically serious area of mainstream Italian cinema, whose potential for international earnings was recognized. A pattern emerges of directors' adroit manipulation of existing structures and social practices in the industry in order to continue making films.

The Impact of Commercial Television

Morrione (1978) has shown that the occupations of Rai premises, strikes and calls for change were but the start of a period (1969–76) of intense political activity with the aim of reforming State television organization and putting its finances on a firm footing. Aldo Grasso (1992: 234–40) identifies a move from a model (in the 1950s and early 1960s) where television used old cinema productions indiscriminately to fill its schedules to a model (in the late 1960s and early 1970s) where cinema became a cultural event on television with films presented in seasons arranged around directors, themes, schools, screenwriters, actors, and interpreted by a growing army of critics. In a third phase (1970s and early 1980s) television sought to combat crises in the cinema industry by producing films that would have a conventional cinematic release as well as televisual transmission. The projects chosen were those of established directors – Fellini's *I clowns* and Bertolucci's *Strategia del ragno* in 1970, from the quality or art film end of production, culminating in the 1978 Cannes Film Festival awards to the Taviani's *Padre Padrone* and Olmi's *L'Albero degli zoccoli*. State television investment was made on the basis of commercial return (Gallo 1986: 95–6). RAI also made

other important cultural interventions such as over forty hours of
television directed by Roberto Rossellini, and the prestigious series
of experimental film on RAI 2, which launched the careers of several
young film-makers.

If the Italian art film sector had polarized, so too had the rest of
the industry. State television lured away the mass audience from its
launch in 1953, and some of its favourite genres/*filoni*, such as the
musical review, the *giallo* or detective fiction, and the family drama.
The projected audience is a key factor in the success of a mainstream film. The Doxa Inquiries showed that, by the early 1970s,
the cinema audience had changed and was now predominantly
urban, educated and middle class, and therefore able to appreciate,
and 'read' the complex narratives of art films. That this audience
also existed internationally meant that there was a market for
political cinema, which, in turn, led to increased budgets for film-
makers who had proved themselves able to communicate ideas
clearly (Wood, 2000a).

Increased production costs, tight credit at high costs, the limited
size of the market, difficulties in exporting and lack of forward
planning in the sector contributed to the crisis of the 1970s. In
1976 there were 8,799 films in circulation in Italy (56 per cent of
which were foreign). Although different types of exhibition catered
for different products, the market as a whole was inadequate to
absorb all the films in circulation. The 560 new films contributed to
53.7 per cent of cinema receipts, showing that producers expected
to make most of a film's return rapidly in first-run cinemas (SIAE
1976: 197–200). Angeli claimed that, in 1975/76, 60–70 per cent
of Italian and foreign films took more than 60 per cent of their total
takings in the first two weeks of release and that high production
costs had led to a loss of production and commercial autonomy,
and to an increasingly standardized product (1979: 7–8). There was
a tendency to produce more films at the cheaper end of the market,
costing less than Lire 300 million, thus avoiding competition with
imported American blockbusters like *Jaws*. Many new directors
started out (and continued in) this 'Z-film' area of low-budget
comedies, exploitation and sex films at this time. Miccichè identifies
matching graphs of the slow decline in numbers of spaghetti westerns
(from 108 in 1970–2 to twelve in 1975–8) and the corresponding
increase in erotic comedies and soft porn films (around 250 in the
decade) (1995: 378). Among the many reasons for the explosion of
sex films, the phenomenal growth of commercial television from
1976 must be a factor. Before the satellite sector opened up, sex
films had to carve out their own distribution networks.

The relationship of cinema to television also developed over
time. In 1975 control of the State television networks, the three
RAI channels, was transferred from government to a parliamentary
commission. Although theoretically independent, they were *lottizzati*,

shared out politically After 1976, attempts to beat off competition from private television, particularly Berlusconi's Fininvest group, resulted in policy swings as networks frantically copied private television models, or swung back to the public service model. These swings were reflected in investment in film production. By the end of the 1970s the RAI channels were aware of the cultural capital that could accrue from co-producing quality cinema, allowing the production until the mid-1980s of films whose subjects were not considered commercial enough for film distribution. Other areas of programming were then prioritized when competition with private television channels increased.

The deregulation of broadcasting had the most profound effect, resulting in the decimation of the film industry, while paradoxically favouring the proliferation of private television stations, which, by the early 1990s, together with RAI, consumed 11,000 films a year (Marcotulli 1993: 7). Cinema blamed television for robbing it of audiences, while relying on the sale of television rights to supplement the inadequacies of the cinema distribution market.[4] In addition, by the late 1970s, American direct investment in Italian film production had decreased and, to fill the vacuum, films were increasingly made with television as a co-production partner.

Art Cinema and Prestige Production

Television was not the only culprit in the problems of Italian cinema. What happened to art cinema is interesting and important because it confirms all the difficulties of controlling its own market that the Italian film industry has had since the silent period. Events in Italian society, such as the expansion of televisual offerings and fears of terrorism changed the cinema experience from a collective social experience to a domestic experience. Whereas (at the high point) Italians went to the cinema 16.8 times a year in 1955, this had fallen to twice a year by 1984 (Zaccone Teodosi 1986: 56). The number of cinemas operating started to fall, from 9,439 in 1970 to 8,431 in 1980, massively dropping to 4,143 in 1985 (Brosio and Santagata, 1992: 332). Film production started to decrease, but still remained at over 100 by 1984. Had art cinema remained a low- to mid-budget activity, as in the 1950s, it would have been in direct competition for screen space with low- to mid-budget popular cinema by the mid-1980s, and would have retired hurt from the competition. The alternative route was to aim for the first-run cinema circuits and to compete with other international productions.

Clues to Rosi's success in co-productions with television lie in Grasso's typology of the characteristics of television in the 1980s – fragmentation, archaeology and the domestic (Grasso 1992: 249). The episodic structure of *Cristo si è fermato a Eboli* (*Christ Stopped at Eboli*, 1979) and the shifts from present to past time in *Tre fratelli* (*Three Brothers*, 1981) lend themselves to broadcasting. They are not, however, innovative in form in the way that the work of film-makers formed by RAI 2's 'L'altra domenica' were. Nor are they for a young, cult audience. 'L'altra domenica' launched the careers of, amongst others, Roberto Benigni and Maurizio Nichetti. The series was marked by rapid cutting between items, interactivity with the audience, self-referentiality and a sort of knowingness or complicity between presenters and audience (Veltroni 1992: 15–17). Rosi's films might appeal to the buying public on the basis of the book or opera on which the film is based – or on the basis of choice of director or subject, but the name of the director has become only one element among the many involved in the production equation, which inevitably includes a variety of co-producers, some of whom will be television companies, banks, State contributions, besides the traditional film distributor. Although very detailed statistics are still kept that chart the progress of a film in various sectors of the film market, the whole system has since the mid-1980s been overtaken by developments in other sectors of the audio-visual industries. The majority of returns on a film's production will not nowadays be received from film distribution, but from broadcasting co-production pre-sales, videocassette and other media deals and sponsorship. These are very much more difficult to assess.

The trade press tried to come to a definition of the quality film genre, realizing that this was no longer strictly identifiable with the committed or political film or with the 'difficult' film, or even strictly with auteurist or art cinema, but the dramatic subject matter and the presence of an 'author' are identifying factors. The serious art film had been absorbed into the category of the quality film genre, the alternative being the low-budget avant-garde film. Art cinema was now mainly funded by television, so cliché and self-referentiality formed part of the communication of the older generation of Italian cinema with its television audience. At the same time, the contracting film industry and the increasing interlinking of sectors of the audiovisual industries resulted in the commodification of the director, and a restriction in the range of opportunities open to a film-maker. Although there was still a spread of genres, Italian production increasingly clustered around comedy, drama, pornography.

In the drama category the producers' desire to cover their risks coincided with commercial imperatives of increasing vertical integration in the media (rather than cinema) industries. Alternatively the producer needed 'a good image with the advertising industry and popular comic and/or female stars' (Sabouraud 1987: 46). The increasing cost of production was also an important factor in the future of a film. Carmine Cianfarani (1984: 14) estimated that the cost of a 'good' film increased between 1979 and 1984 from Lire 350 million to Lire 1.5 billion. Such costs inevitably destined the quality film to television co-production and international production and distribution arrangements. Gianni Amelio's complaint that a director's options were predetermined by diminishing audiences and the marginalization of certain genres within film production for the big screen were justified (Schlesinger 1982: 14). The independently produced film had little place to go because, unless the film-maker had managed to attract critical attention, and the film's subject had international interest, it would have to amortize its costs in Italy alone. This might be possible for low-budget comedies or sex films in the 1980s, but not for a film whose form or serious subject might not appeal to the first-run cinema audience.

Between 1979 and 1990 Rosi made four, big-budget films, co-produced with international and television partners. *Cristo si è fermato a Eboli* (*Christ Stopped at Eboli*, 1979) was a four-part co-production including Gaumont and RAI 2 (which put up half the production costs) and was made in two versions, one for the cinema and a four-part television version. It was an adaptation of a prestigious book by Carlo Levi, which is a constant feature of school and university syllabuses. Like Ermanno Olmi's *L'albero degli zoccoli*, *Cristo si è fermato a Eboli* was part of a groundswell of interest in Italy's rural heritage and was much more lyrical in tone than his earlier political films. Both films had a long exploitation period, and are still in circulation on video and DVD. *Tre fratelli* (*Three Brothers*, 1981) combined Gaumont France and distribution agreements with RAI, German and Austrian television partners. It was nominated for an Oscar, which ensured its success abroad, both critically and financially. Chosen to open the Cannes Film Festival, critical articles praised its treatment of the personal and political issues of emigration from the South of Italy. Its success enabled *Cristo si è fermato a Eboli* to find distribution in Britain and America.

Rosi's *Carmen* (1984) was a Franco-Italian co-production, also produced by Gaumont. Gaumont has been an important force in the European film industries growing from a family firm to an international operation practising vertical integration on a modern industrial model by integrating production, distribution and exhibition. As such it is a good illustration of what David Harvey (1990: 147) terms 'flexible accumulation', the defining character-istic of postmodern, globalized economies. New ways of providing financial services and information have made it possible to open up new markets and to 'greatly intensified rates of commercial, techno-logical, and organizational innovation'. By the 1970s, Gaumont, for example, had moved from the production of 'family' cinema to more 'auteurist' projects, combining, under the direction of Daniel Toscan du Plantier, art and commerce. It had formerly avoided art cinema but, for various reasons including the growth of higher education worldwide, increased prosperity and demographic factors, this niche market is now a large one in global terms. This policy was both a strategy to fight the United States majors, and an acknowledgement of changed audiences and patterns of leisure.

Until 1984, Gaumont was a considerable force in the European industry. It was also said unkindly of it that it was an elephants' graveyard, producing glossy films by quality but ageing directors! Rosi's *Carmen* was exceptional in its success and was rumoured to have saved Gaumont France. By the early 1980s, Gaumont had clearly taken several factors into account in evolving its production policy. Firstly, that the cinema audience was now middle to upper middle class in social origin, so that an opera film would have mass appeal to the contemporary, educated, international cinema audience who would pay higher ticket prices and buy the video. Gaumont was used to operating on an international level through co-productions to spread the costs. The average life of an Italian film was two years at this time and most made 90 per cent of their returns in the first year after release (Ferraù 1984: 14). Rosi's film has lasted for almost twenty years, on celluloid, then on the shelves of the video shop (and frequently re-released), in the racks of music shops on vinyl and CD, on videodisk and recently released on DVD (with twenty different language subtitle options). The audio and the visual aspects of filmed opera allow a double exploitation of the film as product and the music as product (Toscan du Plantier 1987: 14).

Rosi's career after 1985 was affected by trends identified in the foregoing sections, and by the Legge Lagorio, which became law in 1985–6. This legislation aimed to reform State intervention in entertainment – cinema, music, dance, circuses – with a common fund for all of them and quotas assigned to each. It aimed to revitalize the national cultural industries by providing tax shelter terms to investors, provided that reinvestment in technological updating, restructuring the industry and renewing cinemas took place. For the first time, television film production was included. The late 1980s were characterized by a fear that the cinema exhibition sector was now completely obsolete, and the cinema-goers' desires correspondingly unimportant (Rossi 1988: 4; Picard 1989: 40). It was also suggested that so successful was the vertical integration practiced by Berlusconi's Fininvest group, that a Penta-distributed film did not have to have a successful cinema release in order to cover its costs. These could be amortized through the sale of advertising slots which interrupt the broadcast of the film, by sales to other Fininvest channels in France, Spain, Germany and so forth, through videocassette pre-sales, and through spin-offs in the form of books, records. However, cinema exhibition is still viewed as essential to stimulating public interest in the film, and as a positive factor in negotiating good prices for advertising space, and the fullest possible exploitation of the product (Della Sala 1988: 19). Rosi's *Cronaca di una morte annunciata* (*Chronicle of a Death Foretold*, 1987) had a complicated production history. It was postponed in 1984 when Gaumont Italia collapsed, so that the preliminary location work in Colombia was a cost that had to be borne by subsequent production arrangements at a time when interest charges could form almost a third of the final production costs.[5] The film was an exploration of personal and cultural relationships in a multicultural Caribbean society, and of the causes of violence within society. Another adaptation of a book by a prestigious author (Gabriel García Márquez), the film's six co-production partners included RAI 2 and French television. Although it was considered a financial success, and attracted good television viewing figures, its reviews were mixed. Critics disliked it as an adaptation and found some of the casting choices – Rupert Everett as Bayardo San Roman who rejects his wife (Ornella Muti) on their wedding night because she is not a virgin – somewhat strange.

Dimenticare Palermo (*To Forget Palermo*, 1990) was a Franco-Italian co-production of the Cecchi Gori company, Berlusconi's Reteitalia television channel and Gaumont. It uses the device of an Italo-American's honeymoon visit to Sicily to discover his roots to explore the Mafia's control of drug trafficking. It was released at the same time, and with the same distributor (Penta) as Fellini's *La voce della luna*,' but Fellini's stars, the well-known comedians Roberto Benigni and Paolo Villaggio, ensured that his film was more successful from first run to provincial cinemas. Rosi's film had similar distribution but less success, going on to sell-through video via Berlusconi's pay-television channel, Telepiù, but failed to find international distribution.

Given the uncertain success of Italian films in this period, State finance had a crucial role as 50 per cent of Italian film production applied for assistance in the 1980s (Brosio and Santagata 1992: 335–6). The first law to cover production, distribution and exhibition was Number 1213 of 1965, to which were regularly added Articles usually entitled 'Extraordinary Interventions in order to...' revealing the uncertainties of the market (Rocca 2003: 105–6). State subventions were obtained from two sources – the Ministero del Turismo e dello Spettacolo, and the Ente Autonomo Gestione Cinema (Eagc). The Eagc came under the Treasury and operated through Cinecittà and the Istituto Luce-Italnoleggio. A prey to the endemic *lottizzazione*, it is not surprising that in 1992–3 subventions had to be managed temporarily by the Ministero dell'Industria, with a resultant stagnation in production. The Ministry of Tourism and Entertainment was abolished in 1993 in the wake of the bribery and corruption scandals and the election of Silvio Berlusconi to government in 1994 had profound effects, resulting in the suspension of mechanisms for subventions to the film industry while alternative structures were put in place. Directors criticized the Eagc for financing films by well-known *auteurs*, with the addition of two or three first films by young directors each year, ignoring anyone in between (Sabouraud 1987: 46–7).

Until new legislation in 1994, Article 28 of the Law set out State support, including a contribution to producers, prizes to producers for quality (13 per cent on exhibition income), contribution to directors (0.4 per cent on exhibition income), prizes to directors for quality, reduced-rate loans (at 5.5 per cent interest) for production costs, reduced rate loans for the exhibition sector, contributions to festivals and seasons, the Venice Biennale, promotion abroad; assistance to organizations and film clubs, the *cinema d'essai* circuit, and for the running of the CSC and the Istituto Luce-Italnoleggio. To obtain access to these reduced-rate loans, a producer had to have a distributor who had agreed to acquire the film, with a contract providing the minimum guarantees, or a minimum plus a percentage of the box-office takings. The distributor's advances took the form of bills of exchange given to the Banca Nazionale del Lavoro, whose cinema section administered the fund. A producer without a distribution deal could not have access to reduced-rate loans, and therefore had to rely on Article 28 money. In addition, a producer who had obtained a reduced rate loan was entitled to apply to the Ministero del Turismo e dello Spettacolo for further contributions towards interest. Article 28 provided for a grant of not more than 30 per cent of production costs of a film designated as 'quality' – that is, 'inspired by artistic and cultural aims, produced with a production formula which took into account the directors, writers, actors and workers' share in the production costs' and was awarded after a film's launch (Silvestretti 1988: 21). For Barile and Rao (1992: 279), Article 28 finance did not always hit its target of helping quality directors, also being abused to subsidize mediocre productions. Requests for all these subventions had to be scrutinized by the censor in order to avoid subsidies to the pornographic film industry.

American media companies bought into Italian distribution from the 1960s, using Italian earnings blocked from export. From 1985 American films dominated the box office and distributors' charts. Blockbusters had longer first runs than Italian films, at higher ticket prices, and appealed to the mass youth market identified by the Doxa Inquiries. Italian films were only able to maintain any position in their own market by concentrating on typically national forms – comedies and sex films. Distribution companies like Academy and Gaumont exploited the often profitable art film niche, but the industry found it very difficult to predict response at the box office. The trade paper, *Giornale dello Spettacolo*, evolved a system of symbols indicating the warmth of reviews in key newspapers. The *La Repubblica* review appeared to be particularly important for art or 'quality' films, since the 1987 Makno market research for Fice (Federazione italiana dei cinematografi d'essai) identified the 'strong' cinema-goer as well educated, well paid, and a high user of other media, especially that newspaper (Zaccone Teodosi 1987: 16–17).

Younger film-makers had to contend with critical snobbery which maintained that the realist style and the serious themes inherited from neorealism were the only valid characteristics of art cinema, and the lack of role models engaging with the everyday, lived reality of Italy (Miccichè 1988: 256). Nanni Moretti's diatribe in *Caro diario* (*Dear Diary*, 1993), railing against the characters in the film he watches for being middle class, pessimistic and self-absorbed is a caricature of one type of unadventurous film. For those who made the jump from working in television, there were many others who were unable to do so. As a result, there were few films about terrorism but a proliferation of *gialli*, crime films rehearsing public concerns. Comedies with carabinieri or firemen heroes harked back to earlier models of gender relations. Films that had an in-depth distribution in the 1980s were high- to mid-budget features that (with the exception of Dario Argento's films) did not usually travel outside Italy. Made by small independent production companies, often in association with Cecchi Gori, they provided career continuity for comics Adriano Celentano, Paolo Villaggio, Lino Banfi, Luigi Proietti, Carlo Verdone, Enrico Montesano amongst others, female stars Eleonora Giorgi and Ornella Muti, and their directors. Below them lay layers of critically despised Z-movies.

Cinema at the Barricades

By the early 1990s the increasing globalization of the media industries led to fundamental difficulties for Italian cinema in gaining access to its own screens – big or small. The crash of Gaumont Italia in 1985 created a vacuum in the distribution sector, which American companies hastened to fill. The Gaumont exhibition sector consisted of fifty-three first-run theatres in the main cities, a total of 49,396 seats, which was bought by the Cannon group for a rumoured $15 million (Rossi 1985: 23). This represented a noticeable change in the equilibrium of the Italian film as Cannon's production profile had generally consisted of low-quality genre films. This circuit subsequently formed the basis of Berlusconi's Fininvest Group's Cinema Cinque chain, enabling their distribution arm, Penta, to compete in first run cinemas with the big American companies.

Imports of films and television programmes for the whole of Europe in 1990 (publicized during the 1993 GATT talks) were $3,719 million, and $247 million. Some idea of the profound consequences for European cinema can be gauged from Roddick's analysis of the situation in 1989. In that year, in eleven European countries with a combined population of over 350 million people (Austria, Belgium, France, Germany, Greece, Italy, the Netherlands, Norway, Spain, Sweden and the UK), 96 million people saw American films.

36 per cent saw European films... Of those European films, a further 9 per cent were entirely American financed. So, four times as many people saw American films as saw European ones. And, for the films in the sample, (43 in all), the vast majority of the tickets sold – 87.2%, or nearly 114 million people – were for films which were distributed by American or American-owned companies. (Roddick 1990: 37–8)

In this situation it became very difficult to make films, even as a well-known, quality director.

Not being a box-office success became a pattern in the Italian film industry. Some films waited a considerable time for release after the granting of their exhibition licence, their poor distribution making very little money. Giacomo Martini (1992: 25) called these the 'ghost films', which proved that investing in Italian cinema was a big mistake. Negotiating with multiple co-production partners including television demanded skills which changed the producer's role and led to the emergence of the power of the rights holder who would acquire packages of films with which to make deals with television (Cosulich 1987: 4).

What are the Chances for Italian Cinema in the 2000s?

Apart from films on the festival circuits, 'quality' film is the main form of Italian film that the 'ordinary cinema-goer' outside Italy is likely to see. This is not to say that other Italian film productions lack creativity or technical excellence but, for the reasons explored here, they do not reach a large, international audience.

Italian cinema has moved from a relatively simple capitalist model of production to an increasingly fragmented and complex model as the media industries developed their contemporary, globalized form. A very individualistic, unconventional film has to be made within the low-budget sector of the media industries usually with State support and/or by making a co-production agreement with television. Mid-budget productions, also made with television finance, must appeal to 'mixed audiences comprised of both art-house and mainstream elements' (Ilott 1996: 19). High budget films have to be exploited in as many territories as possible, that is internationally, and in as many forms as possible (cinema release, pay-television broadcast, satellite then terrestrial broadcast, videocassette, games, music cassette, DVD and so on). Big-budget films inevitably have complex financial arrangements including finance from major production and distribution companies in more than one European country and, if they are aimed at United States and worldwide distribution, the presence of Miramax has been crucial.

For Italian films, as for other European films, the achievement of a Miramax partnership has meant the potential to achieve good profits on worldwide distribution. In 1993 the Disney organization took over Miramax, the independent US distributor that had specialized in co-production and distribution arrangements with independent, foreign-language and English-language art films. Although Miramax, headed by the Weinsteins, has so far been able to retain its separate identity within the Disney organization, its absorption enabled Miramax to take advantage of elements of the vertical integration of the parent company. In particular, it has been able to draw on the marketing and publicity expertise of Buena Vista, so that any Italian film that included Miramax in its production arrangements was assured of international exploitation in depth.

The year 1993 marked a watershed both in terms of how Italian film-makers had to conceptualize their world on screen, and also as a symbolic moment after which the Italian film industry had to fight for its own autonomy faced with the consequences of increasing media globalization. Italian film-makers had to decide, at a fundamental level, who their projected audience was and how, therefore, to tell their stories. For a film-maker, the choices represented by accounts of how we in the West experience the world in the late twentieth and early twenty-first century translate into economic models at the level of production, and political models at the levels of subject matter and audience address. Big-budget films must conform to mainstream, that is, American styles of film-making, using international stars, aiming at audiences in American-dominated cinema chains. The alternative, for Italian film-makers aiming at an international audience, is to develop stories that will appeal to sections of the population that, although small in terms of the vertical slicing of the market in one nation, add up to a significant audience horizontally across many markets. Such an audience can consist of Italophiles who have studied Italian, or art history, or who holiday in Italy, or who are members of the large and significant Italian diaspora in North and South America, Europe and Australasia.

European states, and the European Union have attempted to combat the accumulative tendencies of global media companies by creating a space for expressions of local and national identity. Italy's Article 28 State subventions were superseded in 1994 by the new Law Number 153, Article 8 which set up the *Fondo di Garanzia*, intended to free Italian films of reliance on television co-production deals. It would advance up to 90 per cent (later 70 per cent) of a film's budget. In return, the producer had to return 70 per cent of the income from pre-sales and box-office receipts. Although technically this enabled film-makers to make films of greater risk and originality, it still did not address the problem of access to the market (Corsi 2001: 144). There are simply not enough Italian cinemas to absorb the level of Italian, let alone American products.

Morever, the exhibition sector has, since the 1980s, been dominated by a vertically integrated oligarchy, the Cecchi Gori company and Berlusconi's Fininvest. Financial problems in the Cecchi Gori company, and the imprisonment of Vittorio Cecchi Gori in 2002, worsened the situation for independent producers such as Elda Ferri, who are obliged either to make deals with these owners of the largest exhibition chains, or risk a long wait for a release and little box-office returns.[6] Italian film-makers are also adept at taking advantage of the European Union's MEDIA programme. Film directors cannot but help, therefore, having to engage with not one but many cultural industries and institutions in order to continue making films.

Rosi's *La tregua* (*The Truce*, 1996) was unfortunate: Miramax bought distribution rights when they had also bought the rights to Robert Benigni's *La vita è bella* (*Life is Beautiful*, 1997), deciding on saturation marketing for the latter film. Benigni provides another example of big-budget 'quality' cinema and a different response to the realities of global film production. Like Nanni Moretti, he is an actor/director with production and distribution interests so that the guarantee of quality that both represent is that of the experience of communicating with the actor's ideas and creative vision. Both are identified as film-makers who successfully differentiate themselves from television production by appealing to intellectuals (Repetto and Tagliabue 2000: 20). In Benigni's case he pulls off the difficult task of also appealing to another large target audience: children.

It is a truism of the film industry and film studies that comedies and comedians do not find success outside their national borders, so that the phenomenal international success of Benigni bears scrutiny. From success in television Roberto Benigni took control of his career by moving into production and direction and well-chosen appearances in English-language films such as Jim Jarmusch's *Down By Law* (US, 1986) brought him to international attention. He owns his own production company, Melampo Cinematografica. The case of *La vita è bella*, however, shows the importance of production flair in moving into larger scale, 'quality' cinema. The independent producer, Elda Ferri, was instrumental in developing the subject and the rights, preparing the co-production arrangements and the creative 'package' and then selling it on. In the case of *La vita è bella*, Miramax partnership meant multiple prints of the film and access to lucrative United States and world markets. Making a comedy about the Holocaust guaranteed the film notoriety and much free publicity from debates in the media (Viano 1999: 158). Hailed as Italy's best loved comic, Benigni's style is now more universally 'popular' than it was in his early television work, reflecting a deliberate intention to widen his audience appeal.

At the narrative level, the film falls into two parts. The first is characterized by spectacular, sweeping shots of 1930s Tuscany, bathed in golden light as Guido courts and marries his wife. The second part is altogether more monochrome and visually limited as Guido constructs a fantasy explanation of life in the concentration camp for his son, Giosuè. The film won three Oscars in 1998 and was phenomenally successful financially, enabling Elda Ferri and Benigni to put together another package, this time for Medusa (Berlusconi), Cecchi Gori and Miramax, *Pinocchio* (2002). The film was hyped as Italy's most expensive production at €40million ($40.2million) and was Italy's Oscar candidate. It was released in one-third of Italy's cinemas in October 2002 with 940 prints, making $31million in Italy by mid-November 2002. *Pinocchio* was both a big-budget adaptation of a widely translated classic of children's literature and very Italian in its setting and cruel humour. As such, it fulfilled Montini's criteria for international success, quality and Italian stereotypes (F.F. 2002: 4). Other 'quality' film directors also draw on universal human events and experiences, on the cultural capital of familiarity with Italian art history, culture and landscape, or the prestige of Italian fashion.

The *European Cinema Statistical Yearbook*'s material on vertical integration between distribution and exhibition and analysis of the trend towards multi-screen cinemas indicate a continued polarization in the European film industry. The ideal of the modestly financed film which brings in many times its production costs becomes more difficult with the development of the multiplex cinema, which is usually owned and programmed by an American company. The contemporary cinema-going audience in Italy is young (66 per cent are under 35) and well-educated, the most loyal categories being students and the well paid (Casetti et al. 1998: 51–2). They are also consumers of film in other media often compiling their own *videothèque* (Zacconi Teodosi 1987: 16–17). The international, quality cinema is one solution to the problem of maintaining European cultural presence. Its form, however, provides a metaphor for the increasing loss of national specificity. Predictably enough, 'quality' films have not pleased critics. 'Such films look spectacular, feature high-profile stars, and sometimes rake in returns at the box office ... but they're always likely to lack the conviction that film-makers can bring to more modest projects, made in their own language and rooted in their own culture' (MacNab 1997: 52–3).

The difficulties involved in film-making were spelled out starkly in an industry analysis of Italian cinema in 2002 (ANICA 2003: 14). Of the 130 Italian films produced in 2002 (including co-productions), fifty-two attracted state subsidy. Only sixteen of them made more than €1 million at the box office and, moreover, 87 per cent of the total box-office take of €116.5 million was concentrated on those sixteen titles, leaving the remaining 200 films (including 100 new releases) to share not much more that €15million. Those film-makers wishing to develop beyond the confines of national, low-budget film have the choice between the commercial, family film, or the 'quality' film genre. Once in the 'quality' sector, it appears to be difficult to return to modestly financed production. Successful film-makers become trapped by the structures of the industry, with the result that they are offered big-budget, international, complex projects where polemical debate and incisive critiques of society are inappropriate. These projects, characterized by technical expertise, set pieces of showy mise en scène, complex narratives, serious ideas, Italian stereotypes, and the personal signature and commitment of one person, the director/author, provide definitions of this type of film.

The international business strategies of companies like Miramax, combining the power of Hollywood's production and marketing with European culture and creativity, have been called 'Globowood' by *Newsweek* (quoted in Rodier 2002b: 1). Miramax, like Berlusconi's Fininvest companies, has relied on a constant stream of quality film products to feed its international cinema, satellite and media interests. Italy's current economic problems and the difficulties in obtaining finance from traditional sources, government funds and pay television, have favoured the development of international co-productions, such as Gianni Amelio's €5 million family drama, *Le chiavi di casa* (*The Keys of the House*, 2004) staring Charlotte Rampling and Kim Rossi Stuart, and other established directors and producers are being courted by international partners (Rodier 2002a). It remains to be seen what effects the film funding Silvio Berlusconi's government put in place will have, and whether Italian film-makers will be able to make films addressing their own reality and the contemporary world – and whether we will see them.

2

Popular Cinema and Box-office Hits

Genres have always been important commercially to Italian cinema, and their codes and conventions, drawing on previous cultural traditions such as the *commedia dell'arte*, epic, melodrama and opera, were established in the pre-sound era. Categorizing films by type or genre developed as a strategy for reducing the commercial risk involved in investing large sums of money in a product which would hopefully make a profit some months later. As described in Chapter 1, box-office popularity was central to the identification and development of Italian genre types. This chapter will therefore explore the nature of Italian popular genres, and which genre elements have a local or an international appeal. Nonetheless, the sheer volume of Italian films described as 'popular', that is (with notable exceptions such as the *commedia all'italiana* of the 1960s) not given critical value or described in terms of quality, indicates their importance, to their Italian audience, in constructing views of everyday reality.

Italy has never had an established studio system on the American model. The large production companies of the silent period, such as Itala, Ambrosio, Cines, were influential, international and had their own studios, but they did not last. Later attempts, such as that of Dino De Laurentiis and Dinocittà, to create a studio were unsuccessful. Italian producers and distributors have held the power to decide what films were made and which projects would never see the light of day. Their roles have evolved in the face of external commercial and political factors such as the market hegemony of American distributors, the proliferation of commercial television and the contraction of the number of cinema screens. Italian producers and distributors aimed to present an annual slate of different types of film, to minimize commercial risk, but some producers, notably Dario Argento and his brother Claudio, found a niche and specialized in one genre, and other film-makers have maintained lucrative careers out of the critical gaze in the production of soft porn films.

Italian producers, directors and distributors have responded creatively to changes in public taste and to the dynamic development of Italian society. Historical changes are, however, difficult to integrate in Giuseppe Perrella's (1981) attempt to construct a structuralist model of the Italian film industry, in which fixed categories of individual producers, distributors, directors, stars varied in importance according to the genre of film. For a popular, big-budget Italian drama, producer, distributor, stars and creative team would be important factors in its success; for a low-budget comedy the star would be the key factor, whereas for the porno film, the star, director, creative team and producer would be of considerably less importance than the promise of the subject matter itself.

Some commercial genre categories were so wide that formulating a set of common themes, styles, iconography, conventions, typical stars, audience address and typical audience is impossible. The industry category 'drama', for example covered films as diverse as Michelangelo Antonioni's *La signora senza camelie* (*Lady Without Camelias*, 1952), an 'art film' which made very little money, and Rafaello Matarazzo's melodrama, *I figli di nessuno* (*Nobody's Children*, 1950), which was hugely popular, coming third in that year's box-office list. Themes such as the avenging hero appeared in popular mythological films and the *giallo*, or detective fiction. Typical style was often difficult to define given the fact that Italian creative workers tended to work across genres and budget categories, so that a low-budget comedy could be marked by creative and spectacular filming of location in excess of generic expectation. Well-known writers also worked across genres. Suso Cecchi D'Amico, the doyenne of Italian screenwriters, worked on neorealist films and most of Visconti's films, but also wrote comedy screenplays, Luigi Comencini's *Le avventure di Pinocchio* (*The Adventures of Pinocchio*, 1972) and family melodramas. Italian stars of whatever level of fame often migrated from one genre to another. Character actors such as Tomas Milian, Gian Maria Volonté and, more recently, Anna Galiena and Stefano Accorsi, like international stars such as Claudia Cardinale and Marcello Mastroianni, worked on popular comedies and genre films as well as art cinema productions. Mythological genre films used international stars, familiar stories and logical, linear narratives to conquer a mass audience (Spinazzola. 1974: 330). These elements ensure that some of these films survive on mass delivery systems such as satellite and cable, but they also now have an international, cineliterate, cult audience that appreciates the camp aspects of hypermasculinity, cheap sets and the ideological values of fifty years ago.

It should also be noted that, although Italian directors presenting their films at international film festivals almost always complain about the difficulties of film-making in Italy, there are several directors who have had extraordinarily prolific careers in the industry. Augusto Genina's career lasted from 1912 to 1954, and Carmine Gallone's from 1914 to 1962 (Redi 1999: 56). In the 1940s and 1950s a small group of film-makers, Mario Mattoli, Anton Giulio Bragaglia, , Riccardo Freda, Stefano Vanzina, Giorgio Bianchi, Camillo Mastrocinque, and others, made anything between three and four films a year. In the drama category, Mario Monicelli has made films well into his eighties. At the pulp fiction level, Umberto Lenzi, Michele Soavi, Lucio Fulci have made large numbers of low-budget films, moving from genre or *filone* to *filone* reflecting changes in public taste. Dino Risi, Ettore Scola and Luigi Comencini have also had long and prolific careers. Alberto Sordi, Totò, Adriano Celentano, Carlo Verdone are comics with tens of films to their name.

Although the economic context is key, any study of Italian popular cinema therefore has to take into account a multitude of contextual factors. Italian genres are flexible structures, reflecting the fact that the Italian film industry has traditionally been a precarious enterprise and, until the late 1970s, the bulk of its production fell within the mid-budget category. As Chapter 1 has shown, producers have attempted to offset the risks involved in covering their costs by jumping on the bandwagon of a successful production and copying its characteristics, leading to the *filoni* phenomenon. At the same time as a *filone* is exploited, a level of product differentiation will take place in order to test the market for change. Thus, within the mythological genre, there are collections of sub-*filoni* – stories set in a Roman, Greek, Carthaginian, biblical or Egyptian historical past, stories of pirates, saracens and the crusades, and stories revolving around individual, mythical figures (Spinazzola. 1974: 330). Elements of these could be combined with the norms of the comedy, or musical, to provide *filoni*, which an audience would interpret on the basis of past knowledge and expectations, resulting in *Ercole contro Moloch* (*Hercules versus Moloch*, Giorgio Ferroni, 1964) (Greek versus Carthaginian), Riccardo Freda's *Maciste alla corte del Gran Khan* (1964, the gentle giant of *Cabiria* goes to the far east by a master of suspense films), *Totò contro Maciste* and *Totò e Cleopatra* (Fernando Cerchio, 1962 and 1963, comedy parodies of the genre). Other genres fragment in this way. Dino Risi's *In nome del popolo italiano* (*In the Name of the Italian People*, 1971; comedy political thriller) and Roberto Benigni's *La vita è bella* (*Life is Beautiful*, 2001; comedy heritage film/holocaust film). The *filoni* phenomenon to a large extent explains why Italian film genres are such hybrids, and why elements considered to be characteristic of postmodernism are present from the 1950s onwards. The apeing, for example of *Star Wars* (George Lucas, United States, 1977), *Cleopatra* (Joseph Mankiewicz, 1963), or *Il Decamerone* (*Decameron*, Pier Paolo Pasolini, 1971), in Italian films with a fraction of the budget, inevitably led to a high level of pastiche, parody and ironic quoting of the original. *Il Decamerone*, in particular, led to many films featuring naughty nuns. Italian popular cinema therefore presupposes an audience for whom making sense of disparate generic regimes is a factor in their pleasure, and training in the skills of making hybrid narratives comprehensible to the mass audience has enabled some film-makers to conquer international markets. Giuseppe Tornatore's *Cinema Paradiso* (1989, comedy/heritage/family film) and *Malèna* (2000; war/coming of age/soft porn), and Marco Tullio Giordana's *La meglio gioventù* (*The Best of Youth*, 2003; historical epic/weepie) are examples.

Prestige Production and Literary Adaptation

The appeal of different genres is class based. Entrepreneurs could aim for the mass market, or for the 'quality' audience who would pay more for their tickets in return for a 'quality' experience. The much-publicized collaboration of the writer, Gabriele D'Annunzio in devising the look and grandiose language of the intertitles of Giovanni Pastrone's *Cabiria* (1914) is an example of Italian producers' annexation of high culture forms in order to snare an educated audience.

In the 1920s competition for Italian cinema in its own markets from Hollywood increased greatly. This threat was undoubtedly a factor in 1926 in the choice of a prestigious adaptation of a Pirandello play, which would be likely to deliver the 'quality' audience necessary for the film to cover its costs. The second title credit of *Enrico IV* (Amleto Palermi, 1926) firmly establishes the film's credentials as 'A poem by Luigi Pirandello'. The form of the film owes as much to commercial considerations as to the individual vision of Palermi. It combines the use of exterior long shots, elaborate interiors and costumes, multiple sets and an established star, Conrad Veidt. The story of a nobleman who, after an accident, takes refuge in madness, believing himself to be Henry IV, the film's mise en scène also delivers spectacle, predominantly through framings in depth, such as the early shot of horses in several planes on the road by the river, the cavalcade in which Enrico's accident occurs and particularly the scene of his accident. Enrico falls off his horse in a beautifully composed extreme long shot. The winding road, bare hills and spiky trees all convey a sense of desolation. On the one hand these spectacular long shots are rather excessive, especially when contrasted with the interactions between Matilde and Belcredi, or the servants. On the other, audiences would admire the artistic success of the *mise en scène* in the staging of the story.

Filming the classics of Italian and European culture rapidly established itself as a commercial strategy to attract an international, educated audience. When the Italian film industry experienced the crisis of the mid-1970s, cinematic adaptations of literary classics increased to such a degree that most art film directors made one. Visconti, Fellini, Bertolucci, Bolognini, Pasolini, the Taviani brothers, Rosi all chose to adapt well-known novels. Giovanni Verga, Vasco Pratolini, Luigi Pirandello, Gabriele d'Annunzio, Alberto Moravia are among the well-known names. Stalwarts of mid- to high-budget Italian film dramas, such as Dino Risi, also sought out popular books for much the same reasons. Many of these literary adaptations were made with the collaboration first of Italian state television, RAI, and later with multi-national television input. In the case of RAI, the strategy of commissioning literary adaptations by established film-makers was intended to consolidate channel prestige and reach a mass audience, especially if the texts adapted were widely studied in schools and universities. Since 1980, vertical integration in the media industries has favoured this type of cinema. The owners of television stations usually also own, or have commercial arrangements with, newspapers, magazines, recorded music interests and publishing houses, so that film/book tie-ins can be exploited. In the wake of the unexpected success of Silvio Soldini's *Pane e tulipani* (*Bread and Tulips*, 2000), the screenplay was published as a boxed set with the video (Soldini and Leondeff 2000). More recently, the international appeal of the texts adapted has been important and authors, such as Gabriel García Márquez, Leonardo Sciascia, Carlo Levi, Pirandello, whose work has been translated into many languages, have been targetted.

The Opera Film

Opera films were amongst the most popular cinema entertainments in the pre-sound era, and a genre that allowed cinema to beat off competition from theatre and the new technologies of radio and recorded music by offering a visual as well as an aural experience (Spinazzola 1974: 56). Local singers could provide the sung accompaniment to sets and decors that would be out of the financial reach of a provincial theatre. Italy's musical heritage of opera and melodrama was a source of national pride, soundly rooted as it was in both national and popular culture. Spinazzola (1974: 57) suggests that the resurgence of opera and musical drama in the aftermath of the Second World War satisfied the emotional needs of the Italian population in a way that imported American films never could, and the presence of this type of film in the annual box-office top ten between 1945 and 1950 bears this out. The singers Tito Gobbi and Gino Bechi made many films in this period. Mario Costa's *Il barbiere di Siviglia* (*The Barber of Seville*, 1946) and *Pagliacci* (1949), starring Tito Gobbi and Gina Lollobrigida and Carmine Gallone's *Rigoletto* (1947) all delivered famous performers and, for the time, sumptuous sets. Carmine Gallone was one of the most prolific and successful directors of popular films whose *Casa Ricordi* (*The House of Ricordi*, 1954), produced by Ricordi to celebrate their 150th anniversary was ninth in that year's lists. It featured extracts from classic nineteenth-century operas sung by established stars of the day, and gave Marcello Mastroianni his first role, as Donizetti.

Musical films of all sorts were a popular genre aimed at audiences in southern Italy up until the 1960s, marrying stereotypical plots of love, misunderstanding, sacrifice, stern fathers and happy ends, with regional popular songs. Ettore Giannini's *Carosello napoletano* (*Neapolitan Roundabout*, 1952) was one of the best examples of this genre. Starring Sophia Loren amongst others, it used the form of the theatrical review to introduce a varied succession of songs and sketches.

In the late 1970s and 1980s, opera films became a significant genre again. It would have been an important consideration when putting together the production package of Francesco Rosi's *Carmen* (1984) that it was a classic opera, and therefore not likely to go out of fashion, or be a passing fancy. This gave Rosi's film what the film business calls 'legs'. Opera films are successful financially on their first runs and have a virtually infinite shelf life amongst 'opera buffs', in the same way that classic vinyl or CD recordings have. Producers noticed that opera audiences were getting younger and bigger and, being visually (or at least televisually) literate, were able to appreciate the constantly changing spectacle and emotional charge of opera (Allsop 1989: 22). On a more basic level, *Carmen* could be said to contain its potential of sex and violence, then as now a staple of mass cinema entertainment Moreover, the 'legs' phenomenon is assisted by the previously mentioned vertical integration

Rosi's *Carmen* used the full resources of his film language to make the 'story' of the opera clear and understandable to his international, mass audience, delivering spectacular images while suggesting a deeper level of complexity and interpretation. Most of the film was shot in Ronda, which not only has one of the oldest bull rings in Spain, but is also divided into two, having an upper and lower town. This allowed Rosi to shoot in several planes, which is one of his prime tools both to vary the visuals during the songs and to connote other levels of meaning. The casting of the principals mainly reflected the iron necessities of the marketplace, but the stars were also essential in making the story comprehensible and here cultural and gender clichés are brought into play. The two male leads were played by established opera stars, Placido Domingo and Ruggero Raimondi, whose world-wide reputations sell records. Tambling (1987: 17) suggests that the cinematic close up emphasizes Domingo's miscasting in terms of age and looks, but it can be argued that these provide a metaphor for the rigidity of Don Jose's world view and guiding principles, motivating the challenge which he represents to Carmen. Rosi and his producers chose the American soprano, Julia Migenes Johnson, for her physical appearance and performance. She fitted with Rosi's conception of Carmen's character, combining 'intelligence and independence, eroticism and sensuality', which would appeal to a mass audience (Wood 1998: 293).

Arias from classic operas are integrated into a wide variety of Italian films, constantly recurring in classics of art cinema. Visconti's *Ossessione* showed how rooted opera is in popular culture in scenes where Giovanna's husband, Bragana, takes part in local singing competitions. Visconti used the words of the arias as an ironic counterpoint to the story of adulterous passion, a technique taken up in *Senso* (1954), and by Bertolucci later in his film, *La luna* (1979). Part of the audience pleasure is the recognizing of the arias and deducing their significance narratively. With vertical integration in the entertainment industries, the soundtracks of more recent Italian films gain considerable marketing significance. The rock star, Luciano Ligabue's first feature *Radiofreccia* (1998) recreated a small 1970s radio station. Some of the anarchy, the lure of sex and drugs and rock and roll, is conveyed, mainly via the character of working-class, heroin-addicted Freccia (Stefano Accorsi). However the main protagonist, who structures the narrative and provides the voiceover, is the one who sells out to commercial influences on radio and, as he says at the end, 'people like me always end up marrying a girl called Ilaria and having a couple of children'. Saying that, and swathed in clouds of nostalgia, he signs off on the airwaves for the last time and closes the radio station. It is left to the emblematic soundtrack to suggest the passions and emotions of 1970s youth and the issues of cultural protest are not developed. Relatively cheap and portable audio recording equipment, pop music and the photocopier were the technologies used to empower young people in the 1970s. Relatively cheap and portable digital audio and video equipment, the cheap personal computer and access to the Internet are being seized by the disempowered young of the early 2000s.

The success of *Fuori del mondo* (*Out of this World*, Giuseppe Piccione, 1999) depends in equal part on the performances of Silvio Orlando and Margherita Buy and Luigi Einaudi's score. In the case of contemporary film, a good soundtrack is not only a strategy to

deepen the resonances of the contemporary setting, but a sound
commercial ploy.

Melodrama

Music was, of course, an integral part of the dramatic form that
became known as melodrama, which, as Peter Brooks (1976: 15)
noted, 'became the principal mode for uncovering, demonstrating
and making operative the essential moral universe in a post-sacral
era'. The musical score's emotional content helped to make meanings
absolutely clear. As Marcia Landy (1998: 11) has suggested, affect,
the articulation of emotion on the screen, allows connections to be
made, through experiential recognition, to 'a conception of world
and life'. Social values and practices that often remain unquestioned
may thus be recognized uncritically, and function in the construction
of commonly accepted values in society at large, that is, Gramsci's
concept of hegemony. The presence of Einaudi's haunting score in
Fuori del mondo conveys a sense of loss which was echoed in the
film's publicity – 'The things we want always happen at the wrong
moment, too soon, too late'. The sense of loss – loss of opportunities
for passion and self-fulfillment, loss of caring values in Italian
society – is made 'visually present' to the audience (Brooks 1994:
18). Caterina (Margherita Buy) is a young nun whose grey habit
signals her outsider status in terms of passion but licences her to
evoke religious principles. A dry-cleaning ticket in a foundling's
clothing leads her to Ernesto (Silvio Orlando), whose hypochondria
and loneliness indicate the self-absorption that have prevented him
from achieving his potential, or a family. The search for the baby's
mother therefore becomes a search for the healthy re-constitution of
the family, and of healthy values in society. The interesting tensions
in this melodrama revolve around the disappearance of the mother
and her reluctance to assume the traditional maternal role, which
was always lauded as the bedrock of Italian society. Repetitions of
instances of selfishness in random characters encountered during
the search, and Ernesto's reluctance to assume the traditional male
control over the family, hint at the damage that traditional gender
roles inflicted on both men and women, while the physical presence
of the baby and its needs asserts the necessity of the family for a
healthy society.

Melodrama is linked to the development of modernity. Argentieri
(1998) makes some very interesting observations about melodrama
in Italian cinema under fascism. His analyses of plots, in particular,
uncover repeated returns to themes of women leaving their husbands
or children, of inconvenient pregnancies and illegitimate children,
of train journeys and quests. Women acquire a greater narrative
agency in wartime films but are still all too often punished in the

last reel for acting autonomously. However, in their explorations of the reception of melodramas in England and Spain respectively, Janet Thumim (1992) and Jo Labanyi (2000: 167) identify the skills of the female spectator of reading against the grain of patriarchal ideologies. Melodrama is usually considered to flourish in times of social change, and to provide through intensity of emotional involvement the opportunity to rehearse safely and work through new ways of acting and being in the world. As Chapter 4 will explore, melodrama was a particularly popular and important genre in the late 1940s and 1950s, becoming known as 'pink neorealism' in recognition of the fact that social inequalities were being rehearsed but through the emotional rather than the intellectual agenda of neorealist films.

Comedies, Comics and the *Commedia all'italiana*

Comedies have always been a staple of Italian film production, their success indicating that varieties of Italian humour touch deep chords in the national psyche. In attempts to categorize the vast output, critics have suggested the mid-1970s as an important turning point in the history of Italian comedy. Up to that date they observe a clear linear development from pre-cinematic models, and regular patterns of production, themes and exploitation (D'Amico 1985: viii). After that date, the explosion of commercial television makes the picture more complicated, with a completely symbiotic relationship between the small and the big screen, and a new generation of comics, Roberto Benigni, Maurizio Nichetti, Nanni

Moretti, Massimo Troisi, Francesco Nuti and others. In fact the situation is more complex, with a greater degree of continuity from earlier models than is generally recognized. Significantly enough, those comics illustrating a high degree of continuity with traditional models are not those exported outside Italy, neither do they make any claim to the status of high culture.

The grotesque and the excessive are located in plot, performance and gags in Italian comedy, by their targets, or structured absences, indicating contemporary preoccupations. Although the Golden Age of Italian film comedy is considered to lie between 1962 and 1969, modern Italian comedies had their roots in theatrical traditions of the *commedia dell'arte* and 1930s American comedies. Italian comedies of the 1930s were generally set in lower middle-class milieux and rehearsed new behaviour patterns. In *Batticuore* (*Heartbeat*, Mario Camerini, 1939) the heroine, Arlette (Assia Norris) is the star pupil of a school for thieves in Paris. She robs the ambassador of a vaguely Central European country and, when he apprehends her in the cinema in which she has taken refuge, her thieves' patter about sick mothers and wind whistling through the windows is inconveniently mirrored by an identical scene on the big screen. Arlette is recruited to steal watches and is groomed as an aristocrat in order to be able to attend parties and rob her target, an English lord (John Lodge), with whom she falls in love. Arlette lacks confidence out of her own social circle but her innate goodness, and grooming in how to wear beautiful evening dresses, secures the desired outcome of lavish wedding to the English lord in the final reel.

Similar preoccupations with modernity and new possibilities for women can be seen in *La vita è bella* (*Life is Beautiful*, Ludovico Bragaglia, 1943) where the heroine, Nadina (Maria Mercader) is contrasted with her eccentric sister, Virginia (Anna Magnani). Nadina is pale, blonde and active, usually dressed in jodhpurs as she runs her farm, incorporating modern agricultural practices. By her example and kindness she rehabilitates the young Count Alberto (Alberto Rabagliati) whose gambling has reduced him to tramping the road. Virginia is starting her singing career with lessons from Leone (Carlo Campanini) who is in love with her. The dress codes of the two women indicate the contrast between restraint/purposeful work and excess/entertainment but, although they both marry in the final reel, Magnani's performance is so colourful and energetic as to cast Mercader into the shade. Performance cues suggest the attractions of freedom and eccentricity.

Stylistic variations, jumps in comic tone occur even in conventional comedies. In Mario Camerini's *Il signor Max* (*Mister Max*, 1937), in which the characters return to their 'rightful' social stratum at the end, changes in tone reveal the desire to transgress boundaries of behaviour, class or taste, which is a common factor in Italian comedy (Viganò 1995: 29). De Gaetano (1999: 10) explains how the grotesque, deriving from this constant transgressive impulse, is used to emphasize the constructedness of most social representations. As such, it occurs in many comedies during and after the Second World War, such as *Campo de' Fiori* (Mario Bonnard, 1943) in which Peppino, a fishmonger in the market of the title (Aldo Fabrizi) has a romantic adventure outside his class, only to return to Elide, the vegetable seller (Anna Magnani) at the end.

In the wake of the forces of liberation, American films were imported in great numbers, conquering an enthusiastic audience for whom popular fascist cinema of strong heroes and class conflicts seemed increasingly old fashioned. The Italian political system as it evolved after the Second World War with its succession of coalition governments was, in fact, government by an élite class. The perception of the mass of the population was that they were not represented, and their views not considered. In addition, the economic boom that started at the end of the 1940s changed Italy from a predominantly rural, geographically and socially static country to a modern, consumer economy. Access to a modern infrastructure of water, electricity, education, roads, meant exposure to new experiences and internal immigration fuelled the process of industrialization. Traditional social and gender power relations were inevitably questioned. A sense of unease with rapid social change and the lack of convincing role models finds its expression in the complex plots and heightened emotionality of Italian comedy.

Masolino D'Amico's (1985: 6–7) analyses of the period from 1945 to 1975 show that cinema-goers in the immediate post-war period preferred American comedies but that, as Italian production increased, Italian comedy's market share rose to a regular 20 per cent to 30 per cent of annual production. Comedies topped the box-office lists fourteen times in this period, in spite of competition from American films. D'Amico suggests that a calculation of the profits of comedies is impossible but that, as a general rule, they cost less than serious films. They usually used realist conventions, contemporary settings not requiring elaborate sets or costumes and did not feature numerous characters. The largest part of the budget therefore went on the main protagonist, or a few famous names in the ensemble films, so that even modest box-office returns represented a good profit. Adding up D'Amico's estimates of the number of comedies produced between 1945–6 and 1974–5 results in a grand total of 966 films. Several *filoni* can be identified in this huge output. This section attempts a synthesis of the main currents in this important area.

In their study of the history of the *commedia all'italiana*, comedy Italian-style, Adriano Aprà and Patrizia Pistagnesi (1986: 17) make the point that comedy can be considered a genre in that there is a 'recurrent presence of directors, actors, screenwriters and producers in the many films produced from the 1950s to the 1970s', but not a genre in the Hollywood sense. Stylistic variations, the intrusion of serious issues, historical settings, authorial stylistic flourishes, the use of realist conventions, and the presence of stars were all absorbed. Federico Fellini started his cinematic career writing sketches, gags and comedies, and his story reveals a post-war world of virtual workshops of gags centred on the columns of comedy papers such as *Marc'Aurelio*, or particular cafés or *trattorie*. The most famous writing duo, who signed some of the best regarded Italian comedies, were Age and Scarpelli (Agenore Incrocci and Furio Scarpelli). Comedies have always provided career opportunities for stars. Sophia Loren impinged on public consciousness as the beautiful and deceitful pizza seller in Vittorio de Sica's *L'oro di Napoli* (*The Gold of Naples*, 1954); Gina Lollobrigida's career took off after the phenomenal success of *Pane, amore e fantasia* (*Bread, Love and Fantasy*, Luigi Comencini, 1954), while Vittorio Gassman (whose early film roles had been as heroes of adventure, or villains) widened his range with Mario Monicelli's hit, *I soliti ignoti* (*Big Deal on Madonna Street*, 1958). The most respected of the often prolific comedy directors were Vittorio De Sica, Mario Monicelli, Luigi Comencini, Dino Risi, and Ettore Scola, and more recent directors such as Massimo Troisi, Carlo Verdone, Roberto Benigni. Within this vast category, a host of comic actors have flourished by accentuating their regional characteristics, effectively forming *filoni* in themselves. Like Italian *film noir*, Italian comedy insinuates itself into more serious types of films – the elements of slapstick in De Sica's neorealist *Ladri di biciclette* (*Bicycle Thieves*, 1948) for example – and engages with contemporary events in ways which would have affected the distribution of more serious films. Mario Monicelli's *Vogliamo i colonelli* (*We Want the Colonels*, 1974) uses farce and grotesque comedy to tell the story of the attempted coup d'état led by Prince Valerio Borghese in 1970. As Accardo (2001: 383–7) has noted, Monicelli's film makes it quite clear that the actions of politicians and factions of the extreme right and left of the Italian political spectrum ultimately benefit the centre, the Christian Democrat Party, which was quite happy to take advantage of atrocities in order to frighten the population and obtain consensus for the status quo, and no change.

The popular comedies of the 1940s and 1950s are comedies of social aspiration and integration. In the hugely popular romantic comedy, *Pane, amore e fantasia*, rural remoteness and poverty are emphasized by location shooting and long shots of rolling valleys, ruined walls, cobbled streets. The heroines are the local midwife (Marisa Merlini), who has worked hard to get her diploma in order to support her illegitimate son, and the equally voluptuous Marina, the *bersagliera* (Gina Lollobrigida), a doughty fighter whose home is a peasant hut with only one bed for the family and bare wooden walls. Both use their physical beauty, wit and intelligence to net their suitors, the carabiniere Major Carotenuto (Vittorio De Sica) and the shy, northern carabiniere youth. The comedy lies in the usual misunderstandings in the path of true love, and the mistakes made by outsiders (from Naples as well as the north). However, whereas the two, cross-cultural happy ends in the formation of the two couples constitutes narrative closure and some recognition of modern social mobility, powerful representatives of traditional society have important narrative functions. The couples are constantly observed (even with binoculars) by local villagers, and the local Catholic priest intervenes regularly to indicate appropriate conduct.

Accardo (2001: 15) identifies a variety of comedy categories; the 'neorealist' comedy, such as Gennaro Righelli's *Abbasso la miseria!* (*Down with Poverty!* 1945); the ensemble comedy consisting of a large cast and several sketches, such as Luciano Emmer's *Parigi è sempre Parigi* (*Paris is Always Paris*, 1951) which follows the adventures of a group of Italians on a trip to Paris; the 'pink neorealist' comedies of *Poveri ma belli* (*Poor But Handsome*, Dino Risi, 1956), *Pane, amore e fantasia* and *Don Camillo e l'Onorevole Peppone* (*Don Camillo and Peppone*, Carmine Gallone, 1953) and their spin offs. Other categories include Totò and Sordi's 1950s films; the numerous comedies set on beaches, among football fans, tourist trips or in carabinieri barracks; the 'Golden Age' comedies of the period of the economic boom and centre-left politics; dark political comedies of the years between 1968 and the 'years of the bullet'; the grotesque comedies of Lina Wertmüller, Paolo Villaggio and Marco Ferreri; apolitical erotic comedies; and the 'new' comics, Verdone, Troisi, Moretti, Benigni, Nichetti, Nuti. To this list must be added the male wish-fulfillment comedies of Leonardo Pieraccione, in which he plays a young, provincial male where narrative pretexts and the clothing of the bevy of female characters are equally flimsy; the low-budget, grotesque comedies of Ciprì and Maresco, and the postmodern, international comedies of Benigni and Nichetti.

In the 1960s, some unwelcome effects of rapid economic expansion were explored on screen in darker, mysogynistic narratives, where grotesque elements are constantly present. *Divorzio all'italiana* (*Divorce Italian Style*, Pietro Germi, 1961), *Una vita difficile* (*A difficult Life*, Dino Risi, 1961), *Il sorpasso* (*Easy Life*, Dino Risi, 1962), *L'armata Brancaleone* (*For Love and Gold*, Mario Monicelli, 1966) are amongst many films that explore the clash of modernity with tradition and the breakdown of community into individual selfishness. With a few exceptions, the heyday of the Italian comedy is over by the 1970s (Aprà and Pistagnesi 1986; De Gaetano 1999). Apart from competition from television, the main reason given for the decline was the effect of terrorist attacks. Italian comedy has always engaged with social realities but, during the period of the 'strategy of tension' and the 'years of the bullet', comedy was not considered an appropriate form for exploring such serious events as bomb

outrages and massacres. In the 1970s, comics who had achieved
fame in the 1930s and 1940s either died (De Sica) or appeared to
be coasting along with well-worn routines. Alberto Sordi and the
post-war generation still had good careers but a younger generation,
honed in public taste through television, would dominate Italian
comedy from the 1980s. The younger comedians fell into two camps;
firstly, comedians closely identified with a particular geographical
region of Italy, often using dialect speech and generally exported
only to Italian diaspora communities; secondly, a more avant-garde
group (Benigni, Moretti, Nichetti) who established a following on
television and achieved fame and international recognition in the
1980s. Less influenced by Italian cultural traditions, their comedy
has proved more exportable.

While some performance elements of younger comedians have
a wider appeal, their firm grounding in Italian reality, their use of
slapstick, the grotesque and irony situate them in the Italian comic
tradition. Thus, in Pietro Germi's *Sedotta e abbandonata* (*Seduced
and Abandoned*, 1962), the use of extreme close-ups of grotesque
male faces, aggressively pursuing Agnese (Stefania Sandrelli) across
the piazza when the forced marriage with Peppino (Aldo Puglisi)
hangs in the balance, opens up a reflexive space in which archaic
social and gender relationships can be judged.

Other *filoni* are entirely structured around the personae of
popular comics. Any video shop in any city in Italy (and any city of

Figure 2.2
The aggressive pursuit
of Agnese (Stefania
Sandrelli) in *Sedotta e
abbandonata* (Pietro
Germi, 1962).

the Italian diaspora) features a shelf of videocassette reissues of films starring Italy's most famous comic, Antonio de Curtis, better known as Totò. New technology has assisted the survival of his reputation and his popularity and there have been many attempts to analyse the roots of the his continued appeal (Fofi 1972, 1998; Caldiron 1980). Totò's persona drew on early twentieth-century traditions of farce and review, made memorable by the physicality of his performance and the grotesqueness of his gestures. The eccentricity of his persona and early ability to draw on American models marked him out as more modern and international than his contemporaries, and comprehensible to wider publics primarily by using references to popular, cinematic culture in his stage reviews. His Neapolitan accent, use of made-up words, and parody of Italian character types make his work difficult to understand for non-Italian audiences. His performances were honed in the review tradition in which a series of sketches was linked together by a tenuous theme, or generic parody (Accardo 2001:168). His comedy was frequently based on doubling or mis-recognition. Typically, Totò plays a lower class character mistaken for an upper class person or someone holding institutional power. Totò's efforts to perform the superior's characteristics would lay bare with a sharp scalpel the petty subterfuges, pomposity, bullying, mystificatory language by which the superior subjugated the inferior. In *Totò al giro d'Italia* (*Totò's tour of Italy*, Mario Mattoli, 1948) he plays a professor who sells his soul to the devil in order to marry the girl, the catch being that he has to win the famous cycle race, the tour of Italy. From much moustache-stroking and pomposity, he changes into 'one of the lads', clean-shaven and hobnobbing with cycling heroes of the time. His performance was physical and gesturally expressive, indicating the appropriate audience response by his poses, bodily contortions and the gaze of his hooded eyes. He also portrays a sort of predatory virility by his famous trick of sniffing his female co-stars from top to bottom.

Totò was 'rediscovered', shortly after his death, by the rebellious youth of 1968 when his public was that of the periphery, of small, provincial cinemas in the south and the islands. Gianni Borgna (1998: 12) identifies Totò's appeal in the implied social criticism evident in his jokes about all those in power, their hypocrisy, pomposity, cowardice and banality. The anarchy and rage at the basis of the Totò persona are symptoms of social and existential malaise, and the ability of the little man to resist and turn things to his own advantage. Consumers of videocassettes and satellite channels are similar to his former public, and his exposure of the abuses of those in power have ensured that Totò has continued to have a topical appeal right up to the present. He made ninety-seven films, thus ensuring that elements of his theatrical performance have survived. Governi (1998: 135) identifies Totò as representing a sort of archaic *italianità* (Italianness) which he connotes across generations, via television and video, so that he is both part of Italian cultural history, and part of the individual and personal experience of his successive audiences.

Given the major social changes which took place in Italy after the Second World War, the popularity of the comic, Alberto Sordi, is not surprising. The ordinary citizen from the peasant, proletarian or lower middle classes, directly experiencing population movements from countryside to city, increasing prosperity, the slow opening up of new areas of employment, new educational advantages, the influence of international culture, had mentally to position himself or herself in a new configuration of economic level, personal tastes and desires, which Bourdieu defines as a *habitus*. While Italian comedies show the accommodation to these social changes, at the same time they reveal the presence of limitations to change. Thus, whereas Marcello Mastroianni's roles move from the proletarian to the middle class, reflecting one effect of increased prosperity, characters only move to the upper middle classes or aristocracy by virtue of luck or subterfuge, criminality (*Abbasso la richezza! Down With Riches!* Gennaro Righelli, 1946) or beauty (*Pane amore e fantasia, Poveri ma belli*). Climbing class is represented as fraught with anxiety and, more often than not, doomed to failure. The majority of Italian comedies are predicated on dramas of class antagonism reflecting the feeling of exclusion from the exercise of power. Sordi's film characters are typified as lower middle class, devoid of political integrity and only interested in personal survival. *L'arte di arrangiarsi* (the art of survival) and *fare bella figure* (presenting oneself to best advantage) form the basis of his comedy, but his films' plot events indicate a rejection of his lack of moral values and anxieties about 'getting it wrong'. Viganò (1995: 58) suggests that the root of Sordi's comedy lies in the grotesque nature of his performance in situations common to large numbers of Italians. His manic delivery, domination of the frame, address to camera, slightly excessive variations on conventional costume, indicate him as different from his audience, while the difficulties he encounters in making a living engender self-recognition in the audience who laugh at him and with him at the same time.

Paolo Villaggio, Adriano Celentano, Ugo Tognazzi, Carlo Verdone, and Aldo, Giovanni e Giacomo have made low-budget films that cover their costs in Italy and have the occasional big financial success. *Filoni* also cohere around another phenomenon, the director/actor/producer, exemplified by Maurizio Nichetti, Nanni Moretti and Roberto Benigni. Nichetti and Benigni have created a persona around their instantly recognizable faces, Nichetti as the bumbling everyman whose gags draw him into a mire of extraordinary situations. Part of his appeal is to a cinephile, educated audience that can appreciate the references to other texts, such as Vittorio De Sica's *Ladri di biclette* (*Bicycle Thieves*, 1948) in *Ladri di Saponette* (*The*

Icycle Thieves, 1989) which is partly a parody of classic neorealism, and partly a biting satire of Italian commercial television and its constant interruption of films with adverts. In *Volere volare* (1991), Nichetti is a cinema sound recordist who finds himself turning into a cartoon character at the same time as he meets and falls in love with a girl (Angela Finocchiaro) whose occupation is to satisfy the sexual fantasies of rich clients. Roberto Benigni's persona is that of the outsider, the little man, as in his *Johnny Stecchino* (1991) where he discovers that he is the double of an infamous mafioso, whom he has to impersonate and whose wife (Nicoletta Braschi) falls in love with him. Comedy based on a character who is the double of a more successful character was a staple of Totò's gags, imitated by many others (notably Carlo Verdone) since. The strategy creates sympathy for the underdog, usually lower middle class, and a space to revile and ridicule those with greater social or economic power. Although not doubled, Benigni's character in *La vita è bella* (*Life is Beautiful*, 2002) is an outsider by virtue of his race and occupation. His targets are therefore the middle-class collaborators and fascists of his Tuscan town, and the Nazi military in the concentration camp, while the beauty of his wife (Nicoletta Braschi) and the citiscape connote the fundamental goodness of *italianità*. Despite its huge budget and Miramax support, Benigni's *Pinocchio* (2003) has not been an international success. Going back to original elements of Collodi's famous story and shorn of the cute and saccharine accretions of the 1950s versions, Benigni's film has clearly been considered too strange and idiosyncratic for international consumption.

Leonardo Pieraccioni and Carlo Verdone achieve enormous financial successes on the Italian market alone. Verdone's *Viaggi di nozze* (*Honeymoons*, 1992) made Lire 24,306,730,000 at the 1995–6 box office, whereas Pieraccioni's *Il ciclone* (*The Cyclone*, 1997) beat Hollywood films, *The Hunchback of Notre Dame* (Gary Trousdale/Kirk Wise, 1996) and *Independence Day* (Roland Emmerich, 1996) and others by a long chalk with a box office of Lire 53,441,667,000. Verdone draws on the tradition of Sordi and Totò, creating an ironic distance for his audience in characters who are less perceptive than his audience, or less able than the important person for whom they are mistaken. Incompetent these characters might be but female characters rarely get the better of them, mainly having to put up with the consequences of extremes of male stupidity (Panero 1998: 203–18). Leonardo Pieraccioni has tailored his persona to his audience, that of middle- to lower-class, educated, single males, and their fantasies of controlling a variety of stock characters from rural farming fathers, to bus loads of scantily clad performers.

The Sicilians, Daniele Ciprì and Franco Maresco's black-and-white films appeal to a minority, cult audience, aware of cinematic conventions and appreciative of grotesque and transgressive elements. De Gaetano (1999: 112–13) considers these the life-affirming and subversive consequences of the banality, repetitiveness and lack of authenticity of televisual and media culture. Ciprì and Maresco's films can be considered attempts to reconquer the meaning of the human condition, shorn of ideas of mediation and representation, of psychology and social identity, in which the carnevalesque, in the Bakhtinian sense, overturns the seriousness of official culture and re-establishes the fundamental ambiguity of life. De Gaetano sees nothing obscene in the sexual penetration of the donkey in *Lo zio di Brooklyn* (*The Uncle from Brooklyn*, 1995), the hen in *Totò che visse due volte* (*Totò who lived twice*, 1998), or in the spitting, urine, faeces and parade of grotesque human faces, merely that human beings are animals and that all other representations are constructs. Only through considering the whole narrative, rather than isolated, grotesque parts, does a sense of the infinite inventiveness of human beings, and hence a sense of the sublime and mythic, emerge. *Il ritorno di Cagliostro* (*The Return of Cagliostro*, 2002) is more linear and accessible than usual, its subject being Italian cinema itself through the figures of two incompetent, Sicilian builders, the La Marca brothers, who start the first Sicilian production company, Trinacria films. The socio-political and economic basis of their enterprise is emphasized in the frequent meddling of their bankers, the Bin Ladenesque Cardinal and the bloated capitalist Mafia chief (both played by Pietro Giordano), the Cardinal's smelly mother, and the aristocrat who proposes the project, *Il ritorno di Cagliostro*. The last named recalls the great Totò in his striking of grotesque poses, if not precisely in his dissolving in floods of pale vomit. The economic basis of media production is also alluded to in the washed-up American star, Errol Douglas (Robert Englund), representing the use of American B-grade stars in 1950s Italian cinema. The internal narrator, direct to camera, of the second half of the film is a dwarf with a boyish, ravaged face and high voice, who intervenes in each scene, populated by the ugliest people the film-makers could have found. An excessive number of grotesque faces, lots of vomiting on shoes and other people, a proliferation of odd, inconsequential events, signal the power of the carnevalesque to establish its own 'reality'. By contrast, the total incomprehension of the American actor and his girlfriend, the limited understanding of the film's backers and makers constitute an ironic distancing from a world and an ideology that are usually represented as 'natural' but which are, in reality, totally bizarre.

Italian comedy has always embraced the grotesque, its excesses allowing those who stand in for 'the ordinary person' to get their own back on those in authority, or the tyrannies of social and economic orders.

The *Giallo*

In the 1970s a number of low-budget films, aimed at an early-evening, male audience, and drawing on these earlier traditions acquired the label, *film giallo*. The word *giallo* entered popular vocabulary to denote mystery stories from 1929 when the publisher, Mondadori launched detective fiction in yellow covers. The word has come to be used both as a shorthand term for any type of detective fiction and, more widely, as a generic term for stories with any mystery element; hence the genres of the *giallo erotico*, the *giallo politico*, and the use of saturated yellow tones on film to connote hidden realities and to introduce the intertextual frames of generic conventions into the text. Many have achieved cult status and are marketed on video with garish illustrations on a yellow background. There is no space here to attempt a detailed discussion of these films beyond mentioning that one of their distinguishing characteristics (which is also visible in more upmarket *gialli* and the horror genre) is their misogyny and noticeable elements of sadism and sado-masochism. In *Non si sevizia un paperino* (*Don't Torture a Duck*, Lucio Fulci, 1976) a slightly unhinged village wise woman is tortured and beaten on suspicion of luring local boys to their death when the perpetrator is actually the local priest. These pulp *gialli* are obsessed with liminal or enclosed spaces and their story worlds typically feature a culture clash which indicates anxieties about modernity and the pluralism of city life (Koven 2003). These 1970s *gialli* are able to indicate disaffection with traditional authority figures, while their sadism and misogyny signals the level of anxiety about increased female power without examining patriarchal power itself.

In the same period the *giallo poliziesco*, detective story or police procedural thriller flourished through a succession of popular *filoni*, such as those with city names, *Milano violenta* (Mario Caiano, 1975–6), *Torino nera* (Carlo Lizzani, 1972), *Roma bene* (Carlo Lizzani, 1971), *Roma drogata: la polizia non può intervenire* (*Drugged Rome: The Police are Powerless*, Lucio Manaccino, 1975–6), *Napoli violenta* (*Death Dealers*, Umberto Lenzi, 1976), and titles featuring the words 'police', 'justice', 'violent', 'investigation' in various combinations, and starring Maurizio Merli or Tomas Milian as the detectives. As Enzo Natta (2002: 17) has suggested, these *filoni* have now migrated to become a staple of television in series like 'Il Maresciallo Rocca' and 'Commissario Montalban'.

Social élites were targetted in a lighter vein in Luigi Comencini's hit film *La donna della Domenica* (*Sunday Woman*, 1975) as Commissario Santamaria's (Marcello Mastroianni) investigation of sordid architect Garrone takes him into upper-class Turin society. He discovers their predilection for kitsch art (a major exhibition features an enormous painting of a man having sex with a large swan) and bizarre murder weapons (an enormous stone penis, manufactured with great pride in the workshop of the local stonemason). Night shooting, shadows and chases uncover a louche, amoral society of extreme wealth, sexual pluralism, exploitation and prostitution which the detective has to handle with 'silken hands in velvet gloves'.

Since the political murders and terrorist attacks of the 1980s, there has been an explosion of publications, from comic book adventures, to detective novels and thrillers, and Internet sites. Italy now has a very wide *giallo*, and particularly *noir* culture (Wood 2005). Some examples of films with a more *film noir* edge are explored in Chapter 8.

The Italian Western and International Export

Opinion differs as to whether 300 or 400 Italian westerns were produced, reflecting the huge popularity of the genre, and the spinning out of its life in many sub-*filoni*. The genre evolved from the ashes of the mythological genre when the public grew tired of the embarassing excesses of hyper-muscular noble heroes and narratives set in historical settings, which required a classical education to fully understand the nuances. The western had the advantage of being extremely familiar to audiences following the saturation releases of American films onto the market after the Second World War. However, by the 1960s, the American western was showing signs of tiredness. The iconic stars of the 1930s were now rather elderly to make convincing love-objects for the nubile American starlets of the 1950s, and the urban world of work and family provided more topical narrative concerns than the settled, patriarchal stories of conquest and community of classic American westerns. Schooled

Figure 2.3
Clint Eastwood (left) in *Per un pugno di dollari* (Sergio Leone, 1964)

in the excesses of the ancient world, Italian audiences were ripe for a fresh take on the west, and the second-rank stars of the *peplum* epics migrated to the western.

There was, of course, no suggestion of filming in the United States itself. Italian production companies had been badly burned by attempts to set up business there. Instead, the dry, empty landscapes of southern Spain ensured cheapness and easy audience recognition of place, and facilitated export to the lucrative Spanish and Latin-American markets. The usual Italian strategy of hiring B-grade American actors was used to enhance box-office appeal, and ensure some authenticity in the presence of Anglo-Saxon facial characteristics. A spurious authenticity was also provided by the very Anglo-Saxon names of the creative teams of director, cinematographer, scriptwriter, actors, although their Italian basis rapidly became known and part of the cult experience. Bob Robertson is more familiar as Sergio Leone, for example. From the start the American stress on landscape in order to emphasize the huge nature of the pioneering task of taming the wilderness and establishing community was shorn of its mythic dimensions. Spectacle, and a very Italian exploration of the *mise en scène* of space and place produced representations of landscape surplus to narrative requirements, whose excesses indicated that concerns quite other than the establishment of order and community were being rehearsed. Christopher Frayling's analyses of many spaghetti westerns shows the complete absence of community or society, but he goes so far as to suggest that certain plot strands represent 'the first explicitly political form of popular cinema in Italy since the Mussolini era' (Frayling 1981: 56). For Frayling, the main clue here is the southern origin of film-makers and the characteristics of southern society, which allow concerns about the American influence on Italian society, and male fears about failure and victimhood to be sublimated in narratives of violence, escape and revenge (Frayling 1981: 57–65).

In Italian westerns, male characters are usually presented at narrative conjunctures where they have become unfettered from the ties of convention and community. The mythological genre preferred heroes whose hyper-masculinity and musculature indicated difficulties of reconciling strong leadership with the exercise of democracy in the First Republic, and the firm rebuttal of the feminizing characteristics felt to be threatening traditional patriarchal Italian authority. The characters of Italian westerns, however, represent a step into the void of post-patriarchal society. Male characters are represented as operating at the margins of society, rejecting religious dictates of obedience, respect for authority, women and children, owing loyalty only to themselves and indulging their personal whims and desires. Grotesque elements signal the psychic investment in throwing off the shackles of convention, and these are enhanced by the dubbing necessary for the international market, resulting in communication that takes the form of facial grimaces, violent action, grunts and other phatic methods of expression.

The genre featured regularly in top box-office grossers in the 1960s, but, following the laws of the life and death of *filoni*, fragmented into a myriad of sub-*filoni*, before mutating into the horror genre and political cinema in the 1970s. Some *filoni* revolved around a particular tune and set of characters, *The Good, the Bad and the Ugly* team; or around a particular character, such as Django, or Satana; or around well-known combinations of actors, such as Bud Spencer, Terence Hill. Grotesque elements lay in the stress on the facial characteristics of the actors, on the hyper-violence, represented as unmotivated and excessive, the lack of convincing personal relationships, including that with female characters. There seems to be no necessity for narratives to be coherent or production values of the highest for some of these westerns to have achieved cult status, and therefore additional sources of revenue from reruns on cable and satellite. In fact, the less motivated and uglier the violence, the less logical the plot, the more appealing the film to cult audiences. These films ensure a steady income for rights' holders with media re-runs, and re-issues on video and DVD. Cheaply made, they have earned their keep many times over.

The Italian Contribution to Horror: Style and Visual Flamboyance

Excess and the grotesque are also characteristics of the Italian horror genre. Riccardo Freda's 1940s and 1950s low-budget films were often shot back to back on sets built for other films, high contrast lighting and areas of shadow making a virtue of necessity. Influenced by British horror cinema, his and Mario Bava's films used *film noir* conventions to give a gothic edge to tales of mystery and horror. As Freda remarked, 'vampires are around us all the time even if they don't have recognisable teeth ... they're older people who "feed off" young people, sucking their vital spirit and ideas' (Faldini and Fofi 1981: 200). The generational conflict is at the heart of the underlying concerns of Italian *noir* horror, that is anxieties about the breakdown of traditional Italian class and gender power relationships. Italian women got the vote in 1946 and the economic boom of the late 1950s drew them into paid employment, disturbing previously held certainties about women's mental and physical limitations. Antonio Margheriti's *Danza macabra* (1963), Bava's *La frusta e il corpo* (*The Whip and the Body*, 1963) and *La maschera del demonio* (*Mask of the Demon*, 1960) make spectacular use of shadows and architectural features (often reused on subsequent films) to create worlds in which the focus of horror constantly returns, usually associated with extreme female sexual desire.[1] In *Danza macabra*, Alan takes a bet to stay overnight in a haunted house where he falls under the spell of the darkly beautiful Elizabeth (Barbara Steele), despite her telling him she has been dead for ten years. Unbalanced and asymmetrical architectural compositions mirror the cycle of increasingly hysterical sexual couplings, and the constant return of Elizabeth's murderous former lover. Alan wins his bet but goes mad in the process, the ultimate metaphor of loss of power. *La frusta e il corpo* uses *noir* lighting, a colour palette of blues and yellows, visual asymmetry and dramatic excess in a narrative which sets freedom and restraint, duty and desire, in opposition. All the male characters seek to exercise patriarchal power, Kurt (Christopher Lee) by whipping his former lover, Nevenka (Daliah Lavi) into sexual submission, the others in traditional marriage arrangements. Nevenka's apparent passivity is as excessive as the murders she is revealed to have committed.

Film-makers active in the horror film sector by definition work on mid- to low-budget films and are schooled in the *filone* tradition. Italian popular cinema has always had an eye for the next trend and, with the global reach of international media companies, this virtue has become a necessity. Horror film-makers refuse to regard themselves as an 'Italian School' and there is constant creative contact, particularly with American directors such as Tobe Hooper, Wes Craven, Sam Raimi, Aaron Lipstadt, David Cronenberg and Roger Corman (Pugliese 1996: 24). Japanese horror films have exerted a recent influence. In addition, assistant directors, camera operators, designers move from horror film to film so that a style coheres around clutches of films.

Dario Argento's films up to 1982 are considered to be influenced by *film noir* and *giallo* conventions in their use of the investigative narrative and depiction of excessively dark and disfunctional worlds. *Profondo rosso* (*Deep Red*, 1975) is typical in featuring non-detective investigators, Mark David (David Hemmings), a musician, and Gianna Brezzi, a journalist, (Daria Nicolodi), and a mad murderer, the elderly Marta (Clara Calamai), an actress who murdered her husband to prevent him sending her to an asylum. The predominant colour tones are grey, black and deep blue, only relieved by deep red tones of frequently spilled blood and gaping, slashed wounds in flesh. The key to the first murder, of the clairvoyant Helga (Macha Méril), lie in an enormous, excessively art deco villa, haunted by a crying child. The *mise en scène* dwells on the rococo architectural curlicues and ornamentation, which contrast with the extreme high angle shots of the cold, empty, blue tones of the modern square in which Mark's apartment is situated, with its diner *à la* Edward Hopper. Annalee Newitz (1999: 68) locates the narrative logic of serial killer narratives in difficulties with traditional gender roles. In this respect the main female characters are emblematic of aspects of male unease with female emotional competence and female autonomy. Helga mediates the thoughts of the killer to an audience, making her living out of hyper-intuitiveness. Gianna is a journalist whose intelligent and combattive relationship with Mark is that of an equal. The clue pointing to the haunted house is an article written by Amanda (Giuliana Calandra). Photographs of the murderer's youthful film roles as a *femme fatale* indicate that her exchange value in capitalist terms is in conflict with her role as a mother.

Male anxieties and pathologies are more overt in *Tenebre* (*Tenebrae*, 1982), in which an American author, Peter Neil's (Anthony Franciosa) visit to Italy is disturbed by a series of murders, the victims being found with pages of his latest novel stuffed in their mouth. Graphic knife murders are found to be the work of disturbed journalist, Cristiano Berti (John Steiner) but the novelist, too, is revealed as a serial killer whose frenzied axe attacks derive from sexual humiliations revealed by initially unmotivated flashbacks. His luckless fiancée, Jane (Veronica Lario), has the misfortune to wear similar red shoes and white dress to the girl in the flashback, and is rewarded by having her arms cut off in a fountain of blood.[2] In effect, *Tenebre* represents the limit of the appropriation of *film noir* by the horror genre in that its metanarrative level is visible from the title sequence where a voice-off (that of Dario Argento himself) reads a section from Peter Neil's pulp horror novel, which effectively explains why the novelist is a serial killer – killing is a cathartic experience to exorcise an earlier, traumatic crime. The title of Neil's book is also the title of the film. The scene where the lesbian journalist, Tilde, aggressively interrogates Neil about his misogyny, his lack of respect for women, could as easily apply to Argento. Berti, the incompetent television interviewer and first killer, photographs his victims, eroticizing their dead bodies. In her study of the relationship between true crime and fictionalised serial killings, Newitz (1999: 70–81) suggests that the economic dimension is as important as that of gender in understanding the impetus to kill. Thus, serial murders represent both the overproduction of late capitalism, and the desire to see oneself mass-produced in media reports. The former indicates the individual's lack of power in the capitalist system, and the latter an attempt to re-establish power. Argento's narratives are mirrored by his own role as director who manufactures multiple copies of stories of multiple deaths.

Argento's iconography as well as his narratives take *giallo* conventions to dark extremes. Both *Profondo rosso* and *Tenebre* contrast limited chromatic tones of modernist streets, regular architecture and in-teriors, with spaces of excessive decoration and saturated colour. Narrative, emotional and visual excess, complexity of themes and cultural allusions, virtuosity of ideas, *mise en scène* and camera work, all indicate the presence of instability, distrust of modernity, and the breakdown of social control of individual behaviour that is a feature both of *film noir* and neo-baroque texts, characteristics which *film giallo* and *noir* horror also share with political cinema. Argento has always had production control of his films which, from *L'uccello dalle piume di cristallo* (*The Bird with the Crystal Plumage*, 1970) and *Quattro mosche di veluto grigio* (*Four Flies on Grey Velvet*, 1971) onwards, covered their costs on the Italian market alone. Since 1982 Argento has both diversified into pulp film production by the company he owns and runs with his brother, producing low-grade films by film-makers such as Umberto Lenzi and Michele Soavi, and his own film output has moved firmly into horror cinema. He has cashed in on his own reputation, the evolution of the genre into harder manifestations of horror epitomized by Jonathan Demme's *The Silence of the Lambs* (1991). In common with other Italian *auteurs* he has moved into the 'quality' genre and international distribution. His cult, international status ensures that his films maintain premium prices on the racks of video and DVD.

Argento's budgets started to increase with *Trauma* (1993), made in America and distributed in Italy by Penta (at that time an arm of Berlusconi's Mediaset). His three following films, *La sindrome di Stendhal* (*The Stendhal Syndrome* 1996), *Il Fantasma dell'opera* (*The Phantom of the Opera*, 1998) and *Non ho sonno* (*Sleepless*, 2000) were all big budget productions confirming Argento's position at the quality, international end of horror film production. They are also very self-reflexive, quoting plot elements and visuals from earlier films, such as the black gloves and the bold red cloth in which knives are wrapped in Argento's first film, *L'uccello dalle piume di cristallo*. The lack of tension in *La sindrome di Stendhal*, and the straight-jacket of an old story in *Il fantasma dell'opera* makes these films appear slow and visually less complex than earlier films. *Non ho sonno* is a return to his previous pace, with subjective camera work, murders behind glass windows, and stylish *mise en scène*, with plenty of clues for the horror buff to recognize. *Il cartaio* (*The Card Player*, 2003) returns to visual complexity, mixing Argento's hallmark black rubber gloves, and overgrown houses with Baroque exteriors, with modern police stations and, in this case, computer-generated card games. Violent and grotesque elements are limited to the webcam close-ups of the screaming girls, and the post-mortem investigations of dead female bodies. Argento manages to make a typical Italian generic hybrid of the serial killer film and the love story, while offering the visual and narrative inventiveness that appeals to his international fan base.

Below Argento are hundreds of low-budget films by directors such as Umberto Lenzi, Lucio Fulci, Michele Soavi, Ruggero Deodato and Sergio Martino, some of whom adopt American names according to genre. One might suppose that, in the way of most cheaply produced Italian films, these would disappear once exploited to their full in the 1970s and 1980s, but video, DVD and enterprising Internet sales appear to have given them an additional life. Issue 12 (2003) of the cult magazine, *Nocturne*, featured cannibal films and where

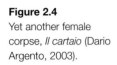

Figure 2.4
Yet another female
corpse, *Il cartaio* (Dario
Argento, 2003).

to obtain them. Umberto Lenzi's *Mangiati vivi!* (*Eaten Alive*, 1980),
whose poster features a naked woman having her breast cut off
at the hands of desperate characters in the jungle, is still earning
money for whoever holds the rights. *Cannibal Holocaust* (1979)
attracted the attention of the courts, but Ruggero Deodato claimed
that it made an enormous amount of money, 'something like Lire
ten million in ten days' (Nepoti 1999: 39). Some additional light
was recently shed on the appeal of this sort of film, which some
might regard as an extremely specialized interest, by the 2003 trial
of the German, Armin Meiwes, who advertised for a victim willing
to be cannibalized but found his videotaped meal of a previous
victim being used against him in court. Gianfranco Galliano (2003:
44) admits the possibility of political metaphor in the cannibal film.
However, besides the theme of cannibalism as mirror of capitalist
consumption, it is also possible to read the theme of man eats man
(or, more usually, man cuts up and eats woman) as a variation on the
vampire theme where the victim represents the ultimate possession
and control by another person.

Soft Porn

Although not precisely box-office winners, films with sexual content have, since the 1970s, been consistent earners for Italian film-
makers. The official censor and the censorship activities of the
Catholic Church held Italian cinema in the grip of respectability
until the late 1960s. Sexual and erotic content had to be indicated in
coded form, their suppression usually resulting in the protruberant
biceps and breasts of Italian actors, indicating the difficulties of
squashing erotic content into conventional representation. Erotic
content became more overt in art cinema. Visconti explored
incestuous family relationships in *Gruppo di famiglia in un interno*
(*Conversation Piece*, 1974), *La caduta degli dei* (*The Damned*,
1969) and his under-the-sheets shots of Giuliana's (Laura Antonelli)
aroused body in *L'innocente* (*The Intruder*, 1976) reveal a sound

understanding of the interplay of the desire to see and its deferral that underpins erotic texts. Antonioni's, Fellini's, Pasolini's, Cavani's and Bertolucci's films include nudity and sexual content, aiming to shock and sometimes provoke statements about contemporary society. Their position as quality directors ensured exploitation in first-run cinemas internationally.

In the wake of 1968, two things happened. Censorship was relaxed, and social uncertainty and terrorist activity made the second circuit of suburban cinemas increasingly unattractive for an entertaining night out. Amongst the results, cheap sex films became an attractive commodity to replace the Italian western, which had reached the end of its cycle in a plethora of similar, far-fetched stories. Italian cinema was ready to subject its actors to trials and tribulations of a different order. The Italian industry developed both the suburban cinema circuits at home into *luci rosse* (red light) cinemas, and their traditional distribution networks in the Middle East, and the Europe-wide, art cinema networks to take their products. Producers of porn cinema have not looked back. The gradual increase in media outlets from the beginning of the 1980s ensured that the market for soft and hard porn films grew exponentially, with video, cable, satellite, DVD, and specialist outlets being energetically developed. As public tolerance increased, soft-porn films aimed at middle-class sensibilities featured at the top of box-office listings (Minella 1998: 162–7). Tinto Brass (*Salon Kitty*, 1976), Salvatore Samperi (*Grazia zia, Thank You, Aunt*, 1968), Gianfranco Mingozzi (*L'iniziazzione, The Initiation*, 1986), Gabriele Lavia (*Scandalosa Gilda*, 1985) and others established their careers in the 1970s.

The pornofilm industry is virtually a mirror image of the officially sanctioned industry, with its own star system, production companies, and differentiation into *filoni*. Alba Parietti claimed that an erotic role was obligatory for her film debut because there were few other opportunities for television actresses (Rombi 1998: 44). In an almost parody of the careers of silent film stars, a significant number of pornostars have managed to impose their names on the public (Rocco Siffredi, Moana Pozzi, La Cicciolina, Selén) by dint of appearing in many films. Bruno Ventavoli (2000: 151) claims that more than 1,000 Italian porno films are released each year. This perhaps explains Selén's complaint, after leaving the hard industry, that she was appearing in films she had never made, assembled from off cuts (Bogani 2003).

The Italian pornographic film industry often found its products excluded from yearbooks such as the *Catalogo Bolaffi*, and its revenue (as befits a barely respectable genre) is difficult to establish. However, as a genre, the erotic film has never been prey to the falls from fashion of other genres, guaranteeing continued revenues when exploited in other media.

Conclusion

Competition from television was blamed for killing the medium-budget drama but, in fact, production deals with television have ensured its continued presence. Comedies survive, covering their costs through national theatrical and satellite release. Distributors' agents with networks of export contacts have been crucial in developing audiences for the work of Benigni, Moretti, Nichetti. The gentle comedy of *Il Postino* (Michael Radford, 1994) used Massimo Troisi's southern characteristics, but subordinated them to a universal story of the shy underdog who writes poetry and gets the beautiful girl (Maria Grazia Cucinotta) in the end. This film also indicates the role and current importance of foreign distributors, especially Miramax, in ensuring in-depth exploitation abroad. Science fiction, horror and the erotic film have all built international and cult circuits of exploitation with the Internet assuming increasing importance.

The sheer volume of Italian popular entertainment films precludes neat conclusions, not least because it is impossible to see them all. High- to mid-budget films span an ideological spectrum from acceptance of the status quo to more or less profound disquiet at social changes, feminist ideas, terrorism, State secrets, globalization. Popular genres such as the *giallo*, horror film, spaghetti western or pornofilm are stamped by more overt difficulties about gender power, which will be explored further in Chapter 7. The impossibility of constructing a completely modern consensus of Italian values results in continuing narrative and visual tensions in popular cinema, characterized by emotional and visual excess, elements that will be explored in the following chapters.

3

The Epic and Historical Film

The epic and the historical film have made regular appearances in charts of box-office popularity in Italy and this chapter will argue that the form that they take, and the historical periods that come and go in fashion, are indicative of the complexities of Italian notions of identity and nationhood as they have evolved over the last century. Italy became a nation in 1870 after centuries in which regional identity, centred on historical cities, shaped the allegiances and self-image of its inhabitants. Recourse to representations of ancient history in the peninsular, and to the struggles to establish the nation, have surfaced at key points in cinematic history, such as the early 1900s, the 1930s and the 1950s when a combination of external threats and social and economic change provided an interested audience for the renegotiation of national values. Films set in earlier historical moments, however, occur in every decade, sometimes so obsessively as to constitute a mini-*filone* (films of the 1990s and 2000s about the death of Aldo Moro, for example). This chapter will also explore commonalities between other forms of popular Italian cinema, such as the particular combination of realist conventions and visual spectacle, which indicate the traumatic nature of social change and the psychic difficulties of coming to terms with painful events. Disasters (natural and man-made), State repression, bomb outrages, assassinations, murders, corruption, kidnappings, military blunders and defeats, mass migrations pepper Italian history at regular intervals and, for many of them, no responsibility is ever established and no State intervention is effective.

Angela dalle Vacche (1992: 26) attributes the interest in history, and the themes of national unity and historical continuity to the philosopher, Benedetto Croce's influence in the Italian school system. Croce argued that the function of the historian is to represent the actual, that is to examine evidence (which can include documents, or other evidence of what people thought, believed and felt) and construct a narrative of how things might have happened. Historical accounts, however, were inevitably partial because, if the study of the past was the result of concerns or interests in the present, then these concerns had an impact on the sort of evidence that would be considered important, and therefore the form of the historical narrative.

Francesco Rosi's *Cristo si è fermato a Eboli* (*Christ Stopped at Eboli*, 1979), is based on Carlo Levi's book, written in 1945, about his experiences of internal political exile to a remote area of Campania during the 1930s. Levi uses his position as a northerner, a doctor and an artist to record the words, beliefs and actions of peasants and villagers, of those who have returned from America, and of the lower middle classes who have embraced fascism's promises of prosperity. He then makes sense of what he has found by constructing a narrative around the premise that these remote, rural areas have always been ignored by Italy's rulers and by Christianity so that they have effectively been outside the historical process. Levi's account reflects the prestige of the post-war, left-wing indictments of fascism and concerns to stress the vitality and value of a pagan, ancient culture and its continuity with the past. Fidelity to the original book was one of Rosi's concerns, but his film is both influenced by the work of Antonio Gramsci, which began to be published and debated after 1947, and by the groundswell of interest in rural life at the end of the 1970s. Rosi's film is a quest narrative, centred on the figure of the intellectual, Levi, who observes strange rural practices and listens to the voices of the inhabitants, coming to understanding in small steps in a series of episodes. Women, and particularly his servant, Giulia, represent gateways to the understanding of arcane rural lore, yet, although as a prisoner Levi lacks power, as a male intellectual he appropriates information. In exploring this archaic, rural world, Rosi highlights the impact on the *Mezzogiorno*, the south of Italy, of the emigration that resulted from poor government and lack of State investment in education and industry.

In Emanuele Crialese's *Respiro* (2002), set on the remote Sicilian island of Lampedusa, concerns about the disruptive effects of female autonomy on conservative and patriarchal societies result in a series of attempts to contain the free-thinking young mother, Grazia (Valeria Golino), and to constitute her as deranged. In Croce's terms, each film seeks to know the world it depicts and the historical agenda is always incomplete because it is not possible to know how rural Italy might be interpreted in the future. We can however come to an epistemological sense of how we know what we know, and therefore perceive how 'common sense' assumptions arise and shape our views. Influenced by Gramsci, Rosi's film shows how class interests structure beliefs, while being part of the hegemonic shift of giving value to non-urban life, represented as more vital and authentic, but still patriarchal. Crialese's film, influenced by feminism, represents an evolution in the presentation of ideas about patriarchy but rehearsed in the isolation of a remote island where the consequences of patriarchal power structures are made visible on the body of the female protagonist. These films also show the tension between the idea of a unitary Italian identity and the experience of Italian life as one of regional differences. Regionalism is part of the process of fragmentation into class, geographical, political, gender identities in postmodern culture. They illustrate the fact that evocations of the past cannot be viewed uncritically, but betray the interests and concerns of the present through cues to reading contained within the narrative structure.

Pre-sound Epics on Classical Subjects

Between 1910 to 1919, Italy dominated national and world film markets with its grandiose epics, epitomized by *Cabiria* (Giovanni Pastrone, 1914) and *Quo vadis?* (Enrico Guazzoni, 1913). Between 1909 and 1911, films increased in length, entailing higher investment in terms of more complex stories, more film stock, sets, costumes and actors, and the hiring of lyric theatres, where middle-class audiences would feel comfortable in spending their time and money. In their search for the 'quality' audience, producers rapidly hit upon historical tales from Italy's rich past as a source of respectable subjects that would be comprehensible to, and interesting for, a lower middle-class as well as an upper middle-class audience. Ivo Blom (2001: 19–28) has demonstrated the extraordinary longevity of what have become stock images of the ancient world.[1] Tales of adventure and heroism, cruelty and spectacle, and allusions to popular engravings are typical of the mingling of high art, bourgeois and popular culture that is so characteristic of the epic film.

Some of the short, ten-twelve minute, films produced before 1913 already show characteristics that will be developed in longer epics. The actors in *Patrizia e schiava* (*Afra, Patrician Slave*, Cines, 1910) use behaviour and gesture to indicate psychological states and character in the *commedia dell'arte* tradition, which focuses on the human problems of daily life, rather than the macrohistorical world view. There are interesting visual patterns in the staging, similar to the use of the proscenium arch by opera directors, and the tendency to forward the narrative through tableaux recalls nineteenth-century history paintings. Marcella's servants either react to her in a group, or are placed in painterly compositions that draw the eye, by means of diagonal, visual arrangements to the apex of a vanishing point in which she is situated. This will be developed in more ambitious films, thus setting in motion technological experimentation with equipment and sets.

Interestingly early Italian cinema also used depth of field and movement to indicate off-screen space, which is one of the conventions of realist cinema. Many Italian films of this period are staged on several planes. Often these deep spheres of action serve no narrative function; nothing happens in them that will change the direction of the story; the objects may be insignificant but the accumulation of illusionistic detail has the function of contributing to the effect of the real, which is important for films set in a historic past, and which seek to suggest the authenticity of the recreation of that past. Costumes, even of minor figures, are exquisite and finely detailed in their suggestion of 'Roman-ness'. Similarly, the painted walls of the interiors, the atrium of Marcella's house, the beautiful details on the boats, have a dual function, suggesting both authenticity and Latin superiority. In another one-reeler, *Il Cid* (Mario Caserini, 1910) the opposition of an individual love story to the macro conflict of nation and duty to one's country is made more intense by Rodrigo's gestures. The depths of his despair, his quandary, have to be suggested by gestures conveying his huge passion for Climène, his deep love and respect for his father. As he becomes a hero, his stance, the rigidity of his body, increases. The set is painted to suggest depth and grandeur – a hall that might also be a cathedral, hung with heraldic banners, evoking a medieval world where heroes undergo suffering in the name of duty to tribe, clan and nation. Moreover, the importance of the larger conflict is indicated by repetition and numbers of actors in frame, or by the staging of action in several planes in the battle scenes, where corpses lie in the middle ground, horses gallop into the background, fights and capitulations take place in the foreground.

At the same time as Roman and Latin virtues triumphed, many other epics used the past as an excuse to depict political conflicts or torrid love affairs, but Brunetta (1993a: 156) has suggested that, after 1911–12, the emphasis on large collective movements functions to re-launch a nationalistic ideology. Since the late nineteenth century Italy had been attempting with limited success to establish colonial possessions. After the defeat of Adowa in Abyssinia in 1896, Italian governments targeted North Africa, particularly Libya, some of which was part of the Ottoman Empire. Italy declared war on the Ottoman Empire in 1911, unleashing great patriotic fervour. This colonialist agenda is visible in *Cabiria*, in which conventions of the cinematic epic coalesced. After the success of his film, *La caduta di Troia* (*The Fall of Troy*, 1911), Pastrone determined to repeat big-budget productions that would appeal to the new, middle class audience, and which would bring him in large sums of money. *Cabiria* was publicized as a lavish, epic production and its public relations campaign was very cleverly orchestrated. It was billed as the work of the poet, Gabriele d'Annunzio, based on the history of the Second Punic War, a period familiar to Italians from their schooldays. This period was especially significant in 1913–14 because of the parallels between the Romans' struggle with the Carthaginians, which resulted in Roman victory and Sicily's return to the national territory, and the twentieth-century State's attempts to annex areas of North Africa. The actors' performances would have been totally adequate without Gabriele d'Annunzio's grandiose, poetic intertitles, and without the specially composed music of Ildebrando Pizzetti. However, given the envisaged mass audience, and foreign export, the intertitles, visual images, performances and music form part of a rhetorical whole. They are designed to repeat information and to complement each other. This is essential because the film's action spans several years, two continents, several historical events (Hannibal crosses the Alps; Archimedes destroys Marcellus' fleet by focusing mirrors on the boats' sails; Massinissa helps the Romans in the battle for Carthage), and labyrinthine plots and subplots.

The traditional epic conventions of mingling historical and fictitious characters is used. The Roman child, Cabiria, and her nurse Croessa are kidnapped by pirates, taken to Carthage and sold to the High Priest, Karthalo, where Cabiria is destined to be sacrificed to the god, Moloch. Meanwhile, Croessa has met the noble Roman spy,

Figure 3.1
The temple of Moloch
in *Cabiria* (Giovanni
Pastrone, 1914).

Fulvio Axilla, and his faithful servant, the giant, Maciste (Bartolomeo Pagano), who resolve to rescue Cabiria. These stories – the abducted slave girl, the low-born strong man who saves the weak, belong to popular culture. The more powerful and evil the enemy, the greater the triumph and validation of Roman society. Carthaginian crowds, therefore, are wild and emotional and their size is foregrounded by their containment and channelling by architectural features, most notably the spectacular temple of Moloch, shaped like a giant, staring head.

The interior of the temple is full of movement, with exotic dancers in the foreground, and the enormous furnace in the background statue into which little girls are being thrown. The injustice and cruelty of a city that sacrifices little girls (and for an Italian audience, whose children are the sacred heart of the family, indulged and loved, this would have been an abomination) sets up dramatic oppositions, law/disorder, justice/injustice. From quite early in the film, the connotations of good, worthiness, and civilization stack up on the Roman side; Africans and Orientals are bad.

The costumes and props of the Romans are equally detailed and elaborate but, whereas Carthaginians lounge about and are insensitive to their daughters, Romans are busy, working, planning the siege of Carthage. Scipio's physique and face are powerful and pugnacious. This stereotype of the forceful, intelligent, Roman leader was utilized not so many years later by Mussolini. On an ideological level, the film suggests that the Carthaginians would benefit from some self-discipline and direction from a superior society. Roman soldiers are intelligent and disciplined, in contrast to the wild mobs of Orient.

The rich variety of tales from the ancient world provided ample material to explore the concerns of the 1910s. As Maria Wyke (1997: 37–9) has shown, the Spartacus story was appropriated 'for the articulation of Italian political struggles' in *Spartaco* or *Il gladiatore della Tracia* (*The Thracian Gladiator*, Giovanni Enrico Vidali, 1913), becoming associated with the fight for liberty, equality and national independence. Films like *La caduta di Troia*, *Marcantonio e Cleopatra* (*Mark Anthony and Cleopatra*) (both Enrico Guazzoni, 1913) were conveniently narratives of colonial conquest of the eastern Mediterranean and North Africa in which the representatives of other countries are orientalized and feminized, geographical conquest of a land being 'naturalized as sexual possession of a woman's body' (Wyke 1997: 80). Tensions around the role of the Catholic Church, which had initially refused to recognize the Italian State, were also played out in narratives of Christian struggle, such as *Nerone* (*Nero*, Luigi Maggi, 1909) and *Quo vadis?* Extolling the virtues of Roman civilization, values and conquests created narrative difficulties with plot elements of Christian sacrifice and moral triumph. Analysis of film periodicals of the time has shown the complex nature of the nationalist rhetoric, making connections between film as an art, Italy's artistic heritage and its power as a nation (Rhodes 2000: 309).

Epic Films of the Fascist Period

Italian pictorial traditions were plundered again under fascism, a period intensely conscious of the role of the past in constructing a unifying cultural memory. One of the most spectacular epics of this period was *Scipione l'africano* (*Scipio Africanus*, Carmine Gallone, 1937), celebrating the strength of the Roman leader in combating both domestic problems and difficulties inherent in preparation for a war in Africa. The film is visually spectacular, evoking the power of Rome through its monumental architecture and the presence of a brave and industrious population. Scipio's role as embodiment of the collective will is constantly stressed by his positioning within crowds and the number of close up shots increases the affective impact of his leadership. Amidst all the detail, the contrast between the muscles of Maciste and the ascetic look of the leader, Scipio, is used to effect the transformation of the leader's body 'from the physical to the heavenly', into a cult, kitsch object (Dalle Vacche 1992: 42–3).

Similar processes can be seen in other historical films. *Un'avventura di Salvator Rosa* (*An Adventure of Salvator Rosa*, Alessandro Blasetti, 1940), in which the hero-painter leads a double life in order to protect the peasants from the exploitation and neglect of the local aristocracy, also places the protagonist within, but slightly apart from the collective. Rosa aims to enable the peasants to control the water on their land, his modernizing agenda rhyming with Mussolini's contemporaneous draining of the Pontine marshes. Here the period evoked is the Renaissance and, as Landy (1998: 140) suggests, 'the preoccupation with the … need for a strong leader to reclaim and reinvigorate the land is central'. Only the leader is allowed warrior virility. Male as well as female characters are under his control, passively accepting his actions in a depolitizing strategy similar to that identified by Jo Labanyi (2000: 164) in her study of early Francoist Spanish film. Dictatorship denied the mass of Italian citizens active participation in the public sphere, activities being limited to projects sanctioned by the leadership.

Sword and Sandal Epics of the 1950s

The epic pattern of combining stories of fictitious characters with great historical events became a box-office staple between the late 1940s and early 1960s. The prospects for a profitable *filone* were

Figure 3.2

A spectacular return to the ancient world, *Fabiola* (Alessandro Blasetti, 1948).

identified by the huge success of *Fabiola* (Alessandro Blasetti, 1948), which topped box-office lists for 1948–9.

In its depiction of the brutal persecution of the early Christians in Rome, it performed many functions for the population of 1948, providing analogies with torments endured during the Second World War, and the demonization of communists who had taken part in the resistance (Wyke 1997: 55–6). The American army of occupation's fear of communists had led to the rapid reinstatement of many fascist officials into positions of power, which the start of the Cold War had solidified. The Christian Democrats' huge 1948 election victory effectively excluded the Left from power, leading to a continual perception of political exclusion for large parts of the population. Many interesting tensions are played out in these films. Fascism's re-working of the symbols of Roman-ness created ambiguities for post-war suggestions of the superiority of Roman civilization. The Catholic Church, which had collaborated with the fascist regime, was co-opted in the post-war period by the Americans to administer the Marshall Plan in order to marginalize the impact of communists, or the political Left. If many 1950s comedies are structured around attempts to transgress Catholic teaching on sexuality and acceptance of one's lot, the epics of the period are similar in their enjoyment in depicting sexual and other wickednesses, which are, of course, defeated in the last reel. A significant number of them contain a St Peter figure who counsels resistance to imperial authorities, and sexual abstinence. Many of the epics described as 'sword and sandal' or 'peplum' (after the short skirts of both male and female characters) feature tales of Christian suffering and moral triumph, contrasted with the wickedness and violence of their persecutors. Ironically, the censorship efforts of the Catholic Church had as one effect the development of *filoni* where sexual adventures, sadism, violence and the erotic might be safely depicted in narratives of the evil and perversions of ancient empires. Moreover, the consolidation of the Cold War provided ample opportunities to develop metaphors around the characteristics of another evil empire in the East.

The historical epics which rapidly cashed in on *Fabiola*'s success in the 1950s and early 1960s were mid-budget productions, often co-produced with French companies. They combined basic studio sets with location shooting, often using the grottos of Castellana outside Rome, and the beach of Torcaldara where a small stream ran through low cliffs and across a sandy beach. American technologies of new colour processes and widescreen filming were appropriated by Italian film-makers. Although aimed squarely at a new Italian, post-war, mass audience, the peplum epics found markets around the world. David Forgacs (1996: 53) suggests that rural Italy was largely unable to access modern media until the 1950s and 1960s – radio, books, newspapers, magazines – through lack of distribution outlets and money. The spread of third run and parochial cinemas in the 1950s meant that a rural population with minimal schooling was now exposed to cinema, the choice of melodrama and stories from antiquity being accessible forms for this new audience.

A new generation of directors successfully mined the epic genre: Duccio Tessari, Antonio Leonviola, Riccardo Freda, Vittorio Cottafavi, Giacomo Gentilomo and others, such as Mario Bava, Sergio Leone, were trained within it. The male leads were generally played by American B-grade actors or body builders – Reg Park, Steve Reeves, and Gordon Scott – as the American fashion for body building spread to Italy by the early 1950s (Della Casa 2000: 792). If productions could not afford big stars, they would employ large stars, distinguished by the hyper-muscularity of their bodies, the devotion of their followers, and the ubiquitous peplum which displayed their muscular thighs and calves. Carefully made-up, with elaborate hairstyles and flowing costumes which accentuated their bust and legs, the actresses display a stylized glamour far removed from the 'natural' girls of 1950s' comedies. Stars such as Gianna Maria Canale, Daniela Rocca and Moira Orfei were too southern in their physicality to play in the aspirational comedies of the period leading up to the boom but, with their exotic and florid looks, they embodied the temptations of a traditional type of Italian sensuality, or could play the dark and evil priestess who threatens the innocent, blonde heroine. Metaphorically, the image of backwardness of the *Mezzogiorno*, the south of Italy, was equated with the excesses of uncivilized regions.

Omar Calabrese's attempts to explain the strong presence of excess, virtuosity, the monstrous and grotesque, violence and disruption in cultural texts, defines as neo-Baroque those complex texts that work on the forms and contents of the past, restoring a sense of ambiguity to certainties of the present (1992: 179). Besides the visual disharmony and asymmetry, which is explored elsewhere, excessive bodies and violence are also features of the neo-Baroque. These disruptive, destabilizing elements coexist with simple internal narrative structures that validate conservative social relationships. For Christine Buci-Glucksmann, the Baroque represents the validation of an alternative system to the order and rationality of modernity. Modernity's threats to traditional society were represented visually and narratively.

L'Eroe di Babilonia (*The Beast of Babylon Against the Son of Hercules*, Siro Marcellini, 1963) has a typical structure with a hero, Prince Nippur (Gordon Scott), invited to return to his country by rebels in order to reclaim his rightful inheritance of the throne of Babylon. The tyrant, Belshazzar, has usurped the throne, oppressing the population with great cruelty, assisted by the high priestess of Ishtar, Ura (Moira Orfei). Despite many heroic fights, Nippur is imprisoned in the dungeons below the temple. He manages to escape and, although wounded, joins the Persian army as it marches on Babylon, overthrows Belshazzar and regains the throne. Minimal sets with unpainted walls are offset by colourful costumes for the villains and the obligatory dancing girls. In the dungeon scenes Nippur is the focus of the gaze of his Christian servant, Tibis, and the other prisoners, low-angle shots dwelling on his swelling muscles and grotesque facial expressions as he wrestles with neck and body chains. Sado-masochistic conflicts occur in most of these films. In *Nel segno di Roma* (*Sign of the Gladiator*, Guido Brignone, 1959), General Marcus Valerius (Georges Marchal) is captured and tortured by the forces of the Assyrian queen, Zenobia (Anita Ekberg), his sweaty, semi-naked body displayed in mid-shots. Significantly, Valerius wears trousers matching his scarlet tunic for the final fight with the evil Palmyran minister, thereby becoming active and less the object of erotic contemplation. Zenobia, who has worn a succession of green and blue frocks during the film, is reunited with Valerius in Rome at the end, wearing white and red to match her lover. Divested of her regal power, Zenobia is consigned to a traditional role, with patriarchy firmly re-established. As Steve Neale (1993: 17–18) has explored, both the voyeuristic and the fetishistic looks intertwine in films of male conflict. The heroines are typically colourless and reduced to screaming loudly; violence and the erotic, in the form of fetishized female characters, dancers, excessively muscular men, slow the narratives down, indicating by their interpellation of the audience to involvement in pleasure, the attractions and dangers of alternative ways of being.

There have been many attempts to explain the popularity of peplum epics, Michèle Lagny (1992: 178) identifying the instructive function (battles to establish democracy) while having fun 'while letting off steam'. As John Foot (2003: 45–6) has pointed out, the fascist dictatorship carried Italy into the Second World War with 'muted' opposition and the rapidly following defeat and disasters in Greece, Africa and Russia led to the events of 8 September 1943, when Italy changed sides mid-conflict. Italians were faced with acute choices between different versions of duty. The battles set in the ancient world in cinematic epics of the 1950s all rehearse wartime conflicts at one remove – whether to follow the usurper, how to reconcile one's Catholic belief with supporting rebels, in what circumstances to become part of an army, at what point would one change sides. The size and attraction of the actors are indicative of the size and complexity of the problems rehearsed, resulting in conflict narratives of gender power, wartime resistance and threats of annihilation.

Bertolucci's Epics

The expressive and political possibilities of the epic also attracted art film directors. Bertolucci's *Novecento* (*1900*, 1976) is the product of a particular moment of the early 1970s, when the political upheaval of 1968 had caused Gramsci's ideas to be re-evaluated. There is no space here for detailed consideration of how an Italian Marxist managed to make a two-part, epic film with the financial assistance of Paramount, United Artists and 20th Century Fox (Kolker, 1985: 68–77). The Italian title signifies both the year 1900, and the century, thus implying something altogether more significant and powerful than the English title. The subject, the rise to political consciousness of the peasants of Emilia Romagna between Summer 1900 and April 1945, is framed by Pelizza da Volpreda's painting, 'The Fourth Estate', and by the prologue set on Liberation Day, 25 April 1945. The painting shows the purposive movement forward in collective action of peasant figures and sets the style and expectations of the following narrative. Bertolucci's Marxism informs the most minute artistic choices. He uses the device of following the lives of two boys, born on the same day, one into the peasant and the other into the landowning classes to represent class struggle symbolically. The meaning of the story, the truth of class relations and how and why the upper classes supported fascism, is suggested not only by the informative dialogue, but by the visual organization and emphasis. The *mise en scène*, for example, repeatedly draws attention to the fact that the peasants, the Dalcò family, only have natural light, thus eating quickly. Their collective solidarity is stressed by their compression into one space, as well as by the heroic figure of Leo Dalcò (Sterling Hayden), who delivers the lesson of family (and metonymically, class) solidarity. By contrast, the landowner's family occupy many rooms, and use artificial light. The personal is always political. As in all of Bertolucci's films, the exploration of sexual relationships is fundamental to that of social and political relationships, repression being associated with political oppression, anality and sodomy used as metaphors for the exploitative, consumerist relations of capitalist society (Loshitzky, 1995: 188). In *1900* sexual perversion is used to indicate the decadence and degradation of bourgeois society in the fascist period, its adherence to fascism in order to maintain its own power.

Bertolucci's interest in a Marxist view of history, and in Freudian analysis also meant the inclusion of the occasional sex and violence, and sexual perversity, none of which ever hurt in box-office terms. However, Bertolucci left analysis in 1984, and the crises of socialism and communism, culminating in the fall of the Berlin wall, left a great void in his life. From the mid-1980s Bertolucci's films question the values of European society and explore other cultures and belief systems, and his track record led to large budgets to do this – $25 million for *The Last Emperor* (1987), which won nine Oscars and grossed $93 million, and *The Sheltering Sky* (1990), and $33 million for *Little Buddha* (1993). These are sumptuous, wide-screen epics whose striking and sensual use of colour and composition lend interest to the ideas expressed. For Bertolucci, Western societies, under the influence of multinational business corporations, and the media, which they control, are becoming more similar, more monocultural; class struggle has been ironed out and most Europeans live in an ideological desert.[2] These films are both quests for personal authenticity, embodied in the non-Western Other, and explorations of other sexualities. In all of them, narrative conflicts (wars, revolutions, lack of certainties) are also expressed through excess – the virtuosity and visual beauty of Bertolucci's (and his cinematographer, Kim Arcalli's) film-making, and the presence of extreme violence and grotesque characters and incidents.

Returns to the *Risorgimento*

Key events in Italian national history have regularly been visited. The Risorgimento, the struggles for national unity in the 1860s, gave rise to many potent myths, such as the notion that an active minority could succeed in heroically founding the nation (Foot 2003: 17–18). Fascist cinema evoked the Risorgimento to cement the idea of continuity for the regime. Post-war, Goffredo Alessandrini (who had actively supported the fascist regime) depicted Garibaldi's retreat to Venice in *Camicie rosse* (*Red Shirts*, 1952). There are many evocations of Second World War resistance in the use of actors, Anna Magnani and Raf Vallone, who had achieved fame in neorealist films, and in images of reedbeds, boats and marshes, and especially in the shooting of the marshland family by the German-speaking soldiers, recalling Rossellini's film, *Paisà* (1946) visually and narratively. There are also frequent uses of conventions of the cowboy film and the war film, which Forgacs (2001: 271–4) attributes to the film's agenda of recovering collective pride at a time of deep national crisis at the transition from fascism to the Republic. Affective elements are used to erase any sense of failure and to link the sacrifice of the few to the higher good of the nation; the repetition of extreme close-ups of the suffering faces of Garibaldi and his wife Anita, interspersed with sequences in which Anita rallies the red shirts or cares for young soldiers; vignettes of red shirts speaking in different regional accents; long shots of the land, all indicate the pain and difficulty of unifying the nation.

Influenced by Gramsci's writing on the Risorgimento as a failed revolution in which revolutionaries and their ideas were absorbed into the ruling classes, Luchino Visconti's *Senso* (1954), and *Il gattopardo* (*The Leopard*, 1963) are subtle and complex narratives that use representative characters to epitomize this historical process (Nowell-Smith 2003; Marcus 1986). This process is known as *trasformismo* in Italian history and can be seen in *Il gattopardo* epitomized in the person of Tancredi's (Alain Delon) adherence first to the Garibaldians and then to the Piedmontese army, and in his courtship and marriage to Angelica (Claudia Cardinale), the daughter of a rich, provincial bourgeois. In *Senso*, Count Serpieri's pragmatic changes of political allegiance reflect the same historical movements, which are generally suppressed in official historiography. In exploring the complexities of *Senso*, Millicent Marcus (1986: 186–7) acknowledges the working through of Gramsci's ideas so that Livia and Serpieri come to embody the cynicism of the class which survives by adaptation, but is troubled by the film's spectacular elements for which Visconti was criticized at the time. However, his spectacular use of colour and texture, decor and location, his virtuosity and the accumulation of illusionistic detail are, as we have already explored, also characteristics of the Italian postmodern, the neo-Baroque, which works to problematize fixed interpretations of history.

The Shield of History

Setting a film's narrative in a historically remote moment is a trope derived from literature which allows contemporary concerns to be rehearsed at a safe distance or indicates the presence of 'unfinished business' in the form of mysteries whose lack of resolution offends in the present. Enrico Mattei's (the Head of the State Hydrocarbon body, ENI) death was only one of many unexplained accidents, murders, assassinations that litter the history of the Italian Republic. Cumulatively these events constitute constant affronts to belief in democratic ideals, and are evidence of wounds to the Italian body politic. Recent work in the film studies area on trauma theory is useful when examining cultural texts, such as films that

seek to explore reasons for these violent events in Italian history. As
Susannah Radstone (2001: 192) has argued, trauma theory is less
useful as a term which 'refers' to a catastrophic event, than 'to the
revised understandings of referentiality it prompts'. This is especially
relevant in the case of Italian cinema with its constant references
to the 'real' world of Italian politics or social life. As with Irish
cinema, the relentless pull of referentiality to an exterior context
is an indication of the psychic investment of engagement with
contemporary history. There is too much at stake not to attempt to
make sense of everyday reality. In Rosi's *Il caso Mattei* (*The Mattei
Affair*, 1973), *noir* elements and visual excess are used to indicate
a dissatisfaction with official versions of Mattei's death, and/or
to evoke a dysfunctional world, but the codes and conventions
of expository cinema are also constantly used to persuade the
audience of the accuracy and authenticity of his reconstruction of
events. The film's mise en scène associates traditional politicians
and industrialists with Baroque architecture, complexity and lack
of clarity, and Mattei with buildings and industry associated with
modernity. Mattei's death was traumatic precisely because he
represented an attempt at the introduction of modern governmental
practices (of all sorts) into Italian civic life.

A similar dichotomy is visible in *I cento passi* (*The Hundred Steps*,
Marco Tullio Giordana, 2000), centred on the conflict between the
Sicilian mafia and young political activist, Peppino Impastato, killed
by the Mafia in 1977. Grotesque elements of Peppino's behaviour,
and his use of local radio, contrast with the corruption and
mediocrity of the local Mafia. From his viewpoint of the late 1990s,
Giordana connects Mafia and legal power in the contemporary and
the historical worlds, and contrasts the passionate convictions of the
late 1960s and 1970s with the inertia and lack of a sense of history
of contemporary youth. Another film which makes the contrast
between commitment and conformity, but this time evoking anti-
fascist ideas and the rejection of bourgeois conformism, is Guido
Chiesa's *Il partigiano Johnny* (*Johnny the Partisan*, 2000). Based
on a prestigious book by former partisan, Beppe Fenoglio, Chiesa
describes Johnny's story as a 'search for authenticity' and 'small acts
of greatness for the mediocre time awaiting us' (De Gaetano 2000:
121). In this respect, the film attempts to be an accurate record of
an ambiguous and contested history, and a reflection in the present
on the difficulties for young people of achieving maturity and moral
stature in a time of corruption and compromise.

The Family Drama and the Nation

Metaphorical constructions of national unity are fraught with tensions. The idea of *italianità* or 'Italian-ness' always seems incomplete
in that landscapes and bodies are either regionally specific, or

vaguely generic. As we have seen, comedies of the fascist period often featured someone of a lower class either 'marrying up' and therefore signalling the successful uniting of class interests in a modern country, or attempting the performance of upper-class roles but returning to their previous station in life in the final reel. The latter scenario was rehearsed repeatedly in the melodramas of 'pink neorealism' in the 1950s, in which desire for the lower-class woman was often consummated, but the formation of the successful, cross-class couple was thwarted in the final reel. The most successful solution to the problem of exploring the nature of the Italian nation and Italian history was to use a family reacting to historical events as a paradigm of the nation.

Dino Risi and Ettore Scola based their careers on dramas of this type of generational and family conflict. Scola's *La famiglia* (*The Family*, Italy/France, 1987) follows the life of Carlo (Vittorio Gassman) from his birth to his eightieth birthday party. The film's action never leaves the large, upper-class apartment and the extended family is used to illustrate how historical events impinge on different types of people. In its loving recreation of domestic interiors and costumes, and particularly the textures of glasses and tableware on the table around which the family congregates, the film both offers uncritical enjoyment, and a metaphor for the national family. The only major family row is over how Italians came to support fascism, to which Scola's camera's obsessive return to the apartment's central corridor supplies the answer, stressing the inward-looking dynamic of the Italian family and the self-interest resulting in decisions not to contest fascism.

Roberto Faenza's *Marianna Ucrìa* (1997), on the other hand, uses spectacle and the archaic family rituals of a Sicilian aristocratic clan to arrest any tendency towards nostalgia. Based on a well-known book by Dacia Maraini it is set in the early eighteenth century. The protagonist, Marianna, has been deaf mute from the time of her rape at the age of six by the man her parents force her to marry at the age of thirteen, her uncle, Duke Pietro (Roberto Herlitzka). Freed from her circumscribed life of child bearing by her children's Scottish philosopher tutor who teaches her sign language, Marianna is able to communicate and to move forward to a full place in the world. This is signalled by her taking control of family building projects and her rejection of the brutal and unequal relationship with her husband. Her recovery of the memory of her rape is the final element that enables her to express her personal freedom by leaving her estate to travel. In the film's story of the liberation of one, individual, southern, aristocratic woman, the film asserts the realities of how the suppression of women in Italian familism maintains patriarchal and class power.

The family is again used to explore recent Italian history in *La meglio gioventù* (*The Best of Youth*, Marco Tullio Giordana, 2003), covering forty years in the lives of brothers Nicola (Luigi Lo Cascio) and Matteo (Alessio Boni), their family, friends, and the disturbed girl, Georgia, who affects their lives. Meeting Georgia makes Nicola decide to become a psychiatrist, whereas Matteo drops out and joins the police force. The film, which was made with Miramax and television money, had its cinematic release in two, 3-hour parts, drawing on melodrama and soap opera conventions in its engagement with recent history. Italy itself is firmly integrated into the narrative. Nicola sees the 1966 Florence flood on Norwegian television, returns to help clear up, and meets his future partner, Giulia (Sonia Bergamasco), playing a piano amid mud. They set up home together and have a child, Sara, during the 1968 university riots, in which Matteo is involved in police action against demonstrators. Significant moments in the life of the nation thus punctuate the saga. The film's action traverses the entire country as characters move, marry, find jobs and partners. The function of the visually stunning long shots of scenery are not just establishing shots but, by their virtuosity, they establish a pattern suggesting that their diversity contributes to the unity that is Italy. Beautiful high-angle long shots of Turin with the Alps in the distance are associated with Nicola and Sara; street-level long shots of golden house fronts on narrow streets (the parents); the cityscape of Florence (during the floods and when Giulia meets her daughter, Sara); Tuscany (where their sister, Francesca and her husband convert a deserted farmhouse, using another friend as contractor); Palermo, where Matteo meets Mirella; Stromboli (Mirella's home).

The theme of health – family, physical, mental and national, also structures the narrative. Georgia is mentally ill, but intelligent, kind and undeserving of the abuse in the asylums. Nicola is a doctor, passionate in the support of the human rights of mentally ill people, but often less perceptive than other less-educated characters. Perceptiveness is mainly the province of women (mother, Sara, Francesca, Mirella). Matteo is dysfunctional socially and sexually, reflected in his uncontrolled and violent rages and inability to sustain personal relationships. Giulia is similarly a person of certainties,

Figure 3.3
Rebellious youth and the cityscape of Florence, *La meglio gioventù* (Marco Tullio Giordana, 2003).

represented as a dysfunctional mother (she abandons Sara) and person. She refuses family life and joins the Red Brigades, ending up a rather grey figure working in a library. Health resides in the family and is associated with caring and vitality. Nicola and Matteo's parents marry across classes. The father met their mother, a schoolmistress, when selling Spanish oranges in Campo de' Fiori. He is entrepreneurial, full of schemes and imagination, successful in nurturing all his children. The mother mentions her professional role of nurturing the younger generation, which may not have time devoted to it at home. Through the activities of the brothers and the family, the caring institutions (asylums, schools) are represented as healthier for Italy than the coercive institutions of the forces of law and order. Civic duty finds its ultimate expression in the older sister, a magistrate, who volunteers for Palermo after the murder of the magistrate, Giovanni Falcone, in order to do her duty. Giordana's film is an epic of Italian history of the last forty years, linking the country to positive characteristics of the family.

Excavating the Past

Other films also contest the traditional view of history as the great deeds of exceptional men by putting alternative histories on the screen. *Metello* (Mauro Bolognini, 1970) is the product of renewed interpretations of Gramsci's ideas in the wake of the students' and workers' uprisings of 1968. An adaptation of a book by the left-wing author, Vasco Pratolini, *Metello* follows its eponymous hero's involvement in workers' political struggles in the late nineteenth/early twentieth century when workers' associations were brutally suppressed. Workers' families are constantly threatened and broken up by imprisonment, the precariousness of working conditions, or by accidental death, but the metafamily of male solidarity provides opportunities for mutual support, education and idealism. As in all these films, illusionistic detail is used to anchor filmic actions firmly to historical events, while spectacle and wide-angle long shots of cityscapes and landscapes signal the importance of this working-class history in the construction of the nation.

A small group of contemporary films have returned to the 1970s and 1980s in order to re-enact traumatic events of the holocaust, *anni di piombo* (the years of the bullet), terrorism and political corruption. *Buongiorno notte* (Marco Bellocchio, 2003), financed by Miramax and RAI, re-enacts the kidnapping and murder of Aldo Moro in 1978. It ignores the usual polemics and the temptations of *dietrologia* (the science of speculating who is behind (*dietro*) unexplained mysteries) by concentrating on the kidnappers. The young couple who view an anonymous ground-floor flat with two entrances turn out to be part of a Red Brigade cell. Preparations for the kidnapping are recorded in detail as the false bookcase is constructed to conceal the hidden prison, and daily routines established. The central character, Chiara (Maya Sansa) works as a librarian in a Ministry and struggles with her conscience. The narrative is punctuated by news bulletins and Chiara's dreams/flashbacks, to her father's death as a partisan, to Stalin and early Soviet Russia. The film is ambiguous about the dreams' motivations but, in the authoritarian ranting of the cell's leader, Mariano (Luigi Lo Cascio) there seems to be a rejection of the Red Brigade's political stance. However, the claustrophobic *mise en scène*, the dullness of the appartment and its inhabitants and the lack of contextualizing for a foreign audience fails to excite interest in any moral dilemmas that might have informed those responsible for Moro's assassination.

Ferzan Ozpetek's *La finestra di fronte* (*Facing Window*, 2003) is a quest narrative that uncovers a lost 1940s history of racial and sexual persecution in the Jewish ghetto of Rome, nicely epitomized by the ellipsis between the sepia-tinted past, and the traffic-noisy present in the effacement of Davide's (Massimo Girotti) bloody handprint on the wall. Two impossible love affairs, and the association of appetite and sexual desire structure the narrative. Giovanna's (Giovanna Mezzogiorno) frustration with her job in a chicken factory, her two children and partner finds expression in rages, and relief in her desire for the neighbour, Lorenzo, glimpsed from her kitchen window, and in making cakes to sell in the local bar. Attempts to discover the identity of the elderly and confused man Giovanna and her partner find on the Ponte Sisto and take into their home lead them back to the original murder in the bakery, carried out so that Davide could escape to warn his community of the imminent roundup of Jews. Memory, and recollection of his homosexual lover, Simone, unleashes an orgy of patisserie in Davide in the present. Excavating his past uncovers violent events, racial and sexual oppression conveniently forgotten for fifty years. In the multicultural present, Giovanna is given the opportunity of satisfying her extra-marital sexual desires, only to opt for loyalty to her family. Ozpetek's previous film, *Le fate ignoranti* (*Ignorant Fairies*, 2001) similarly stresses the racial and sexual pluralism of contemporary communities as Antonia (Margherita Buy) discovers that her late husband had had a gay lover (Stefano Accorsi) for seven years. Excavating the past results in acceptance of diversity and an alternative 'family' that represents the nation.

La finestra di fronte, like Liliana Cavani's *Il portiere di notte* (*The Night Porter*, 1974), Roberto Benigni's *La vita è bella* (*Life is Beautiful*, 1998) and Francesco Rosi's *La tregua* (*The Truce*, 1997) are all attempts to represent the trauma of the Holocaust in story form. Like other traumatic events in twentieth-century history, all of these films show what Hayden White (1996: 20–1) has described as 'resistance to inherited categories and conventions for assigning them meanings', that is that the 'facts' of the events tell us less about the attitude we ought to take with respect to them than fictional accounts do. Guido (Roberto Benigni)'s comic narrativization of events in the concentration camp as fantasy relegates the logical consequences of the Third Reich's racial policies to the realms of the grotesquely lunatic and tragic. In Cavani's erotic tragedy, dramas of submission and abjection provide metaphors for the exercise of power and patriarchal control and Rosi's adaptation of Primo Levi's account of his journey from Auschwitz to Turin is an assertion of the value that a sense of the precariousness of life gives to community and society.

Conclusion

The history of modern Italy has been marked by traumatic events and massive social change, events perceived as beyond individual control and profoundly threatening. Elsaesser (2001: 201) suggests that 'trauma theory is not so much a theory of recovered memory as it is one of recovered referentiality'. The films discussed here draw on historical events in an attempt to resolve doubts about interpretation. Narrative, kinetic, performative and visual excess – *film noir* conventions, disturbing asymmetry, *chiaroscuro* lighting, showy visuals – function to draw attention to the presence of events that offend democratic sensibilities, or simple explanations that mask the abuse of power. Neo-Baroque excess is a way of restoring complexity to events represented as open to simple explanation. At the same time, the films draw on realist strategies to lend authority to the director's analysis through the foregrounding of referentiality in repeated, illusionistic detail, authenticity of place and setting, attempts to control explanations through narrative closure. The excess of detail and visual organization signals the importance of the mysteries and the effort that the text is making to persuade the audience that its interpretation is the right one. Each traumatic event in Italian history – war, violence, atrocities, assassinations – represents a failure of the modernizing process and a threat to a successful image of a modern State. In the next chapter we will explore the different styles and modes of realism that became associated with Italian film-making in the post-war period.

4

Realisms and Neorealisms in Italian Cinema

Italian critics have tried to define neorealism since the Parma conference of 1952. At regular intervals since then the bones of neorealism have been picked over by film-makers, academics and critics. A major conference held in Pesaro in September 1974 led to Lino Miccichè's (1975) publication of a volume of documents and papers. There are other factors in the continued interest in neorealism. The influential French critic, André Bazin, devoted several essays to defining it. The main figures of neorealism had long careers in the film industry, their films being regularly evaluated in the context of larger bodies of work. Other directors, screenwriters, cinematographers, started their careers in neorealist cinema, so that critics have had to speculate on the influence of neorealism in their formation. When Vittorio de Sica died in 1975, a large critical evaluation of his work was published, and reassessed by a major retrospective at the 1992 Pesaro Film Festival. Last, but not least, the expansion of film and media studies courses in the 1980s and 1990s, has ensured that films like *Ladri di biciclette* (*Bicycle Thieves*, Vittorio De Sica, 1948) are introduced to new audiences, so that the sheer numbers of people familiar with their names and reputation justify their release on sell-through video. The presence of this chapter is part of that process.

It is difficult, now, to appreciate what was perceived as real and what was new about neorealist Italian films after 1943. Not only were few exported, so that it is difficult to appreciate the range of films that could be labelled neorealist, but critics continue to disagree about which films to include. It is also difficult to gauge the context because films of the preceeding fascist period, and contemporary films that are not neorealist are largely unavailable outside Italy. Many have been released on video, but sporadically, for limited periods, and without subtitles. Nonetheless, successive generations of film-makers and critics have turned their attention to this small band of films produced in Italy in the 1940s in order to assess it and to come to terms with it. It has to be said that one major reason for this interest is the snobbery about popular entertainment that afflicted Italian intellectuals until the 1970s. Realist cinema, and films that explored serious issues or themes, enjoyed critical prestige whereas the director Raffaello Matarazzo, who had made hugely popular melodramas classified as 'pink neorealism' in the same period, had to wait until 1976 for serious consideration of his career (Aprà and Carabba 1976).

The Italian experience of the Second World War was traumatic. Imprisonment, a governmental push for modernization that disturbed regional and traditional identities, mobilization, armed conflict, the break up of families so that women had to enter the workforce, shortages of food and other commodities, were upheavals whose existence was suppressed by the fascist regime and not made public knowledge until 1943. After 1943, foreign occupation by first the German then the Allied armies, the change in allegiance half-way through the conflict, meant that Italians experienced hunger, death of family members in combat, death, rape and displacement of civilians, partisan resistance, and then hunger, homelessness and unemployment. The effects of occupation and the huge changes of the period of reconstruction included voting rights for women, the abolition of the monarchy and the establishment of the First Republic. It is not surprising that there should also be battles on the cultural as well as the political front with Right- and Left-wing movements evolving different strategies to engage with contemporary reality.

Recent critical attention to this post-war period of reconstruction has made a strong case for considering the continuities between the fascist and the post-war periods, with a consequent re-periodization of historical phases (Forgacs 1989: 57–9). With the benefit of time, the critical case was made for a cut-off point around 1960, when the boom period of economic prosperity had transformed Italy into a capitalist economy with a marginalized left-wing culture. Forgacs sees the neorealist period as having more in common with the preceeding period than with the modern Italy of juke boxes, fashion and style, consumer goods such as fridges and cars, and popular culture.

The neorealist label was attached to a small group of films, but there were in fact several realisms, reflecting the fact that making sense of the immediate present, let alone the immediate past, was the site of conflicting accounts, with different film-makers making their bid to interpret events. This chapter aims to introduce the cultural, political and commercial context of neorealist cinema, and to explore these different realisms

The Realist Tradition

As Chapter 1 has shown, films *dal vero* developed early in the silent period. *L'eruzione dell'Etna* (*The Eruption of Mt Etna*, Ambrosio Productions, 1910) is an early example of film documentary, organized to stress the bravery of the intrepid photographer in filming the lava flows and their effects. What is interesting about it is the use of documentary footage to construct a narrative and the intercutting of shots and reaction shots (of peasants attempting to divert the lava flows) to heighten the dramatic impact. Intertitles giving places and dates draw on earlier, magic lantern traditions.[1] Clearly, the realist cinematic tradition was established early in Italy, but did not prevent a good, dramatic story. Rondolino (1993: 25–31) has shown that Ambrosio's films were initially made either for the Lumière company of France, or copied the Lumière format of short films on topical subjects such as military displays, visits of the King Umberto and Queen Margherita, horse and motor races. He makes the point that these subjects went on to form the staple of the *cinegiornali*, the film news programmes that accompanied the main feature in cinemas until the 1960s. A glance at current television schedules shows the persistence of news items of local interest that organize the comprehensibility of events.

Authenticating events were also positioned in fictional dramas. In the late 1910s the actor/director Emilio Ghione copied French film serials, using the investigative format and the figure of a transgressive hero, the *apache*, as keys to a darker world. These figures did not subvert established order but targeted social injustices (Brunetta 1993a: 208–9). Although the story world of Ghione's films has fantastic elements, the backgrounds to the action use working-class exteriors that are striking in their depiction of a poverty-ridden and socially backward country.

Film-makers also took advantage of abundant sunshine to set the action of fiction films outdoors, using scenery and monuments to foreground the picturesque, to suggest a generic Italianicity, or to stress the authenticity of the story world. In doing the latter, the prestige of French realist cinema provided a model. Cesare Zavattini, the influential screenwriter associated with neorealism, started writing for films and journals in the 1930s and was not alone in choosing realist film conventions in order to depict social problems or new milieux. The fictionalized documentary *Uomini sul fondo* (*SOS Submarine*, Francesco De Robertis, 1941), *I bambini ci guardano* (*The Children Are Watching Us*, Vittorio De Sica, 1942), *Quattro passi fra le nuvole* (*Four Steps in the Clouds*, Alessandro Blasetti, 1942) and *Ossessione* (Luchino Visconti, 1943) all used realist conventions and are regarded as precursors of neorealism. De Sica's film uses location shooting in parks and at the seaside as venues where the mother can meet her lover while surrounded by anonymous crowds. Blasetti's film offers interesting glimpses into the realities of the life of the lower middle-class chocolate salesman, living in a new apartment in one of the recently developed housing complexes and having to travel to remote, traditional rural communities.

Luchino Visconti's *Ossessione*, made in 1942, was very different from other dramas of its time and was hailed both as a precursor of neorealism, and as an early example of *film noir*. Although these categories seem on the surface to be mutually exclusive, they do in fact constitute the defining characteristics of Italian *noir* (Wood 2004). Based on James M. Cain's book *The Postman Always Rings Twice*, *Ossessione* shares with later neorealist films quite careful choices of sets, locale and framings. Visconti is concerned to show his characters in their social context, so that their actions are to some extent explained, and always contextualized. Thus the opening sequences of the film contain many long shots showing characters acting and reacting in their environment, and is particularly marked by the use of crane long shots. Early close-ups (and there are very few in the film) are used deliberately to suggest the immediate sexual attraction between Gino (Massimo Girotti) and Giovanna (Clara Calamai). The camera lingers on Gino and his physical presence as much as Giovanna's. The editing is varied, but there is more use of the long take, a feature of European cinema, where the camera follows a protagonist as he/she moves, rather than cutting to speed up the action. Location shooting in *Ossessione* gives a sense of geographic realism, the high-angle shots from the road conveying a sense of the monotony of the Po marshes. Shots through doors and into cramped rooms stress how characters are bounded and trapped by their environment. The diegetic world contains a young drifter, a woman who explains her marriage to a fat, older man as an escape from unemployment, poverty and 'getting men to buy me dinner'. When Gino runs away from Giovanna to the port of Ancona, he meets a cynical young dancer who may be involved in prostitution, and stays with the sexually ambiguous Spagnolo. This is a disfunctional world of privations, of people forced to the margins of society in order to survive, where the precarious equilibrium of 'normal' life is shaken by the arrival of strangers, or overwhelming sexual attraction. On its release in June 1943 it was severely criticized by the fascist press for its portrayal of adultery, amorality, sexual excess and murder and had a limited distribution. *Ossessione* was not as influential as it might have been at the time because, two months later, political events and the Allied invasion dominated national life.

The raw vitality and realism of American writers like Cain contrasted with the 'cultural autarchy' of official fascist aims to create 'art and literature totally free from foreign influences' (Heiney 1964: 54). Besides admiring American writers such as Melville, Dos Passos, Faulkner, Poe, young intellectuals also idolized the Sicilian author, Giovanni Verga. Verga's naturalism, called *verismo*, depended on the evocation of particular geographies of place and atmosphere through the building up of detail.

Chris Wagstaff (1989: 72) has pointed out that the majority of films classed as neorealist were 'produced, directed, written, acted, photographed and distributed by exactly the same people who had made exactly the same kind of film before the war'. However, the idea that those who had experienced the war would be unchanged is not borne out by the films themselves. In his study of Italian films of the Second World War, Mino Argentieri (1998: 297–336) concludes with an exploration of the participation in wartime events of people involved in the film industry. Some of them accommodated to fascism, others were involved in the ferment of ideas and debates about realism and new techniques at the CSC, some formed co-operatives to help each other in the face of nepotism and corruption in the film industry, others left film altogether. Whereas few directors were directly involved in the Resistance, many young partisans chose to go into film or theatre after the war. Stories of artists and film technicians who were murdered by the fascists provide the force behind Argentieri's view that Italian film-makers and screenwriters reached artistic maturity in the neorealist period not because of all the debates around artistic form, or Visconti's *Ossessione*, but because of the lived experience of the war and the need to bear witness to events in ways which stressed their emotional impact.

What is Neorealism?

Neorealist films were produced in the immediate post-war period, that is to say, roughly, from 1945–50, with a few stragglers afterwards. It is important to remember that this was a time of material deprivation; the infrastructures of fascist society had been broken down by the battles that accompanied the Allied advance. To start with, the Germans had taken much film-making equipment with them as they retreated; Cinecittà was used as a refugee camp and there was a shortage of film stock to make films. *Roma città aperta* (*Rome Open City*, Roberto Rossellini, 1945) used these constraints to its own advantage. The mixture of film stocks gives a grainy, documentary feel and the use of real locations all add to the overwhelming impression of reality and authenticity.

On the positive side, there was an enormous sense of freedom and release in the late 1940s, and a desire on the part of film-makers opposed to fascist ideas to record the turmoil of this period of Italian history. Fascist films had, consciously or unconsciously, reinforced fascist values and had played down inequalities in Italian society. Neorealist films had a social agenda, and film-makers wished to differentiate their films from those of the recent past for ideological reasons. Italy was a defeated nation, but the Left-wing and communist partisans had emerged from the war with immense prestige. They were the patriots who had fought against fascism, and who had assisted the Allies. Neorealist film-makers considered that they had the opportunity to say something new about Italy, and to portray sections of the population who had not had much screen time devoted to them – the working class.

For various reasons the wartime alliances of anti-fascist political parties fell apart after the Armistice but, for our purposes, it is sufficient to note that Left-wing views predominated in the neorealist movements in literature, painting and cinema because they represented new and fresh approaches to the evaluation of the turbulent period of history which artists were living through, but that they very soon came under attack from the Catholic Church and more conservative elements in Italian society. That Left-wing cultural strategies failed was, according to Forgacs (1989: 161), because the Left concentrated on traditional conceptions of cultural activity, while the Centre-Right parties and Christian Democrats concentrated on building 'a bureaucracy of political and cultural operators, to occupy the radio and television, to extend their influence into private cultural organisations by offering economic concessions and facilitations'. The Right inserted itself into the capitalist system, while the Left set up parallel organizations, based on Gramsci's notions of the national-popular and the role of the 'organic intellectual', that is, someone who would analyse society from within in order to show how it might be changed (Gramsci 1975). However, Gramsci's *Prison Notebooks* only started to be published from 1947 onwards and arguably influenced film-makers of the wave of critical realism from 1960 onwards rather than those of the late 1940s. Neorealist film-makers of the mid to late 1940s were concerned to bear witness to their time but underestimated popular aspirations to forget hardship and move on. Moreover, the prestige of neorealism abroad and the pride felt by artists in their achievement assisted their mistake of 'abandoning to the right the energies inherent in popular culture' (Elsaesser 1996: 164).

The Commercial Success of Neorealist Films

Initially, Neorealist films were successful financially but, as the economic situation improved in the period of reconstruction, the public became less keen to pay to see hard-hitting social dramas. However, even at the height of their popularity, they coexisted with comedies and melodramas that displayed elements of continuity with films of the fascist period. *Roma città aperta* was the top Italian film of the 1945–6 season, when forty-three films were released. It made Lire 162 million; *Sciuscià* (*Shoeshine*, Vittorio De Sica, 1946) came eighteenth with Lire 55,600,000. In 1946–7, fifty-three films were released. *Il bandito* (*The Bandit*, Alberto Lattuada, 1946) came fourth (Lire 184 million), *Vivere in pace* (*To Live in Peace*, Luigi Zampa, 1946) sixth, *Paisà* (Roberto Rossellini, 1946) ninth, *Il sole sorge ancora* (Aldo Vergano, 1946) twelfth. Fifty-four films were released in the 1947–8 season, of which *L'Onorevole Angelina* (*Angelina*, Luigi Zampa, 1947) came fourth (Lire 264 million), *Gioventù perduta* (*Lost Youth*, Pietro Germi, 1948) fourteenth, and *Caccia tragica* (*Tragic Pursuit*, Giuseppe De Santis, 1947) twenty-eighth. In the 1948–1949 season, sixty-one films were released. *In nome della legge* (*In the Name of the Law*, Pietro Germi, 1948) came third. *Anni difficili* (*Difficult Years*, Luigi Zampa, 1948), *Ladri di biciclette* (*Bicycle Thieves*, Vittorio De Sica, 1948), *Senza pietà* (*Without Pity*, Alberto Lattuada, 1948) were ninth, eleventh and fourteenth respectively. *Germania anno zero* (*Germany, Year Zero*, Roberto Rossellini, 1947) and *La terra trema* (Luchino Visconti, 1948) were forty-sixth and fifty-second (Cosulich 1957). These, and the figures for subsequent years bear out Chris Wagstaff's (1989: 73) contention that neorealist films were neither more nor less successful than other types of film in this period. The statistics also show that, as Italian production increased, so did the number of American films in circulation so that Italian films had to jostle for a diminishing share of the market. There are many reasons for the decline of neorealism; changing public taste, the competition from the influx of the huge backlog of American films that had been unable to be imported into Italy until the post-war period, and the increasing use of censorship by the Right-wing Christian Democrats to refuse State subsidy to films presenting a critical view of society.[2] In the period of reconstruction, the Allies were much more in tune with the Christian Democrat Party than with the Left wing, and they certainly distrusted and never understood the partisan parties and Eurocommunism. Whereas the Labour Party in Britain won the first major, post-war elections, expressing the hopes of the mass of the population for social change, in Italy the Christian Democrats won a key victory in the April 1948 elections, and absorbed many right-wing elements into their party. Through endless coalition governments, they dominated political life for forty years.

Theorizing Neorealism

In 1952 the Paris journal, *Films et documents* published its 'Ten points of neorealism' by which neorealism could be classified. These were '(1) a message; (2) topical scripts inspired by concrete events – great historical and social issues are tackled from the point of view of the common people; (3) a sense of detail as a means of authentication; (4) a sense of the masses and the ability to manipulate them in front of the camera; (5) realism; (6) the truth of actors, often non-professionals; (7) the truth of lighting; (8) the truth of decor and refusal of the studio; (9) photography, reminiscent of the reportage style stressing the impression of truth; an extremely free camera, its unrestricted movements resulting from the use of postsynchronization' (Liehm 1984: 131–2). No neorealist films showed all of these characteristics. Some of the above categories are in effect conventions of cinematic realism, one of the definitions of which is that it is a strategy for suggesting what lies beneath the surface of events or things that have been captured by the camera. Neorealist film-makers wanted not just to record post-war society, but to suggest that events had a meaning.

In the 1950s André Bazin's enthusiasm for the films of Jean Renoir, American and new Italian cinema led to a series of articles in which he attempted to define the elements of what was, essentially, a new style of film-making. In particular, through close analysis of Renoir's films, he elaborated his theory that certain types of film-making were inherently more realistic, because they approximated more closely to his perception of how the active viewer made sense of the world around. That is, that deep-focus composition and lateral reframings during tracking shots in a long take mimicked how a person experienced the world while moving through it, giving the impression of spatial realism. He considered montage and editing as less inherently realistic, encouraging passive spectatorship, while spatial realism was morally superior because the spectator had to actively decode the visual cues revealed by the moving camera. Bazin (1971: 26) recognized that this impression of reality 'could only be achieved in one way – through artifice'. The impression of the randomness of everyday life is evoked in film after film by allowing actions extrinsic to the plot to take over. Moreover, for Bazin, neorealist film-makers went beyond previous realist movements in cinema and literature, by introducing an ethical element into their analysis; that is, they attempted to incorporate a point of view on the human condition described. Thus the tragic conclusion of *Ladri di biciclette*, when Antonio is driven to attempt to steal a bicycle, invites the reflection that the poor must steal from the poor in order to survive. Bazin's theories are still interesting as insights into the conventions of a certain type of realist cinema, even though the films that he admired were far more constructed than he cared to admit.

The idea of how cinematic reality was constructed fascinated Gilles Deleuze (1989: 1) and, in particular, the claim of neorealism to produced an 'additional reality', or interpretation of a situation. In traditional realism objects had a functional reality, that is, that Etna's lava flows provoked reactions in the peasants filmed, or the city dwellings and countryside depicted in *Quattro passi fra le nuvole* shaped the actions of the commercial traveller and his reactions to the traditional rural family. Neorealist cinema rejected this over-determined realism and, for Deleuze (1992: 211), recognized 'the need for a new type of tale capable of including the elliptical and unorganised'. By including insignificant spaces ('any-space-whatever') of wastegrounds and urban cancer, subjective images, memories, fantasies, the clichéd desires of modern capitalism, Deleuze (1992: 212) suggested that film-makers accessed a 'third moment' which explained the thought processes of a social group, or an historical conjuncture. In the Rome episode of Rossellini's *Paisà*, the initial meeting of the idealistic girl and the soldier contrasts to their later mis-recognition of each other when he has become world-weary and cynical and she a prostitute. In Deleuze's model, the two phases of their clichéd yearning for romantic union cue affective understanding of both a political situation (the American occupation of Italy), and a mental attitude towards it. In the fantasy world of *Miracolo a Milano*, the short scene where the homeless crowd together to warm themselves in the footprint of a ray of sunshine is uncoupled from reference to a specific place, existing only to display a lifestyle devoid of material comforts and a yearning both for physical and collective warmth.

The 'haptic' sense of lived space described above indicates or maps the geographic spaces available to the characters (Bruno 2002: 6). One of the ways this is achieved is through a narrative organization that follows a character looking at and experiencing his or her environment so that a sense of how that reality is mentally constructed by those who live in it becomes an integral element of the story world. Fellini's central characters in *La dolce vita* and *Otto e mezzo* are constantly conscious of their mediating roles (as journalist, film-maker). Foregrounding the subjective elements of Marcello's observation of the nightclub's cabaret spectacle, of the prostitute's squalid home in the urban periphery, of the star bathing in the Trevi fountain, enables a grasp of how lives are lived, and might be explained. Antonioni's films can be categorized as neorealist because these indeterminate spaces become part of the mental landscape of the characters (Deleuze 1989: 8–9). In his early 1960s films it is access to the subjective perceptions of women or the working class that functions as the 'third meaning' ignored by the bourgeois male protagonists. Deleuze's model explains the persistence in Italian cinema of this different relationship to landscape and narration. The banal squalor of urban wastegrounds,

Figure 4.1
Angela (Iaia Forte) on her
territory in *I buchi neri*
(Pappi Corsicato, 1995).

concrete public housing and anonymous pavements in Gianni
Amelio's *Il ladro di bambini* (1992) betrays the marks of careless
middle-class attitudes to social planning, the breakdown of any
sense of community or ethics, and the restricted opportunities of
the Italian underclass. Similar areas in Pappi Corsicato's *I buchi neri*
(*Black Holes*, 1995) achieve significance as liminal spaces indicative
of the heroine's (Iaia Forte) marginal occupation as prostitute, and
her zestful rejection of the patriarchally dominated city centre.
Deleuze's work is useful in suggesting links between neorealist film-
makers and their successors, but cannot be applied to all neorealist
films, or to 1960s critical realism.

Later neo-formalist analyses, such as that of Kristin Thompson
(1988: 215–17), stressed that neorealist films were perceived as
more 'real' because their subject matter was new and, certainly for
American audiences, the lack of spectacle, the chance events in the
narrative, the choice of characters and environment, the lack of
stars, made it new and unfamiliar.

Roma città aperta

Roberto Rossellini is typical of film-makers of this period in experiencing 1945 as a wonderful opportunity, in the absence of traditional
film production organization, to experiment, spurred by the sense
that they were doing something which was culturally important
(Faldini and Fofi 1979: 96). Rossellini had started to film his story
of the resistance four months after the Germans left Rome. There is
a consequent, and deliberate, feeling of immediacy, gained mainly
from the initial high-angle long shots of German army trucks on the
streets of Rome. Since the studios had been looted by the retreating

Germans, Rossellini's Rome, shot on location, is that of ordinary people opposing or accommodating to the reality of fascism and occupation.

Anna Magnani plays Pina, a working-class widow with a young son, expecting a child by her friend Francesco, a printer who does clandestine work for the resistance. Pina and Francesco are about to marry. He is a communist and an unbeliever who has already established a good relationship with Pina's son, Marcello. When Francesco hides Manfredi the resistance leader in his appartment across the hall, the two lovers have only the stairs where they can be alone together to express their hopes for the future. Besides being a good story, with a well-constructed script, *Roma città aperta* functions at a deeper level, and much has been made of Rossellini's symbolic depiction of the alliance of catholics and communists to oppose the evil of Nazism (Bondanella 1983: 50; Marcus 1986: 33–53; Brunette 1996: 37). As in all good melodramas, Pina has her opposite, Manfredi's girlfriend Marina, who betrays him for drugs and a fur coat. This dichotomy also indicates a fissure, an area of disruption and danger in traditional culture which reveals power relations, and raises questions.

Magnani's Pina is a stereotype of the good, working-class woman who is prepared to fight for her family and a better world. Brunette

Figure 4.2

Pina's (Anna Magnani) death. *Roma città aperta* (Roberto Rossellini, 1945).

(1996: 50) suggests that it is Rossellini's larger-than-life male characters who initiate the action, female characters being usually seen
as acted upon. Pina is an exception. Manfredi's presence in the block
of flats provokes a raid by the Germans and the fascist police. As
Pina comforts a neighbour, she spots Francesco being carried off
by the fascists and launches herself after him. She fights off various
Germans who try to stop her and is shot as she runs after the truck.
The cutting, camerawork, and Magnani's performance contribute
to the emotional impact of this sequence, giving no doubt of Pina's
feelings about the Germans, or of the intensity of her caring for
Francesco. Just as Rome stands for Italy as a whole, Pina and
Francesco together are emblematic of the moral and ethical strength
of the people. However, Pina's attempt at initiating action, albeit for
good womanly reasons, fails – she dies, falling in a heap in the road
with her skirt lifted to show her suspenders and laddered stockings.
As she dies she is, therefore, objectified, made powerless, and at the
same time eroticized.

There were films in which the female characters were portrayed
as more-or-less equals in the struggle – the partisan-financed films
for example – but *Roma città aperta* is not one of them. There is an
interesting tension between the narrative drive of the dialogue to
present Pina as inferior to Francesco by virtue of her class, education
and gender, and the story events and the actual performance of
Magnani. Pina is represented as mature, active, earthy, strong,
defiant; she is a mother. She may be poorly educated, but projects
considerable native intelligence and honesty. She is, as Marcus (1986:
39) points out, also an activist who organizes the local women.
The portrayal of Pina as the instigator of the women's raid on the
baker's shop also evokes a form of women's protest that had become
a feature of the fascist period but which was played down politically
and certainly never represented on celluloid (Colarizi 1996: 145).
The invasion exacerbated problems of food distribution, mobility
and employment and it is significant that when Rossellini wanted
to typify female protest against the deprivations of fascism it is
embodied in the looting of a food shop. Pina's action is emblematic
of the sense of injustice, of the harshness of life for ordinary people,
of what women are constrained to do in order to feed their families.
Rossellini's film attempts to stop at the delineation of injustice and
to suggest a commonality of purpose for the Italian people, that is,
the need to provide for a new generation, the children seen walking
back into the city in the final shots of the film.

In this respect *Roma città aperta* reflects feelings of optimism in
Italy when the end of conflict was in sight. However, in the film social
and gender hierarchies are firmly in place (Sorlin 1991: 57). Pina is
not represented as refined, and her emotionality is represented as
an integral and essential part of her. It is this forceful emotional
and ethical integrity that is so interesting and that offers additional

explanations as to why Magnani was sought after not only by populist film directors, but also by Fellini, Rossellini, Visconti. Her appeal was both visceral and intellectual. *Roma città aperta* contains a number of dramatic and traumatic events, Don Pietro's carrying money for the resistance through German-occupied Rome, Manfredi's escape over the rooftops, the band of boys blowing up German targets, the search of Pina's apartment block, the arrest of Francesco and Pina's death, the capture and torture of Manfredi and Don Pietro. The film mobilizes melodramatic techniques to increase the affective charge by the use of emotive music, loved ones in peril, abuse of positive characters, violence, heroism and horrific events. Emotional pauses occur in the comic sequences. At the same time, the portrayal of lower middle-class and proletarian Rome enables the emotional perception of events to be apprehended as authentic.

Political Realisms

It is interesting that the National Association of Italian Partisans (ANPI) felt the need to put its hard-earned cash into presenting their own version of wartime resistance in such films as Giuseppe de Santis' *Caccia tragica* (*Tragic Pursuit*, 1945), Aldo Vergano's *Il sole sorge ancora* (*The Sun Rises Again*, 1946) and Carlo Lizzani's *Achtung banditi!* (1949). *Caccia tragica* is set in an agrarian co-operative in Romagna, formed to enable agricultural workers to organize themselves to take advantage of the push for land reform, that is, to break up the enormous landed estates that were perceived to be acting as a brake on equitable, and modern, development. The State subvention to the co-operative is stolen by *banditi*, in an ambush in which the heroine, Giovanna (Carla del Poggio), is kidnapped. Her newly wed husband, Michele (Massimo Girotti), is the focus of the struggle of the peasant farmers to get both back. The photography is very vivid, with open spaces continually occupied by labourers, stressing metonymically the values of the collective and the community. The struggle itself functions as a metaphor for class conflict, particularly by the landed interests threatening the operation of reform.

The first film about the Italian resistance, *Il sole sorge ancora* was filmed in 1945, financed by ANPI. The action takes place around an agricultural estate in Lombardy in 1943. The characters, Cesare, the son of a peasant farmer, Matilde, the blonde, cynical landowner's daughter, represent class positions, particularly the distrust of the middle classes who had collaborated with fascists. Cesare and the partisans try to take the arms hidden in the big house by the Germans. Excess, in the form of the horrific violence of Heinrich, the German officer, acts as an indicator of the psychic impact of wartime atrocities, while the repetition of illusionistic detail (the film was shot in locations near the scene of similar events) insists on the veracity of the story world. The film was praised critically, but poor distribution, combined with censorship and funding difficulties, did not encourage ANPI or the Communist Party to invest their hard-earned money in other productions.

Equally unsuccessful, Carlo Lizzani's first film, *Achtung Banditi!* had a similar resistance theme with partisans working with workers to hide machinery that the Germans had ordered to be sent to Germany. In this film too, an attempt is made to interpret the events depicted in terms of showing the class basis of society as exploitative and criminal. All these films had bad distribution deals and failed to make money. An additional contributing factor to their failure lay in their good/evil narrative oppositions, capitalist consumption being firmly presented as bad. Successful neorealist films operated within standard industrial models of production and exploitation, using genre characteristics to attract an audience.

Ladri di biciclette

By 1948 *Ladri di biciclette* had to fight for a showing in a crowded market, and almost failed to make any impact at all. There is a widely held belief that neorealist films, with their air of improvisation, were cheap. *Ladri di biciclette* cost about Lire 100 million to make (almost £50,000 at exchange rates then) and it was certainly not a cheap production. Financing was haphazard at this time, and De Sica had backing from a couple of private industrial sources, but was relying on the state body, ENIC, for distribution – then as now a crucial equation in a film's success. ENIC suddenly decided to present the film with a restricted launch in Rome and a short run. The left-wing producer, Alfredo Guarini, was influential in ensuring the success of the film, re-launching it with personal presentations by De Sica in all the main cities (Guarini 1953: 320–3).

That *Ladri di biciclette* had a second chance is entirely due to De Sica's star status. De Sica had, by the late 1930s, become an immensely popular film actor. He avoided the taint of fascist culture both because he specialized in comedy and subtly differentiated, lower middle-class characters, and because, by 1943, he was already part of anti-fascist intellectual circles. Thus he not only had the support of critics but had sufficient fame and financial clout to form his own production company to make *Ladri di biciclette*, and then to ensure that it was not ignored. It made over Lire 200 million at the box office, coming eighth in the list of successes for 1948–9. The film was also a huge critical success, winning prizes for best director, screenplay, subject, photography and music at the Venice Film Festival. It therefore attracted attention outside Italy, which has been one factor in the film's survival.

The impetus towards analysis and commentary is visible in the work of Cesare Zavattini, one of the first theorists of neorealism, sharing the best screenplay prize with De Sica for *Ladri di biciclette*. Although Zavattini's ideal film was a camera record of 90 minutes of a man's life, observed in total silence, he modified this in the hundreds of articles he wrote attempting to define neorealism. For Zavattini human life had to be given its historical significance. Ordinary rather than exceptional people had to be the subjects of contemporary stories, and he suggested that, when ordinary situations were depicted in an analytical way, they became dramatic spectacle, going beyond the illusion of reality to suggest a deeper truth. The influence of Zavattini's ideas is visible at many points in *Ladri di biciclette*. Non-professional actors were used in the main roles to contribute to the impression of authenticity. The main character, Antonio, was played by a factory worker, Maria his wife by a journalist, although adherence to the conventions of realism did not extend to using Lamberto Maggiorani's real voice; he was dubbed. The use of crowds in neorealist films is very interesting. Crowds are carefully framed in social spaces – homes, streets, markets, squares, or outside the football stadium, in order to emphasize their size. They may be anonymous, but these crowds function as a metonym for the working classes as a whole. Small but identifiable crowds stand for and represent the masses.

Ladri di biciclette also has a topical script. It tackles historical and social events from the point of view of the working class; that is, we see one effect of the aftermath of war, mass unemployment, on the life of the protagonist and his social position is perceived through delineation of his context and the events that befall him. The film uses detail to suggest the authenticity of this portrayal. The long shots at the beginning of the film, for example, situate Antonio in his surroundings. He sits apart from the crowd of unemployed men and having to be told that his name has come up for the job of billposter; the flats where he lives at Val Melaina are surrounded by wasteground, and by placing a conversation between Antonio and his wife, Maria, around the standpipe where she collects water, we learn not only that he has pawned his bicycle, but that their area is without services like roads or running water. Val Melaina is differentiated from central Rome and, at a deeper level, indicates a social reality where speculative building has not been accompanied by planning, where there is high male unemployment, and more jobs for unskilled, rather than skilled craftsmen. It also indicates that Antonio is an outsider and unpoliticized, because he does not go to his local Communist Party office when his bicycle is stolen (where he would have received assistance, thus ensuring a speedy end to the film), but seeks the help of his friend Baiocco, the dustman. Similarly, the sequence where the couple visit the pawnbroker to pawn Maria's sheets in order to redeem the precious bicycle is tightly structured

as a series of head and shoulder or close-up shots of Antonio and
Maria looking, and answering reverse shots of what they are looking
at. When the camera pans up the laden shelves of pawned sheets it
shows just what the volume of business the shop does – and thereby
generates a further level of meaning and awareness of the level of
poverty of people represented by Antonio.

The film contains very few studio shots; most of the shooting
was done on location in Rome. Pierre Sorlin (1991: 120–1) has remarked that Antonio seems to be an immigrant to Rome, because
he appears unfamiliar with the central districts. This would explain
the reaction of the people Antonio accuses of stealing the bicycle.
They round on him angrily and gang up together, an understandable
response to the threat posed by the massive influx of population to
the outskirts of cities, respresented by the Val Melaina development.
In a reaction against fascist art, which emphasized 'Roman-ness' to
stress its own legitimacy, familiar monuments are absent, allowing
De Sica to suggest a different Rome, far from the centres of political
power. Exterior shooting had developed initially through necessity
as the big studios were unavailable in 1945, but the Italian film
technicians' experience and skill in post-synchronization meant that
the camera was free to move, unencumbered by heavy sound, or
lighting equipment. Aesthetic choice coincided with and developed
from practical considerations.

Filming on the streets contributed to an overwhelming sensation
of realism. The camera may seem to be recording directly a 'reality'
out there in front of it, but, in the scene in which Antonio's colleague
shows him how to stick up a poster the camera is carefully placed so
that, from one angle, the street is clearly visible in the background.
From another angle, a small boy with an accordion and his friend

Figure 4.3
Life on the street. *Ladri di
biciclette* (Vittorio De Sica,
1948).

arrive to stand in front of Antonio and his colleague. The colleague kicks the boy off his ladder; a well-dressed man passes and the boys ask him for money, the camera panning to keep man and one boy in shot as they go up the street. The lines of wall and pavement lead the eye upwards, echoing the movement of the characters, while we hear the voice-off of Antonio's colleague. This scene differs from Hollywood cinema in drawing attention within the frame to characters who are not essential to the story and who are not used to motivate any further action. This example does, however, illustrate some of the conventions of realism at work. The busy street in the background gives the illusion of life going on around the main protagonist, reinforced by figures coming into and going out of frame. This is suggested both visually and aurally as noise, sound, dialogue originating within and outside the frame is used to suggest the existence of a world all around the camera. Encounters like these are used throughout the film to give the illusion of chance. The opening sequences of American cinema generally concentrate on building up characterization and setting in motion a logic of cause and effect that will move the story forward. *Ladri di biciclette*, however, is not interested in individual psychology but is concerned to situate Antonio, Maria and their son, Bruno, in their social and historical context. The quest for the bicycle is prevented from being totally unstructured by regular references to deadlines by which Antonio has to find a bicycle, show up for work, meet Baiocco and find the bicycle again, but within these markers of time passing, the action takes the form of a series of situations that are given the impression of randomness. When Antonio and Bruno follow a suspect, an old man, they find themselves in a church. This allows De Sica both to satirize the behaviour of upper-class do-gooders, and, by long shots revealing the sheer numbers in the congregation waiting for the free meal, to indicate the extent of poverty. This strategy of adopting the point of view of a particular, isolated individual and using him to illuminate contemporary reality has been imitated many times since 1948.

Rossellini uses a similar strategy in the Neapolitan episode of *Paisà*, when the boy and his captive (a drunken black soldier) stumble into a puppet theatre in the slums, which they disrupt completely. It is a little closed world, where ordinary working men are watching large puppets dressed as knights in armour having a sword fight. This is an example of neorealist use of the small but telling detail. 'Carolingian' adventures were just one theme in a massive oral tradition in Italian culture, which survived certainly right up to the advent of mass culture in the 1950s. To the uneducated, these tales of chivalry always seemed as real as recent history. Here, therefore, the director has chosen to show something fleetingly which draws its meaning from a whole wealth of cultural connotations behind it. Rossellini punches home an ironic contrast between the tale of chivalry, personal danger in pursuit of an ideal, and the actual situation outdoors, where men are involved in a life-and-death struggle, not only for an ideal of peace and freedom but also for the means of life itself, food, shelter and warmth.

These telling details are used in a political way to make a comment on social situations, but it is interesting that there is no actual engagement with actual political events, such as the demonstrations that took place in 1947 and in the run up to the 1948 elections. In other respects *Ladri di biciclette* uses the continuity conventions of mainstream cinema, maintaining eye-line matches and screen direction across cuts. The two styles are visible in the sequence in Piazza Vittorio, where tracking shots accompanying Antonio, Bruno, and the group of dustmen through the market, alternate with rapidly cut shots of ranks of bicycles, wheels, bells, indicating visually the scale of the problem of finding the machine.

De Sica also uses editing for suspense in the sequence where Antonio leaves Bruno on the embankment in order to search the banks of the Tiber. Shouts-off indicate that a boy is drowning, but the comfort of recognizing the live figure of Bruno is delayed, first by shots of Antonio running back in a distraught manner, and then by a low-angle, extreme long shot of the embankment steps, dwarfing the figures and making recognition difficult. Suspense is further heightened at the end of the film, where the desperate Antonio is tempted to steal a bicycle outside the football stadium. Antonio's tortured expression, glances off-screen, shots of piles of bicycles are accompanied by music and the roar of the crowds, and orchestrated to increase tension up to the moment when he steals a bicycle himself, and is caught. For Bazin (1971: 51), the 'truth' suggested by the film was that, in a situation of social breakdown, the poor had to steal from the poor in order to survive.

Fantasy and the Political: *Miracolo a Milano*

Pierre Sorlin (1991: 126) has pointed out that *Miracolo a Milano* (*Miracle in Milan*, Vittorio De Sica, 1950) is one of the few neorealist films to be set in a shanty town, although temporary houses of wood and corrugated iron were extremely common in the post-war period. The combination of the fantastic (the boy with the magic dove; the finale where the down-and-outs go to heaven) and the 'realistic' (the shanty town community of homeless people and tramps) make the film difficult to categorize. However, through the combination of realism of place and narrative excess, the film manages to achieve a coherent discourse on poverty and prosperity. As Piero Meldini (1989: 121–5) has observed, the film alternates tableaux delineating the characteristics of poverty with those of riches, so that the fragile solidarity of the poor is juxtaposed with representations of the rich and powerful, usually represented through contrasts in clothing. The things that the poor wish for are significant in their general ordinariness – a sewing machine, radio, wardrobe, a suitcase, a panettone, a pair of shoes, prosperity being represented as having the wherewithall to have a change of clothing, food, contact with the outside world. But aspirations also enter into the equation with requests for an evening dress, a fur coat. Many neorealist films display considerable ambiguity about the trappings of riches. In *Abbasso la ricchezza!* (*Down With Riches!*, Gennaro Righelli, 1946), Gioconda the market trader (Anna Magnani) signals her black market wealth by the variety of her costumes, her fox fur, and her fantastic hats, her paintings and her record player. She is contrasted with the upper-class good taste of Count Gherani (Vittorio de Sica), who wears grey, double-breasted suits with discreet ties. Although contemporary critics disapproved of the Gioconda character, the film was a financial success, probably because of its representations of plenty, epitomized by Gioconda's coach ride through Trastevere in Rome, where she acknowledges the jealous comments of her former neighbours as she lolls back, patting her fox fur. The motif of the robbery of the poor by the rich is common, occurring in *Miracolo a Milano*, *L'Onorevole Angelina* and *Abbasso la ricchezza!* in which poor characters return to their 'rightful' place in society at the end, providing neat metaphors for class struggle. Here there is continuity with 1930s comedies, such as *Il Signor Max* (*Mister Max*, Mario Camerini, 1937).

The heroine of *L'Onorevole Angelina* (Anna Magnani) lives in slum housing in Pietralata on the fringes of Rome with her policeman husband and five children. Circumstances propel her into taking the lead in fighting for better living conditions for her community. Zampa uses montage sequences to illustrate the process of her politicization and to show what is at stake. Shots of newspaper presses rolling with Angelina's story cue her appreciation of the power of the press. Collective action is indicated in scenes of Angelina in the midst of a crowd of women serving pasta. Shots of dry taps are followed by close ups of the feet of women marching off to protest; the tap runs. A mob of women lie down in front of a bus; they get a bus stop. Feet march in the rain to the Assistance Office; they get a nursery for children. These sequences conclude with close ups of Angelina looking at children.

Magnani herself claimed that the roles of Angelina and Gioconda were written for her, and that she thoroughly enjoyed playing 'lovely, authentic characters. I never said I wanted to act great tragedy queens. I want characters I and the public can believe in. Well-constructed characters ... authentic and true to life' (Faldini and Fofi 1979: 125). Angelina is a complex character, having to juggle her role of wife and mother with that of community leader. She is aggressive, raucous, vital, energetic, tender and compassionate, and her performance was praised for its truth to life, its authenticity. However, Angelina's politicization leads to family conflict; her son threatens to turn to crime; Pasquà, her husband bemoans the lack of home comforts; again, she is duped by the upper classes represented by the landlord, and, when her community shout out that they want her as their MP, she declines, saying that she will leave that to those who can speak better than her. She goes back to her place, as wife and mother, although still politically active. Patriarchy has established its rule once again and, metaphorically, the working class has given in to its political masters. The longed-for reforms will not take place in this period (Ginsborg 1990: 82).

The underlying concerns of *L'Onorevole Angelina* undoubtedly reflect worries about women taking power. In 1946 women had the vote for the first time in Italian history and, in the first free general elections for over twenty years, took part in the decision between monarchy and republic and the election of representatives to the Constituent Assembly (Ginsborg. 1990: 98).

Neorealismo nero

There is a very small sub-genre of neorealism called *neorealismo nero* (black neorealism), which dealt with social problems in a very melodramatic way. One of the best known, *Il bandito*, deals with the problem of returning Italian soldiers. The gradual return to Italy of detainees from Germany, concentration camp survivors from Eastern Europe, and thousands of former soldiers from Russia, North Africa, Greece, coupled with the return to the cities of ordinary people who had fled into the countryside to avoid the fighting meant that a largely static and settled population had been shaken up, dispersed, and its ties to family and home (*paese*) severed. As a result, before the Marshall plan swung into effect, there was widespread unemployment, poverty, social and familial disruption and, not least, the questioning of traditionally held beliefs about social and gender hierarchies, about politics. These things were within the lived experience of all strata of Italian society. The excesses of popular film melodramas indicated the difficulty of reconciling traditional Italian stories, based on a certain understanding of social and gender relations, and the lived experience of the world outside the cinema, with which all neorealist artists sought to engage. It is not surprising that, in this period of 'supervised freedom', popular cinema provided an outlet for expressions of a desire for change and freedom (Boneschi 1995: 108–9). The Italian film industry in this period could, for the most part, only express desires for changes in social and sexual mores in coded form. Ernesto the bandit (Amedeo Nazzari) is desperately attached to traditional values, such as protecting the family and looking after the family's honour and name. He is in fact emblematic of an institutional crisis, the destruction of the family and moral turpitude of family members (male and female) representing the destruction of the nation. It has been suggested that former soldiers were an inconvenient reminder of the fascist regime, and that mistreating those who had fought far away, with the Germans, allowed Italians to deflect their own sense of guilt away from themselves (Gubitosi 1998: 85). A visual trope, which recurs in other *noirs,* is that of the staircase, which represents a boundary zone. Ernesto turns to criminality after his discovery that his sister is a prostitute and his killing of the man who shoots her, the whole sequence taking place on a dark and dirty staircase.

Il bandito is also emblematic of other tensions associated with desires in the population not to return to coercive social, political and gender relations, and it is significant that Nazzari plays many outsiders in his films between 1946 and 1949. His co-star in *Il bandito* is Anna Magnani. The narratives of Magnani's post-war films indicate difficulties in reconciling strongly assertive female characters with traditional narratives. Magnani's emotionality is metonymic of the sufferings of women in the period of post-war chaos and the general desire for something different. She occupies as much screen space and as many close ups as Nazzari, in this film but her role as gangster's moll, Lydia, indicates a subordinate position with respect to Nazzari, which is unresolved narratively. Ernesto and Lydia quarrel when she ridicules his postcard from his niece, Rosetta, and he humiliates her by throwing his drink in her face. Lydia betrays him to the police; Ernesto dies in a hail of gunfire trying

Figure 4.4
Gangster's moll, Lydia (Anna Magnani) and gang-leader (Mino Doro). *Il bandito* (Alberto Lattuada, 1946).

to reach Rosetta's family's farm, and the final sequence shows Lydia, clothed in furs and with a smug expression on her face, boarding a train – unpunished. *Il bandito* employs the high contrast lighting and stressed camera angles of Hollywood cinema. Interior shots of Lydia's environment are reminiscent of 1930s gangster films, as are her satin housecoats and feather boas but exterior shots predominate, which draw attention to the reality of run-down, dirty staircases in damaged houses and streets, to urban poverty. Criminality and alien values are associated with the urban environment.

Two examples of *neorealismo nero*, Giorgio Ferroni's *Tombolo paradiso nero* (*Tombolo, Black Paradise*, 1947) and Lattuada's *Senza pietà* were both set in the port of Livorno (Leghorn), 'the debarkation point for American army supplies and for this reason a centre of black-marketeering and prostitution' (Armes 1971: 103). *Senza Pietà*, scripted by Federico Fellini and Tullio Pinelli, gives a remarkable picture of the violence of the time. Livorno is depicted as dominated by Pierluigi, a sinister racketeer who controls the port and prostitution, siphons off shipments, robs convoys, and corrupts American Army personnel. Played by Folco Lulli as a pale, etiolated figure in a white suit and hat, a man without pity, he condemns others to death with a soft voice (Farassino 1989: 145–6). Pawns in his game are Marcella (Giulietta Masina) and the heroine, Angela (Carla del Poggio), both of whom end up as prostitutes and have relationships with black soldiers. Marcella uses her lover to get money to buy a passage to a better life in the United States. Angela meets Jerry (John Kitzmiller) when she saves his life after gangsters ambush her train, and their relationship starts when he takes her to a cafe and buys her something to eat. He falls in love with her but his attempts to steal money for their journey to America fail. During his imprisonment, she becomes a prostitute because, as Pierluigi remarks 'she's pretty and has no money'. In their attempt to steal from the gangsters, the lovers are caught outside a church. Angela is shot as she tries to protect Jerry and he drives his truck over a cliff. Although Lattuada denied having a Left-wing agenda, *Senza pietà* can be read as a denunciation both of the corrupt nature of the bourgeoisie and as a metaphor for the corruption of materialism and alien values.

Many of Pietro Germi's films contain *noir* visual elements as they explore the effects of social change. The most overtly in-fluenced by American style is *Gioventù perduta* (*Lost Youth*, 1949), full of shadows and inky black streets in which a gang of young delinquents, led by student Stefano (Jacques Sernas), commit a number of violent armed robberies. Stefano, the son of a middle-class university professor, is represented as excessively cold blooded. His heart-shaped face and fair hair are lit to stress his lack of expression and glacial beauty, echoed in the perfection of the fit of his light suit and silk tie. His motive is money and his actions excessive, whether planning robberies, gambling, or murdering his childhood friend, Maria, to prevent her betraying him. As the police inspector says, 'these are respectable people who would shoot their mothers for money'. There is a suggestion that the war changed Stefano in some nebulous and unexplained way but his war is implicitly contrasted with that of Marcello (Massimo Girotti), the detective who pursues him – and who falls in love with Stefano's sister, Luisa (Carla Del Poggio) – who enrols late at the university because he was in the army, and then North Africa. Two contrasting spatial paradigms are used in the film. The staircase with its ornate Baroque ironwork is used as a boundary zone between the domestic spaces downstairs in the family home, filled with parents and siblings, and Stefano's room full of dark shadows and hidden guns upstairs. There are a number of beautifully composed, extreme high angle long shots of the modernist architecture of the university, representing the rational world of learning and knowledge. The graphic patterns of the regular panes of glass in the huge windows dwarf and contain the people within. This architecture contrasts with the inky darkness of city streets where Stefano's robberies take place, and the classical architecture of the police station where Marcello works. An uneasiness with modernity is being indicated.

Although there was an opening up to Centre-Left coalitions at the end of the 1950s and, in the wake of the events of 1968, greater presence of Left-wing political appointees to head public bodies, what marks Italian society from the period of post-war reconstruction onwards is a sense that power is wielded by unelected sections of the population, be they Mafia-like criminal organizations, or socially or politically élite classes. Ginsborg (2001: 281) suggests that the Christian Democrats' 'dark side' should not be underestimated, that is, the party's arrangement of the affairs of state to its own benefit, through client relationships 'which recognized no clear laws or limits, no boundaries to possible alliances forged in the name of power, money or votes'. The pervasive use of *noir* elements are part of a response to the political situation and feelings of powerlessness. The codes and conventions of *noir* could be adapted to the Italian style in order to allude to those responsible for crimes, or to work through social preoccupations.

Emotional Realism and Melodrama

The examples described concentrate on building an overwhelming sense of historical authenticity, of realism of time and space, yet neorealism also included comedy, and most of them used the conventions of melodrama. Comedy, slapstick and melodrama are not modes usually associated with neorealism, but all of them occur in *Ladri di biciclette*. The priest in the confessional who hits Bruno over the head, Bruno's jump in the air when his father calls him just when he is about to urinate against a wall, Bruno's reaction to the chatter of the seminarians as they shelter from the rain, Antonio's anguish as he realizes that his neglect may have caused Bruno to drown, and the final sequence when Bruno puts his hand in his father's after Antonio has failed both to steal another bicycle and to prevent his son from seeing that failure – these are all examples of appeals to the emotions. In melodrama, at some point, feelings take over, and the 'real world' depicted is characterized by a heightened emotionality, taking the form of extreme action, violence, heroism, horrific plot details, passion, spectacle. Melodrama is very important in cultural politics because melodramatic events usually reveal and make obvious a malfunction in society. Neorealist film-makers found no shortage of such extreme events in the immediate post-war period (Capussoti 2004: 46). Thus the conflict between legitimate and 'scab' labourers in the rice fields in *Riso amaro* (*Bitter Rice*, Giuseppe De Santis, 1949) is heightened by the use of work songs and the fight between Silvana (Silvana Mangano) and Francesca over an unworthy man. Silvana was played by a former Miss Italy; much is made of her black, thigh-high stockings and tight sweater; and much was made of her 'real life' romance with the film producer, Dino De Laurentiis, whom she later married.

Figure 4.5
Silvana (Silvana Mangano) in the rice fields. *Riso amaro* (Giuseppe De Santis, 1949).

Vigour and sexual energy are frequently represented in dance in these films, reflecting the influence and allure of United States culture. Dance also allows display of the body, both male and female and the exuberant display of sexual energy and the spaces within which this takes place link private behaviour with events in a public and national arena. In *Riso amaro* the dancing of the spiv, Walter (Vittorio Gassman), and the ricefield worker, Silvana, display their physical attributes and the erotic attraction between them, but also indicate the appeal of American popular culture and its spread into the recesses of rural Italy. Gassman the weak villain is opposed by the attractive ex-soldier, Marco (Raf Vallone). Vallone, representing traditional male authority, wears army uniform throughout and stridently attempts to influence and annexe Mangano but singularly fails. Gassman is modern; he wears an American suit, his hat pushed back on his head, and knows how to dance the mambo. Gassman aims to persuade Mangano to help him steal the women rice workers' wages (their share of the harvest) but she repents her involvement at the end and kills herself. Female transgression, associated in Silvana's character as a taste for dancing the mambo, reading comics, fake diamonds, sex and unreliable men, is represented as attractive at the same time as it is punished in narrative terms.

Neorealismo rosa and Melodrama

Neorealismo rosa, pink neorealism, is the name given to the popular cinema of the 1950s that had no pretensions to operating on the cutting edge of Left-wing critiques of society, but instead did address the preoccupations of ordinary people – how women could combine work and family, how to obtain access to the rewards of post-war, industrial society, the conflict between archaic, rural social practices and those necessary for survival in modern Italy. These films used many of the stylistic devices of neorealism – location shooting in recognizable places, working-class characters and themes – but heightened the emotional charge of the narrative and ignored the socialist political agenda.

Raffaello Matarazzo's melodramas had enormous success in the post-war period. Produced by the Titanus studio, *Catene* (*Chains*, 1950) was top of the 1949–50 box-office lists, earning Lire 750 million. *Tormento* (*Torment*, 1950) was second the following year with Lire 730 million and *I figli di nessuno* (*Nobody's Children*, 1951) was third with Lire 950 million. These were low-budget productions aimed at drawing the mass audience away from the American competition (Aprà and Carabba 1976: 21). The main protagonists of Matarazzo's 1950s films were Amedeo Nazzari and Yvonne Sanson.

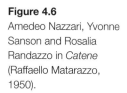

Figure 4.6
Amedeo Nazzari, Yvonne
Sanson and Rosalia
Randazzo in *Catene*
(Raffaello Matarazzo,
1950).

Nazzari was an established star of the fascist period, tall and fair and resembling Errol Flynn, Sanson was Greek and epitomized the mature, self-sacrificing Mediterranean mother. In contrast to American cinema, small children, rather than teenagers or young adults, represented what was at stake for the family. In *I figli di nessuno*, Count Guido Canali is a quarry owner whose mother sends him to London to separate him from the woman he loves, Luisa, daughter of an employee. Luisa's father dies and she flees to a peasant hut to give birth to a son, Bruno. Luisa believes that Bruno died when the hut burnt but he has been stolen on the orders of Guido's mother. Luisa becomes a nun, Sister Addolorata. Bruno runs away from school, finding work in the quarry. Guido's wife tells Bruno his true identity. Bruno saves the quarry from saboteurs but is mortally wounded, dying in the arms of Sister Addolorata and his father.

Although panned at the time by critics, Matarazzo's convoluted plots reflected the experiences, fears and desires of lower social classes and the uneducated. Although complex, plots are linear and characters clearly delineated. Accidents, a malign fate or human wickedness cause the terrible situations in which couples find themselves, and fate or self-sacrifice by the woman offers resolution. In contrast to the heightened reality of 1950s American melodramas with their use of deep focus, saturated colour and symbolic objects, Matarazzo's low-budget films used authenticity of place and tightly organized camerawork to quickly move the action forward, suggest links between complex events, and the impression of inexorable fate. There is a strong sense of the powerlessness of ordinary people faced with adverse events over which they have no control (Marchelli 1996: 126).

Nazzari appears to embody certainties about patriarchal values at times of great social change. His most constant facial expression is one of bafflement. The plots of all his pink neorealist films show a yearning for stasis, for a time when women and the lower classes knew their place. Yet the Nazzari persona is not representative of a brutally forceful masculinity. His violence occurs in protection of his actual or metaphorical family and his openness to affect and emotionality suggest that these qualities were considered necessary to make sense of a changing world, keeping the attributes of the 'old' male hero, but allowing a greater consciousness of the possibilities offered by social change. Change is, however, never successfully negotiated as around these large, dominant, upright male figures, other worlds, usually female, collapse in utter chaos.

The melodramas and comedies of pink neorealism represent a watershed at which some of the ambitions of neorealist cinema were carried forward, but without the realist and political agenda. Increasing economic prosperity, industrial development and popular culture had shaken up traditional beliefs and hierarchical views of society. Rather than resisting change as the underlying discourses of neorealist films implicitly suggested, the pink neorealist films of the 1950s struck a chord with the population because they rehearsed the difficulties of modern life through stories with carefully differentiated protagonists in terms of their age and geographical origin. The younger actors are almost never fathers. Theirs is the generation that has left the fascist period and post-war deprivation well behind. The only bafflement expressed might be at 'what women want' rather than 'what is life all about?' The younger male actors represent, symbolize or are emblematic of aspects of male power in conflict with that of the older generation. Power is seen to be embodied in a certain type of masculinity, characterized by physical energy taken to the level of excess in violent action; mental energy expressed as intelligence and cunning; and personal magnetism or charm – the erotic subordination of rivals. The use of actors from many regions of Italy allowed the question of national identity and change to be explored through a wider range of stories and situations than those seen in neorealist films. The south already connoted archaic social relationships and permitted the problems of traditional patriarchal society to become visible while the use of northern actors allowed a less monolithic and more questioning approach to social change. Covertly the options and courses of action available as models in post-war society are signified through the *mise en scène* delineating a variety of moral positions and social milieux. Far from being emasculated and unrepresentative of post-war reality, the melodramatic form allowed a wide variety of male roles, successful and unsuccessful to be rehearsed and a much broader engagement with the unfolding history of Italy. Interestingly, within the framings of many of these melodramas are bands of younger boys. The choral element, and boys watching the main protagonists, again draws attention to the links between performance and audience, private passions and public histories. In one way the chorus of watchers are there to learn new behaviours, in another, the represent (as Chapter 7 will explore) the force of social control.

Conclusion

There have been many theoretical attempts to understand and define Italian neorealist cinema but, regardless of their philosophical or political point of view, neorealism itself has been an important point of reference for over fifty years for the simple reason that there are still truths in need of exploration in contemporary Italy. The presence of violent events and social upheavals favoured textual hybridity in that realist cinematic conventions were insufficient for the maximum perception of the complexity of the historical context. The affective charge of melodrama, with its consequent visual and narrative excess was important in indicating problems and disruptions which countered simple explanations of events. The concerns of neorealism, and other realisms, were ontological, in that the films make assertions about the nature of the real world. The insistent references to an exterior context is an indication of the psychic investment in the engagement with contemporary history and the traumatic nature of the events depicted. At the same time, spectacular and excessive narratives, performances and/or *mise en scène* prevent total immersion in the illusion of reality. All these realisms influenced later films. Critical realist cinema in the 1960s developed an epistemological claim that it is possible to know the nature of the processes that structure knowledge, and therefore to know why it is that we do not know something. The heightened reality of this type of film forces a reading and interpretation of the image, rather than seeking psychological motivation in characters. In another development, the banality and ugliness of modern cities and their peripheries have provided fertile sources of images for film-makers to explore the contradictions and effects of modernity. Both strategies are part of a new and very Italian relationship to landscape. These strategies are also present, to differing degrees, in that very small sector of Italian film production classed as 'quality' or authorial, which will be examined in Chapter 5.

5

Auteur Cinema

As Chapter 1 has shown, the director as a legal and commercial entity is part of the package for attracting investment and funding in Italy, indicating a particular level of financial success to limit the risks inherent in film-making. From the 1950s, the names of certain film directors became essential to the marketing of their films and to ensuring critical attention. In Italy, specialist journals and academic publishing went hand in hand with the development of *auteur* cinema and the later academic study of film. New technologies have assisted this process by encouraging the collection of films on videotape or DVD by director – the *videoteca* phenomenon.

Several factors influenced the development of auteurist art cinema in Italy after the Second World War. Firstly, although, after their initial popularity, neorealist films did not interest the mass cinema-going public, they excited critical attention outside the country, and were exported with some success. At the same time, Italian producers noticed that the small-scale films of the *nouvelle vague* in France found an audience in specialist cinemas in Italy, and struck chords with audiences abroad. The expansion of education and the gradual opening up to more Left-wing ideas meant that an audience capable of appreciating the formal innovation of modernism and interested in politics was building up for more sophisticated entertainment. Development of this audience was also a commercial strategy to counter American domination of the film industry (Bordwell 1979;

Neale 1981). Exhibition circuits evolved for foreign films, or those not regarded as for mainstream tastes but capable of reaching an audience niche (the *Cinema d'essai*). State support for the Italian film industry grew and included financial assistance for film festivals which were perceived as important for national prestige. A whole critical apparatus of specialist journals, and journalists who would interpret the work of film-makers, grew to draw the attention of a potential audience to films and to assign value, usually on the basis of their subject matter and *mise en scène*. Producers rapidly identified those directors and creative personnel who would deliver these marks of quality.

Seen from the perspective of the previous chapters, Italian *auteur* cinema is not so much a distinct entity in itself, as the intellectual and/or better funded end of national genre production. It shows the same preoccupations with modernity, with social change and political problems as comedy. At the top end of the market, the conventions of the *giallo* or investigative narrative genre were used with great visual flair by directors such as Visconti, Antonioni and Rosi to explore mysteries in Italian life. Auteurist directors use the conventions of popular hybrid genres, and frequently take advantage of contemporary *filoni*, subjects and genres popular at the box office. Elements of *film noir* and soft porn are also found in this sector of the film industry. However, in order to qualify for the additional State funding if a film is retrospectively designated as a 'quality' production, a film must usually stand out by its serious themes and/ or its production values. The former are associated with a realist aesthetic or the working through of a personal vision in the minds of funders and critics, and the latter depend on a budget necessary to put together a quality creative team of director, cinematographer, designer, costume designer and writers. State subsidy requires art cinema to attain high cultural prestige (Dyer and Vincendeau 1992: 8). Following Fredric Jameson's (2000: 128) suggestion to consider the interrelationship of high and mass culture 'as twin and inseparable forms of the fission of aesthetic production under capitalism', this chapter will examine what the *auteur* package consists of and how it has evolved.

In the 1960s Italian cinema had prestige at home and abroad that it was not able to equal afterwards (Sitney 1995: 118–19). One reason was undoubtedly the distribution opportunities that existed then, which targeted a youthful, cineliterate audience world-wide. Another lay in the impact of *La dolce vita* (Federico Fellini, 1960) *L'avventura* (Michelangelo Antonioni, 1960) and *Salvatore Giuliano* (Francesco Rosi, 1961) in terms of their political and social content, innovation and notoriety, which paved the way for other films to court critical and market attention up until the mid-1970s. Another reason for international interest lay in the consequences of the economic boom, whose excesses, in the Italian case, provided narrative opportunities. Social alienation in the form of selfish materialism or psychological disturbance, political and economic corruption and ecological damage provided stories recognizable elsewhere. Serious themes contested the status quo, exploring ideas and events from a Left perspective. Gramsci's work was particularly important from 1968 in giving a role to the Left-wing intellectual who had been politically marginalized by the Christian Democrat grip on power. Discussions of the appropriate forms for this intellectual work were often bitter, and polarized art cinema production between low-budget political cinema with a limited distribution in political or academic circles and perhaps *cinema d'essai*, and medium- to high-budget production with the potential for international distribution. It is not the case that *auteur* cinema in Italy was doomed to financial penury and shown purely in small cinemas. Although some film-makers chose to start their careers in avant-garde, low-budget or political cinema, others came through mainstream genre films, and later television. *Auteur* films have always had a presence in big, *prima visione* (first run) cinemas so that successful directors have conquered more diverse audiences than the educated cinephile of the *cinema d'essai*.

The deregulation of Italian television in 1976 radically changed the film industry, very rapidly displacing cinema from its prime importance in political and social life. In the next fifteen years, auteurist directors struggled to establish a place in the market, resulting in the development of quality cinema and co-production with television that has been explored earlier. From the mid-1980s a combination of political and commercial factors made success difficult. From the fall of the Berlin Wall to the break up the Soviet Union, and the wars in the former Yugoslavia, Marxism and Left-wing ideologies received severe dents in their prestige. The increasing global domination of the media by American commercial practices and vertically integrated companies resulted in less opportunity for any art film to receive a showing in a cinema. Although it can be argued that new technologies have favoured different forms of audience engagement with films through Web sites and niche journals, the low proportion of Italian films issued on video or DVD with subtitles limits their potential in an international market.

The 'Great Director' Phenomenon

The identification of directors whose ideas and artistic flair meant that their films were cultural events, and shown in first-run cinemas, led to the 'great director' phenomenon. The career of Luchino Visconti (1906–76) is an example of this profile and of appeal to a diverse international audience. Visconti was a wealthy Milanese aristocrat whose life was irrevocably changed by working with Jean

Renoir on *Une partie de campagne* (1936) in Paris at the time of the Popular Front. Contact with creative ferment and with communism initiated his Left-wing commitment and an intensely productive life. Visconti chose to work with many of the same creative people on each film, a strategy that both made it easier for a producer to assess the worth of his production package, and made the film-making process easier. It also ensured stylistic consistency. He co-wrote the screenplays of almost all his films with Suso Cecchi d'Amico, both being interested in a strong *scaletta*, the 'ladder' of scenes, each of which was an individual entity but arose from the previous scene, and sustained the following one (Caldiron and Hochkofler 1988: 60). G. R. Aldo was Visconti's cinematographer until Gianni di Venanzo took over after his death. Similarly, Ruggero Mastroianni became editor after the death of Mario Serandrei. He regularly used Piero Tosi as costume designer and Mario Garbuglia for art direction. Although these collaborators worked across the genre spectrum, they regularly won prizes, such as the prestigious David di Donatello awards, and would therefore be identified as part of any 'quality' package. In spite of this strong collaborative team, books and articles stressed Visconti's control of the creative aspects of the production.

Some of Visconti's preoccupations can already be seen in *Ossessione* (1943). In an influential article of the time he stated that his aim was 'above all, to tell stories of living men, of living men *among* things, not of things *per* se. What I am interested in is an "anthropomorphic" cinema' (Visconti 1978: 84). This aim to impart an understanding of a culture, a historical moment or class informs all his work, and is articulated through costumes and sets. The morphology of an actor, the shape of her/his body, their gestures and overall 'look' were therefore expressive of a social, geographic and temporal context, which contributed to the overall meanings present in the film. In Visconti's neorealist films, *Ossessione*, *La terra trema* (1948), *Bellissima* (1951), his ideological viewpoint attempted to make sense of opposing social forces at a time of major social change. Visconti's *La terra trema* shares with other neorealist films a desire to uncover the truth of a situation, but he differs in many significant respects. Rather than treating a contemporary situation, the film is based on a famous book by the realist author Giovanni Verga, *I Malavoglia*. Visconti chose to illuminate the 'southern question' in a historical context by focussing on the Valastro family who stand metonymically for the situation of the south, and Sicily in particular, using non-professional actors and, at the same time, carefully constructed and spectacularly beautiful images.

The film was a financial disaster and its premiere was greeted with massive incomprehension about the lack of plot, stars and the slow pace ('Un referendum su "La terra trema"', 1950: 64). It was later released in 1948 in a dubbed version in standard Italian, supervised by Francesco Rosi who had acted as Assistant Director on it. Rosi's work on the film was to record meticulously what was in each scene as it was shot, what characters were wearing, what was in the background, the focal length and lenses used, weather conditions, noises (Rosi 1977: 9–14). There were no polaroid cameras, no facilities for rushes, and no script, the most minute planning and notes were made to provide a framework within which the non-professional actors could deliver performances which would be perceived as authentic. Authenticity of place and people validated the director's vision and interpretation and *La terra trema* set a pattern of Visconti's extreme directorial control, which was widely publicized on each film's release. Choosing the exact perfume that Countess Serpieri would have used in her boudoir in *Senso* (1954) is one example.

Visconti's third 'neorealist' film, *Bellissima* was equally unsuccessful at the box office. Centred on Maddalena's (Anna Magnani) attempts to achieve a better life for her daughter, the film is remarkable for its choral quality in that she is frequently surrounded by crowds of other women – the mobs of mothers at Cinecittà, or her neighbours. The cacophony of voices offers a representation of social change as the lower classes press at the gates of affluence (Pinna 1997: 174). Women act as the disruptions that reveal difficulties that the narratives have to resolve, and also stand metonymically for the classes excluded from economic and political power. That their aspirations are represented by the meretricious world of the cinema, the world of illusion, allows Visconti to make the political point that the elusive promise of prosperity made by the ruling classes still effectively excludes ordinary people from the decision-making process.

At this stage Visconti's prestige was based on his position in the wartime resistance and three, critically acclaimed box-office failures. His successes in staging theatre and opera productions and his readings of Gramsci suggested a move to more accessible genres would enable him to continue in a film career. Nowell-Smith (2003: 210) identifies a second phase in his career starting with *Senso* up to *La caduta degli dei* (*The Damned*, 1969), in which Visconti explores history through melodrama, and a final phase from *Morte a Venezia* (*Death in Venice*, 1971) to *L'innocente* (*The Intruder* (UK); *The Innocent* (USA), 1976), in which his films appeared inward looking and firmly in the past. Visconti's experience of providing his own interpretation of theatrical texts is visible in his decision to use emotion to aid the perception of historical moments, and he was furiously criticized by the Left for abandoning the realist mode. *Senso* marked a move into international film-making with its use of international stars, a strategy that would be used in every subsequent film except the last. *Le notti bianche* (*White Nights*, 1957) was a blip in his quest for larger audiences, showing that book adaptations (in this case Dostoievsky) did not always guarantee them. The building of the sets of the houses by the canal cost so much that the producer, Franco Cristaldi, had to encourage several other productions to use them, including *I soliti ignoti*. After that, Visconti concentrated on big-budget, spectacular, international projects, on the back of the huge profits of *Il Gattopardo* (1963).

Significantly, his films are all set in periods of major change, present (*La terra trema, Bellissima, Rocco e i suoi fratelli, Vaghe stelle dell'orsa*), or past, especially the period of the creation of the Italian and German States (*Senso, Il Gattopardo, Ludwig* (1973)), fascism and Nazism (*Ossessione, La caduta degli dei*). Visconti is particularly interested in showing how people accommodate, or not, to change. The process of *trasformismo*, accommodation to an evolving new order, is shown in *Senso* (via Count Serpieri's switch of allegiance) and *Il gattopardo* (through Tancredi's support of Garibaldi and his choice of a fiancée, Angelica, from outside the aristocracy). Its opposite, hanging on to outworn traditions, precipitates disaster for the family in *Rocco e i suoi fratelli* (through the figure of the mother, Rosaria, whose insistence on a southern family ideology threatens the marriage of her eldest son, and leads to Simone's murder of Nadia). The family melodrama is a recognizable popular cinematic form but, in Visconti's hands, it is used to explore major social change, such as the place of the family under dictatorship and under advanced capitalism, which disrupts traditional masculine roles. Increasingly

Figure 5.1
Illusionistic detail and visual complexity; Elisabeth (Charlotte Rampling) and her lover (Umberto Orsini). *La caduta degli dei* (Luchino Visconti, 1969).

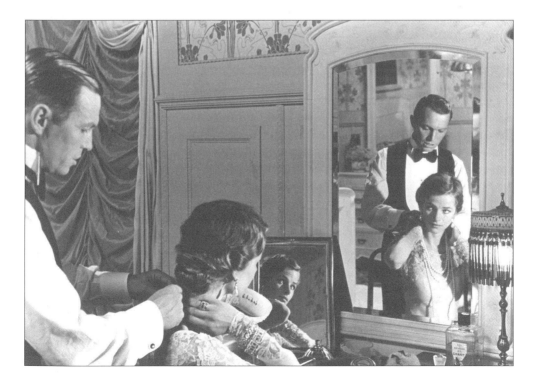

in his films, difficulties within the family structures are signalled by violence, and by performance of sexual excess or homosexuality, or both. Overt homosexuality in the films functions as a disruption to the stability of the ideology of the family, signalling through excess, through *noir* and Baroque elements the instrumental nature of aligning representations of family and nation. Visconti's films, compared to other *auteurs*, appeared considerably less monolithic in their assumptions about gender. Tensions in Visconti's films around dysfunctional male characters and strongly autonomous female characters not only draw attention to masculinity and femininity as performance, but also to the constructedness of patriarchal hierarchies usually represented as natural.

Visconti was able to shape his career into that of a 'great director' through a combination of tremendous visual and organizational cinematic flair, through the lessons of his theatre work, which suggested a move towards melodrama and spectacle, and through occasional favourable commercial results. The notorious overspending on his budgets was tempered by intermittent box-office success in Italy and internationally, which attracted co-production finance and American distribution investments. His films can be appreciated at many levels, with a greater level of cultural capital being required to appreciate the references to events in Italian or European history and culture (Bourdieu 1993). His use of melodrama and plots centred around families generate meanings at a macrohistorical level and make sense as representations of preoccupations in European society about social conflict and change. The generic hybridity of Visconti's films and the visual excess signal Visconti's virtuosity, and an interrogation of the certainties of his class.

Federico Fellini (1920–93) is better known in his directorial persona, in which he appeared to encapsulate characteristics of the Italian male. Childishness, fantastic imagination, fascination with the feminine, and a spectacular *mise en scène*, which gave a more resonant representation of contemporary society than realist cinema, clearly struck chords with his public, even if they did not always understand his films. Fellini always claimed that it was his vocation to tell lies, creating problems with film critics who often delighted in discovering parallels between a director's life and the protagonist of his films (often played by Marcello Mastroianni) (Placido 1993: 29). In Fellini's case, seriousness of purpose was linked to his personal, fantastic and fantasized vision of life, which he also claimed tried to unmask bourgeois values (Fellini 1980: 154). Fellini's career started on Rossellini's *Un pilota ritorna* along with Antonioni, and this contact led to work on Rossellini's films of the liberation of Italy, *Paisà*, and *Rome Open City*. Fellini acknowledged Rossellini's influence on his work, not so much stylistically as morally and artistically, in that Rossellini gave him a vision of the authenticity of artistic experience – that is the moral imperative to take as subjects the dilemmas of modern man or woman, so that the integrity with which they were depicted would make their appeal universal, as well as particularly Italian (Fellini 1980: 46–7).

Fellini's apprenticeship was both with realist masters, and with mainstream comedy writers. He had also had a good training in pitching a story and writing commercially, and in putting his own experiences into words. He could present ideas and stories visually through his cartoons and sketches and was thoroughly in tune with the market when he made his first film, *Luci di varietà* (*Variety Lights*, with Alberto Lattuada, 1950), significantly enough a story of music hall performers. Players, people who perform, who disguise themselves or hide psychologically behind borrowed roles, lies and masks, are a powerful leitmotif throughout all his films. *Lo sceicco bianco* (*The White Sheik*, 1952) shows the effect of the world created by the *fotoromanzo* (cheap comic books telling stories through photos rather than drawings) on a newly wed couple. The bride (Brunella Bovo) leaves her husband for the white sheik of the photos (Alberto Sordi), unable to reconcile the make-believe world of magazines with daily reality. *La strada* (1954) follows a troupe of travelling players. It charts the brutish Zampanò's (Anthony Quinn) road to salvation through contact with the innocent Gelsomina (Giulietta Masina) and the wise fool. *Il bidone* (*The Swindler*, 1955) follows a group of confidence tricksters. *Le notti di Cabiria* (*Nights of Cabiria*, 1957) is the story of a Rome prostitute (Masina) who manages to retain her dignity, even though she is attacked, humiliated and robbed. All of these films were low-budget productions with modest financial returns, but his winning of awards at film festivals indicated international potential. He won a Silver Lion at the 1953 Venice festival for *I vitelloni* (1953); a Silver Lion, an Academy Award and a New York Film Critics' Circle Award in 1956 for *La strada*; and a 1957 Academy Award for *Le notti di Cabiria*.

La dolce vita (1960) represented a marked shift in ways of considering Italian society, exploring a period of transition between the old certainties of traditional Italian society, and a new society that Fellini saw being created by the media. It made a huge amount of money, helped by free publicity from the Catholic Church, which tried to have it banned and advised Catholics not to see it. It made Fellini's career, and, from that point on, he was able to market himself very much as the creator of his films. The addition of his name to the titles of subsequent films, *8½* (1963), *Fellini Satyricon* (1969), *Fellini Roma* (1972), *I Clowns* (1970), *Amarcord* (1973), *Fellini Casanova* (1976), signifies his cultural and marketing importance. Fellini, like Visconti, preferred to work with the same creative teams and, from *La dolce vita* onwards, is associated with quality, auteurist, international film production, while playing with popular genre forms. *Fellini Roma*, *Fellini Satyricon* and *Ginger e Fred* (*Ginger and Fred*, 1985) are comedies that attempt to explore the past which shapes the present of Roman and Italian society. *Amarcord* is a coming-of-age film, and a coming-to-terms-with-fascism film. *Giulietta degli spiriti* (*Juliet of the Spirits*, 1965), *La città delle donne* (*City of Women*, 1980) and *Fellini Casanova* are erotic dramas, the postmodern *Intervista* (1987) is another reflection on Fellini's personal history, and on the role of his films in shaping perceptions of the Italian world view.

Fellini's films are obsessed by the liberation of the individual (and the creative individual above all) from the shackles of the old mythologies. In *La dolce vita* Rome is used as a metaphor for Western culture viewed from the double perspective of the imperial past and the present. Marcello's (Marcello Mastroianni) quests for meaning and personal authenticity result mainly in failures.

Fellini gave considerable narrative space to female characters in his films, as popular cinema was doing, but magnified the disturbance that slowly growing female autonomy occasioned. His early films are interesting as more intellectual versions of *neorealismo rosa*, pink neorealism, in which the cataclysmic changes in post-war society are reflected particularly in male characters whose hyperbolic performances of masculinity indicate the level of effort in the construction of a valid self-image. Erotic relationships are depicted as power struggles for the domination of the other. *Fellini Casanova*, in particular, was bleak in its depiction of the compulsive indulgence in trivial titillation shown as characteristic of both eighteenth-century and our own society.

Casanova is typical in its foregrounding of theatricality of sets, costumes and performances. Casanova (Donald Sutherland), for example, sails to his first tryst with the nun on the island in the Venetian lagoon over a sea of rather obvious black plastic bin liners. There are various distancing effects, such as the self-conscious, stylized performance of the lovers in sexual positions under the gaze of

Figure 5.2
The journey over the Venetian lagoon in *Fellini Casanova* (1976).

the nun's lover. The self-delusion of the protagonist, and the ironic knowingness of Casanova's sexual congress accompanied by the movements of the golden mechanical bird carried around in a black box provide a space for reflection. The bird goes up and down and flaps its wings, a crude metaphor and a Fellini joke (the Italian slang for penis is *uccello*, or bird), commenting on the mechanical nature of Casanova's sexual act.

Elements of the erotic comedy surface frequently in his use of large female figures, whose size and coarse facial features connote a hyper-femininity and sexual voraciousness that both attracts and repels his male characters. However, the explosion of outlets for erotic films from the early 1980s meant that Fellini's cinematic fantasies seemed tame and insufficiently explicit to the soft-porn audience. *Intervista* is emblematic of the fact that Fellini's cinema no longer had the power of startling insights, but relied for its appeal on knowledge of the director and nostalgic recognition of canonic scenes from his films.

The careers of Visconti and Fellini show both the need for directors to engage with the commercial aspects of film-making, and how artistic development depends upon a fruitful creative engagement with others. The formative impact of neorealism is visible in the careers of other well-known *auteurs*. Left-wing critics such as Guido Aristarco railed loudly against any deviation from realist conventions and working-class subjects, areas that had cultural prestige in Left-wing circles. Their cultural intimidation validates Manuela Gieri's (1995: 202) claim that neorealism blighted the careers of Italian film directors from the 1950s until the 1970s.

Roberto Rossellini's (1906–77) cinema did not follow a consistent trajectory. It started with realist dramatic films set in the armed forces' milieux in the fascist period, before he achieved fame and prestige with two of the canonic films of neorealism, *Roma città aperta* and *Paisà*. These films also include elements of broad comedy and moments of tragedy and pathos. Although Brunette identifies chorality as one of their major characteristics and a loss of the choral element in *Germania anno zero* (*Germany, Year Zero*, 1947), the locations and camera movements of his films always link characters to their environment. His films of the 1950s sometimes appeared atypical and were often unsuccessful financially. Over half his output was on historical themes, most of that was for television (Aprà 2000: 126). While Italian critics berated Rossellini for his emotionality and increasingly international productions, he was championed by influential French critics who admired his cinematic skills in delineating the contemporary human condition. There were adaptations of Cocteau in *L'amore* (*Love: Two Love Stories*, 1948) and medieval stories of St. Francis in *Francesco giullare di Dio* (*Francis God's Jester*, 1950). His films with Ingrid Bergman were aimed at an international market and made in English. The sparseness of the sets of *Francesco* prefigures the spare *mise en scène* of his programmes for RAI television. The spirituality or humanism which so many critics identify as a defining element of Rossellini's work is, in fact, an acute visual and narrative exposure of the shortcomings of modernity. As much as Antonioni, Fellini, or the comedies of the 1960s, he is consistently concerned with the power of materialistic culture to divert people from communicating with each other or from holding to values of community. Not for nothing are his television programmes concerned with education and with the struggle for survival ('La lotta dell'uomo per la sua sopprawvivenza', RAI, 1967–9), or with philosophers such as Pascal ('Blaise Pascal', ORTF, 1971–2), who explored how people should live in order to gain most fulfilment.

With hindsight the work of the 1950s and 1960s, *Europa '51* (1952), *Stromboli* (1950), *Viaggio in Italia* (*Voyage to Italy*, 1954), *India Matri Bhumi* (*India*, 1959), *Viva l'Italia* (*Long Live Italy*, 1960) (the latter made to celebrate Italy's 100 years of nationhood), and *Anno uno* (*Year One*, 1974) shows his awareness that the Second World War had changed the 'cognitive map' of the world for ever. Italian film production could not function in national isolation, but was contingent on alliances through co-productions and the use of international stars; and films exploring the loss of traditional values and the sense of one's place in society had a resonance for other European countries. Rossellini's reputation has inevitably rested on his film work as access to the majority of his television output was difficult.

Pasolini's (1922–75) status as one of Italy's leading poets, and author of several fat volumes of empassioned criticism on a wide variety of burning contemporary issues, has meant that he has been regarded as a 'great director' when, in fact, his cinematic output could be considered jagged and uneven.

Pasolini was an outsider, a radical Leftist homosexual. His films always occupy boundary zones, pushing at the limits of taste and trying to jolt his audience into an awareness of all sorts of exploitation, of the constructedness of myths, and of the class interests behind social conventions, by depicting the rude, the vital and the unexpected. Early films, *Accatone* (1961), *Mamma Roma* (1962), *Uccellacci e uccellini* (*Hawks and Sparrows*, 1966), explore the marginal, low-life settings of male and female prostitution and the shanty towns around Rome. An unusual choice for a committed atheist, *Il vangelo secondo Matteo* (*The Gospel According to Saint Matthew*, 1964), is a moving religious picture combining conventions of realism with aestheticized images and investing its peasant setting with enormous dignity and value. Other myths, bourgeois life, sex and religion are explored in his late 1960s films, *Edipo re* (*Oedipus Rex*, 1967), *Teorema* (*Theorem*, 1968) and *Porcile* (*Porcile*, 1969). The inspired casting of Maria Callas in *Medea* (1969) showed him to be acutely sensitive to changes in society through his exploration of female power, the loss of sacred and of moral values, and the importance of what was happening in the Third World to the future of Western civilization.

Pasolini found the hedonism and climate of the 1960s deeply disturbing in its destruction of Italian traditions, regional dialects and rural customs. He also found the political militancy and 'moralism' of 1968 and beyond deeply distasteful, berating students for their arrogance and smugness in fighting the police, who were generally the sons of the poor (Greene 1990: 174). Faced with what he identified as repression and pressure to accept the idea of the bourgeois couple as the dominant sexual paradigm, Pasolini dared to assert the liberating force of sexual polyvalency. The burgeoning sex film industry of the 1970s facilitated filming of *Il Decamerone* (*The Decameron*, 1971), *I racconti di Canterbury* (*The Canterbury Tales*, 1972), whose gay sex scene in the cloisters of Canterbury cathedral created a furore, and *Il fiore delle mille e una notte* (*The Arabian Nights*,1974), popular classics, containing larger than life characters, and a potential international audience. The sexual exuberance which Pasolini depicted spawned a *filone decameronistico* of its own. His adaptation of De Sade, *Salò e le 120 giornate di Sodoma* (*Salò: or the 120 Days of Sodom*, 1975) is a deliberately scandalous film in which Salò, the last Republic set up by the fascist government in 1944 as it fled northwards to avoid the Allied invasion, is represented as a Nazi-porno-erotic fantasy, full of shit, semen and blood. Those who have the stomach for it are forced to watch the literal abuse, torture, humiliation and degradation of naked Italian boys and girls, where sexual exploitation is a metaphor for the commodification of sex in the consumer society. The abusers, an Italian government minister, a duke, a president and a bishop clearly represent one pole of the class struggle. What made Pasolini's last film different from exploitation films was its relentless moral tone but it has been banned, or only shown in limited runs in cinema clubs, since. Shortly after *Salò*'s release Pasolini's mutilated body was found on rough ground near the beach resort of Ostia. At the time of the trial of the young Roman rent boy arrested for his killing, one French critic is reputed to have urged that *Salò* be shown in court as anybody capable of directing such a film was asking to be murdered. Pasolini would have revelled in the hypocrisy of such an attitude. His films are part of a larger body of work, thus demanding that the film-maker's political and cultural agenda be taken seriously.

Sex and the *Auteur*

Critics looking for a continuation of neorealism's concerns rapidly identified Antonioni's films as examples of 'bourgeois realism'. Antonioni's career shows a consistent auteurist profile in his interest in the effects of social change on the new middle class, its seeming inability to find a place in society and to communicate emotionally, and in his visual style. His career was so unsuccessful initially that only critical interest and international appeal could explain investment in his 1960s productions. He started in documentaries in the 1940s, moving on to feature films set amongst the middle classes and exploring the effects of post-war turmoil through *film noir* conventions in *Cronaca di un amore* (*Story of a Love Affair*, 1950) and *La signora senza camelie* (*The Lady Without Camelias*, 1953), both of which made poor box-office returns, although critically admired. As prosperity increased in the 1950s, Antonioni's films chimed more with growing social mobility and its attendant problems. *I vinti* (*The Vanquished*, 1952) and *Cronaca di un amore* are full of moody atmosphere, evoked through desolate landscapes. Both subjects and *mise en scène* signal the presence of an authorial agenda. Italian popular films set in lower-class milieux in the 1940s used prostitute figures to indicate profound unease with rapid social change and the materialistic nature of American consumer culture. Antonioni focuses on the middle classes, so that the figure of the woman who uses her sexuality to move up a class echoes the position of a nation, which is losing its integrity in subscribing to economic prosperity. Elements of American *film noir* style, such as shadows over faces, strong shadows on interior walls, night-time streets, plangent jazz bassoon, are used as the vehicle of the metaphoric transfer. What distinguishes *Cronaca* as Italian *noir* is its creative use of the graphic and expressive possibilities of architecture and landscape. The lovers meet in dark streets, anonymous, modernist buildings or flat spaces, where compositions of insistent, asymmetrical straight lines or wide-angle extreme long shots suggest disturbance and alienation. Two 180° tracking shots in the scene where the lovers plot the death of Paola's husband display the black, crossed struts of the bridge over the motorway, a graphic indication that they are going nowhere.

Subsequently, Antonioni used *noir* elements most effectively in *Blow-up* (1966), where a photographer, Thomas (David Hemmings) investigates a (literal) *femme fatale* (Vanessa Redgrave) in 'Swinging London'. In his darkroom, significantly shot in sulphurous yellow, Thomas attempts to investigate reality, to fix and control it by obsessively blowing up detail after detail. *Blow-up*'s world is *noir* in that it is one of moral ambiguity, where the photographer/investigator exploits everyone around him, homeless men, supermodels, teenage girls. In Thomas's portrayal of crude gender and cultural power exercised by a newly ascendant class, Antonioni suggests that social turmoil masks the continuity of patriarchal relationships. Similarly, a *noir* structure and visual excess in *Professione: reporter* (*The Passenger*, 1975) are used to investigate questions of individual and collective identity and responsibility, the individual standing for the global. Significantly,

Blow-up, Zabriskie Point (1969) and *Professione: Reporter* were all international co-productions by Carlo Ponti for MGM, a company that had invested in successful Italian directors in the late 1960s and 1970s.

Antonioni's access to American finance had come from his increasing reputation as an *auteur*, based on earlier mid-budget, Franco-Italian co-productions, which explored the effects of rapid economic development, ecological damage, urban alienation particularly through their female protagonists. *L'avventura* (*The Adventure*, 1960), *La notte* (*The Night*, 1961), *L'ecclisse* (*The Eclipse*, 1962) and *Il deserto rosso* (*The Red Desert*, 1964), all starred Monica Vitti, whose face and gestures seemed to epitomize a northern, more modern type, whose wide-mouthed, wide-eyed vulnerability could connote both the sophistication of modern youth, and an immaturity that prevented her establishing her place in society. All these films draw attention to authorial intervention, and the organization of meanings through visual elements. Excess, represented by stylistic flourishes, indicates not so much the presence of political mysteries or traumatic events as the psychological damage done by casting people adrift in an alien environment. Fogs and mists recur in Antonioni's later films as metaphors of characters' inability to really see each other.

As a typical *auteur*, Antonioni's films have been the subject of many books and articles offering interpretations of his themes and visual style. His work of the 1950s and 1960s appeared to offer new perspectives on social change but, after his big-budget films and with poor health, Antonioni reverted to modestly budgetted dramas, obsessively investigating female characters. *Identificazione di una donna* (*Identification of a Woman*, 1982) and *Par-delà des nuages* (*Beyond the Clouds*, 1996) contain the beautifully spectacular images that are Antonioni's hallmark, and what Brunette (1998: 23) has called the 'tacky and embarrassing' sexual obsessions of the director. Whereas his narratives of contemporary difficulties in creating community have validity, Antonioni's gender ideology is a source of considerable unease in its occasionally brutal, and very sexual, objectification of his female figures. Marketing of these films is an uneasy mix of authorial celebration of style and attempts to make postmodern readings of fluidity of identities, indicating that this artisanal authorial model is now outdated.

Transitional Careers

Francesco Rosi (1922–) cannot be fitted neatly into definitions of 'art' cinema, but is part of a European realist tradition that seeks to engage with contemporary society. Influenced by a left-wing agenda and Gramsci, his consistent interest is in uncovering how power, legal and illegal, is exercised, and in whose interests. Critical writing and interviews identify distinguishing marks of his style and discuss the films as authored texts. Rosi's films are not primarily interested in establishing psychological realism of characters, and those that engage with political and social issues are more concerned with clarity of argument than with ambiguity. Their use of the investigative format is extremely significant. At its most mundane and pecuniary level this allows Rosi to use a popular literary and cinematic form which will be readily intelligible to financiers, who are able to evaluate the financial appeal of a recognizable genre format, that of the conspiracy thriller. On the other hand, it satisfies Rosi's political and artistic intentions as detective fiction is no stranger to more metaphysical enquiries about the nature of justice, or of crime, and the relationship between the individual and society.

Like Visconti and Fellini, Rosi has consistently collaborated with the same creative team (some of whom he has shared with them) – Suso Cecchi d'Amico and Tonino Guerra as part of the script team, Gianni di Venanzo and Pasqualino de Santis as cinematographers, Mario Serandrei and Ruggero Mastroianni as editors. His collaborators also won prizes at film festivals which, as we have seen, enabled Rosi's creative 'package' to attract finance to move into the 'quality' sector of international film-making. Rosi also takes advantage of popular *filoni*, and his style is both spectacular and

Figure 5.3

The complex evocation of a social world; Naples in *La sfida* (Francesco Rosi, 1958).

generically hybrid. His career also includes a bullfighting biopic, *Il momento della verità* (*The Moment of Truth*, 1965), a fairy tale, starring Omar Sharif and Sophia Loren and featuring flying monks, *C'era una volta* (*Cinderella Italian Style*, 1967), and a war film, *Uomini contro* (*Just Another War*, 1970), in all of which his virtuosity and directorial ability is foregrounded in spectacular set-pieces marshalling hundreds of extras in a complex *mise en scène*.

Francesco Rosi moved into the 'quality' film sector after a series of critically and financially successful political films in the 1970s. Il *caso Mattei, Lucky Luciano* and *Cadaveri eccellenti* all used the *giallo* investigative form and, in the latter case, adapted a successful book. Rosi's stress on the authenticity of his recreations of political situations derived from neorealism, but his use of precise locations and non-professional actors differed. Rather than neorealism's indeterminate locations which indicate characters adrift in an inimical world, Rosi's critical realism is heavily constructed, using the full resources of cinema to indicate layers of meaning and forcing acknowledgement of its readability (Deleuze 1989: 24). Although complex investigations of political events or mysteries, his films were concerned to indicate political truths and it is this clarity of language that enabled Rosi to move into international film-making. *Dimenticare Palermo* (*To Forget Palermo/The Palermo Connection*, Italy/France, 1990) was a big-budget, co-production with Gaumont, the vertically integrated French company, and illustrates the pitfalls of the international, 'quality' film. Aiming to air the problems of the legalization of drugs, the protagonist, an Italian-American politician, leads us into the investigation and his nemesis, the shadowy 'Man of Power', provides an example of the corporate tentacles of the Mafia, whose drugs business is run on the pattern of a multinational company. It did not find critical favour, although the seriousness of the drugs problem would have indicated an international relevance; nor did it succeed financially. Moreover Rosi's style, which includes a flamboyant drawing of attention to the graphic possibilities of landscape and architecture, and a particularly dense *mise en scène* in which meanings can be suggested simultaneously through the visual, kinetic and aural elements within the frame, meant that the pace of his films is slow in comparison to American cinema.

La tregua (*The Truce*, Italy/France/Switzerland/Germany, 1996), an expensive co-production filmed in Poland, Ukraine and Italy, did not have a wide distribution but offset this by deals with TV and satellite and is a case in point. Made with the collaboration of Italian state television, RAI, and Canal Plus, *La tregua* (based on a successful book by Primo Levi) is the story of a journey home of survivors of the Holocaust. It came tenth in box-office returns for Italian national films in 1996, had wide satellite exposure, and appeared as a sell-through video and as an Italian newsstand video title. Its marketing and accompanying articles and interviews stressed the prestige of the film-maker, Rosi, as much as the author, Levi, fidelity to the book and to history, and the authenticity of place and atmosphere (Wood 1998: 279–81). The opening shots of the Red Army riding through the snow to liberate the camp have an epic grandeur, recalling compositions from his earlier war film *Uomini contro*. Even with the picaresque adventures of the mixed group of Italians in which Levi finds himself, *La tregua* was perceived as worthy, rather than entertaining and illustrates the difficulties of successfully combining local culture and global concerns.

However, Rosi's questioning of over-arching explanations of social or belief systems is postmodern in a very Italian way in that his films question events through narrative disruptions, and visual flamboyance. Rosi's career is emblematic of the evolution of a type of art cinema from political contestation to mainstream, international production, and to quality, auteurist cinema whose large budgets mean that too incisive political critique is not appropriate.

Bertolucci's career similarly spanned the crucial watershed of the 1970s so that he was established as an important director before auteurist cinema changed forever. His debut owed much to his personal position in Italian cultural circles as the son of a famous poet, Attilio Bertolucci, with all that this implies in the way of contacts with influential and creative people. His first film, *La commare secca* (*The Grim Reaper*, 1962), made when he was only twenty-one years old, from a subject suggested by Pasolini, was a moderate financial success, but importantly, it was a great critical success, which launched his career.

Bertolucci has also worked for many years with the same people but, since the creative team is never precisely the same from film to film, the constant, controlling talent is that of Bertolucci himself.[1] Moreover, he tends to be involved at several levels, most significantly on the script and the screenplay. Of course, there are financial reasons for a script credit, but Bertolucci benefits both from the input of other creative people, and from stamping his mark on the final film. *La commare secca* is a quest narrative, which uses the familiar device of a death (a murdered Roman prostitute) to explore the reasons for it. Bertolucci's political approach is to make the personal political by sketching out a milieu, that of the poor quarters of Rome, in the repeated revisiting of parks, lower class homes and streets as the characters re-enact their contact with the crime. The characters have no ambition to make their mark on history, but their lives are shaped by power relations within society. The narrative concludes with the identification of the murderer, and that there is not just one truth but multiple explanations for a social situation. However, the film also exhibits the interplay between analysis of events and a desire to know, and an impulse towards composition and aesthetic display. Space is organized both to give a full context to the action, and to display the aesthetic qualities of buildings and perspective.

As the son of a famous man with whom he has had to come to terms, Bertolucci shares with his generation a preoccupation with coming to terms with Italian history, particularly with its fascist past; and with Italian culture and its post-war development. His generation of male, bourgeois, Marxist intellectuals has a complex political past against which to construct their own identity. From film to film, Bertolucci gives us varying representations of his generation's difficulty, personal history and the universal, Oedipal conflict between generations and between artists. *La strategia del ragno* (*The Spider's Stratagem*), made back-to-back with *Il conformista* (*The Conformist*, 1970) (the same year that he started psychoanalysis), is a good example of the RAI film – intellectually and visually spectacular. It was a loose adaptation of a Borges novella, and in it Bertolucci explored the betrayal of the intellectual – both in the past and the present. Young Athos Magnani is summoned to the town of Tara by his father's (also Athos Magnani) mistress, Draifa. He is charged with discovering who murdered his father (who has been immortalized in sculpture as an anti-fascist hero) in the 1930s. It is another quest narrative, using conversations and testimonies in the present to evoke events in the past but this doubling and repetition presents 'a view of history as a past inaccessible to truth' (Loshitsky 1995: 57). In the type of Italian, auteurist cinema typified by Bertolucci, realism and spectacle form a symbiotic relationship to suggest the complexity of contemporary reality, and of masculine identity. It has been suggested that 'the pleasure of texts involving "spectacle" lies in the images themselves; it is a visual, not a narrative pleasure' (Abercrombie, Lash and Longhurst 1993: 121). This provides some explanation of why a director such as Bertolucci has been able to move into international co-production. His appeal combines pleasure at the beautifully composed images, and enjoyment at being able to deploy cultural capital in reading narrative and visuals (Bourdieu 1993: 133).

The critical success of *La strategia del ragno* and *Il conformista*, Bertolucci's virtuosity of *mise en scène*, his ability to handle complex narratives and an international cast meant that he could now become part of an international production 'package'. The enormous financial success of *Last Tango in Paris* (1972) meant that Bertolucci's worth in the investors' league tables shot up several notches, and this was consolidated by *Novecento* (*1900*, 1976) and his three, mega-budget, English-language, international films, *The Last Emperor* (China/Italy, 1987), *Il tè nel deserto* (*The Sheltering Sky*, UK/Italy, 1990), and *Little Buddha* (France/UK, 1993). *The Last Emperor* won eight Oscars, including one for best director, and the film made $44 million at the box office. At this distance in time, these films can be seen as the apotheosis of this mode of 'quality' cinema. They are sumptuous, widescreen films, marketed as Bertolucci films, and marked by striking and sensual use of colour and composition and quests for personal authenticity (Wood 2002: 47). Bertolucci's technical mastery of the visual and aural possibilities of the medium enable him to present ideas and contrasts clearly. In *The Sheltering Sky*, for example, Port and Kit discuss their faltering marriage while sitting on the edge of a precipice in the desert. Sexual ambiguity is expressed visually through feminized male faces and veiled female forms. The quest for the 'Other' and its ultimate unknowability is represented in temporal and spatial terms by the length of time taken for the camel train to return from the desert, and in the high angle, jigsaw movement of the beasts within the mud walls of the town. The strange and beautiful archectural forms of the house through which Belqassim hurries his sexual slave, Kit, hint at the allure of this other life, but, by the *mise en scène* of containment, indicate its limitations for a Western woman. For the most part Bertolucci's representations of these other worlds are spectacular and aestheticized, the name of Bertolucci's cinematographer, Vittorio Storaro, being another guarantee of quality.

Since 1993 Bertolucci has rejected this high concept, big budget mode of film-making for relatively low-budget co-productions with television. *Io ballo da sola* (*Stealing Beauty*, Italy/France/UK, 1996), *L'assedio* (*Besieged*, 1998) and *I sognatori* (*The Dreamers*, 2003) all feature international casts and dramas of identity. The first two are set in contemporary Italy so that characters experience both their own and other identities simultaneously, rather than one or the other. In this respect, Bertolucci's current preoccupations chime with those of the mass, educated, international, multicultural audience, which, as I have indicated, is a significant category. *The Dreamers* explores the interaction of a young French brother and sister with an American student whom they meet at the Cinémathèque on the eve of the May 1968 student uprisings in Paris. Bertolucci's aim was to evoke the atmosphere of enthusiasm and the possibility of change which he considers has been denied to today's twenty year olds.[2] His sensuous composition of cinematic space and architecture in spectacular images, and his sexual frankness deflects attention from narrative progression towards the fluidity of identity (personal, national and sexual) and the role of art and cinema in creating it.

Stealing Beauty made $4.7 million at the box office, more than *Little Buddha* or *The Sheltering Sky*. Bertolucci's current films, although co-produced with television, are still destined for international distribution via globalized media networks, where his serious themes and individual style can be very profitable, without the risks (and stress) involved in big-budget production.

After the Television Revolution

Since the 1970s Italian directors have found it difficult to conquer an international audience for reasons already explored. The older generation of film-makers adapted by building on established reputations but its inability to move beyond the dominant, patriarchal ideologies of traditional Italian society limit their appeal. Ermanno Olmi, Paolo and Vittorio Taviani and Franco Zeffirelli have all moved into 'quality' production, the first two by visual flair and input into several phases of production. Zeffirelli is a director much reviled for his Right-wing views and rarely accorded serious critical consideration, mainly for that reason. Nonetheless, his work can be firmly placed in the 'quality' genre, and is phenomenally successful financially, mainly due to working on co-productions, which have been the mainstay of satellite television. His output has been prolific, including popular opera productions, book adaptations, and numerous biblical epics featuring international stars and a visual richness of composition and *mise en scène*. *Un tè con Mussolini* (*Tea With Mussolini*) (Italy/UK, 2000) has been described as typically sumptuous, but without the director's usual turgid and redundant moments (D'Agostini 2000: 117). A simple story (a young boy in fascist Florence is brought up by a group of eccentric English women), informative dialogue in English, and considerable narrative verve make it comprehensible. Relatively fast-paced tracking shots move the characters through long shots of familiar Florentine sights as young Luca is educated into Italian art, and the ways of the world. There is a quality cast of British and American actors to provide multiple points of narrative interest and to indicate different layers of emotional response.

A similar hybrid appeal (this time of the world of music and opera), and of a talented woman rising above personal heartbreak and tragedy, while wearing wonderful 1960s costumes, is visible in *Callas Forever* (Italy/UK/France/Spain/Romania, 2002), produced with assistance from Canal Plus, the television and satellite giant, and the European Union's Eurimages programme. The film stars Fanny Ardant as Callas and Jeremy Irons as the impresario who hopes to tempt her out of seclusion after her break with Onassis. Irons provides the sub-plot of a gay love affair. The DVD version was issued with selected highlights from Callas's performances, thus appealing to the large niche of opera fans who collect classic recordings. As Rosi's *Carmen* shows, opera films have a virtually infinite shelf life on videocassette and DVD, with regular reissues.

The Younger Generation of *Auteurs*

The younger generations include several well-known *auteurs* who have created careers and international recognition for themselves. Italian film-makers still engage with contemporary society but stories too rooted in Italian political complexities, while cultural events, are destined for local consumption. European Union and

State subventions and co-production with television have ensured the survival of film-makers' personal engagement with serious issues. Gianni Amelio is an example of a film-maker whose cinematic flair and issue-based stories have established his reputation. Although he acknowledges the importance of Italian neorealism, and the impossibility of working in that style now, he uses emotion and melodrama, the family and particularly children, to open up the world of the emotions and feelings to the political (Fofi 1994: 8). In spite of demographic and social changes, Italians still regard the family and children as central to their own self-identity, which is perhaps why rural Italy is still seen as the repository of real Italian values. Amelio is not at all nostalgic about rural Italy and doesn't let provincial Italians get away with being small-minded and hypocritical. *Il ladro di bambini* (*The Stolen Children*, 1992) is interesting in presenting a range of female characters, but is more a road movie, a search for the positive side of stereotypical national characteristics. In many ways this Italy is embodied in the figure of Antonio, the young carabiniere, who, like the judiciary and the police have come to represent the ordinary citizen's sense of justice and right in the face of massive corruption in upper class, industrial and political circles.

This film cost $2 million and 'appealed to the same socially concerned Italian audience that made such a success of *Mery per sempre'* (*Forever Mary*, Marco Risi, 1988) (Ilott 1996: 95). It was a modest co-production, its simple structure and emotional content aimed at a television audience. Designed to break even, it made a return of over 173 per cent on its costs, and, according to Ilott, could have had more international success with a larger budget. The success of Amelio's subsequent films, *Lamerica* (1994) and *Così ridevano* (*The Way We Laughed*, 1998), both of which comment on Italy's post-colonial present and won prizes at the Venice Film Festival, moved him up a production notch for his next production, *Le chiavi di casa* (*The House Keys*, 2004) an international family epic.

Critics are currently attempting to construct a 'Great Director' profile for Marco Bellocchio, based primarily on films targeting the establishment, the media, army, Catholic Church and psychiatric institutions, but also on the success of *L'ora di religione* (*My Mother's Smile*, 2002). Bellocchio maintained that he never caters for a defined audience when making his films (Magrelli 2002: 3), tapping into the myth of the *auteur* who can escape vulgar commercial considerations. From his first success, *I pugni in tasca* (*Fists in the Pocket*, 1965), Bellocchio was praised both for his subject matter and his cinematic flair (Chiaretti 1970: 7). In *L'ora di religione*, Baroque over-decoration and shadows predominate in the milieux of the supporters of Ernesto's (Sergio Castellitto) mother's canonization, whereas his appartment is untidy, but light and modern. Following the atheist Ernesto's quest for the reasons why anyone should seek the beatification of his mother, allows Bellocchio to uncover areas of corruption, self-interest and lunacy within the Church, and resulted in several bishops calling for it to be banned. This success allowed him to impose his own version of the Moro kidnapping, *Buongiorno notte* (*Good Morning, Night*, 2003) on RAI. By concentrating on the moral dilemmas of the central female protagonist, Chiara (Maya Sansa), Bellocchio refuses to speculate on who might be responsible, and joins the groundswell of films rejecting 1970s militancy. Playing down the labyrinthine and specifically Italian political background to Moro's murder facilitates an international distribution at a time when terrorist assassinations have a topical impact. Bellocchio's films consistently invite the spectator to debate their ideas, which are signalled through dialogue and through characters representing viewpoints or institutions. Although presented as 'irrepressibly individual', and therefore the focus of critical attention and a national following, Bellocchio doesn't quite attain the 'product differentiation' necessary for international marketing success (Cook and Bernink 1999: 313). His style does not impose itself and his films are too uneven in their appeal.

Women *Auteurs*

Female directors are generally marginalized in histories of Italian cinema, but two at least stand out, Liliana Cavani and Lina Wertmüller. Cavani has alternated theatre work directing operas with film and, like Fellini, Rosi, Bertolucci and others, one controversial work brought her to the attention of critics. *Il portiere di notte* (*The Night Porter*, 1974) was very successful financially and enabled her to reach an international audience. Moreover, as Gaetana Marrone (2000: 147) has shown in detail, Cavani's career is characterized by a strategy of eroticism, the violation of sexual taboos being paralleled by 'a violation of discursive norms' so how sexual relationships are shown and told clarify the nature of social relationships, particularly where gender power is concerned. Cavani's films have excited consistent critical attention, even if some of them relegated her more explicit films to the *filone porno-soft* (Buscemi 1996: 139–48). She has consistently worked with famous collaborators, such as Franco Arcalli, Gabriella Cristiani, and Piero Tosi. The publication of scripts, serious and/or controversial themes and successful international distribution have confirmed her *auteur* status. Cavani's narrative consistency, in which complex stories exist in a homologous relationship with the visuals, have enabled her to move into international production. The trailer for *Il gioco di Ripley* (*Ripley's Game*, 2002) was filmed to present it as an American product, starring John Malkovich, but the beautifully organized visuals of Palladian architecture, contrasted with Roccoco decoration in Ripley's home, mark it as an Italian film.

Figure 5.4
A complex *mise en scène*. *Il gioco di Ripley* (Liliana Cavani, 2002).

Lina Wertmüller signed her early television films 'George Brown' to avoid the sexism of Italian cinema, worked for Fellini and absorbed the lessons of Italian comedy (Miscuglio 1988). Her international success coincided with the rise of feminism in the 1970s, and she conquered the American market in a way denied to most of her male contemporaries. Her films are hybrids of comedy, drama, melodrama, social problem film, realism and fantasy and she stamped her own individuality on her 1970s films by their typically long titles, her irreverent political stance, and by three Oscar nominations for *Pasqualino Settebellezze* (*Seven Beauties*, 1976). In spite of becoming head of the prestigious Rome film school, the CSC, in the 1980s, she maintained her output and box-office success, shortened her titles, finding that her typical hybridity had now become the norm, and a new raft of political targets (AIDS, education, class, history) provided a fruitful source of topics.

In the contemporary situation where any film-maker achieving international notice is regarded as an *auteur*, several younger women film-makers are constructing careers in the mainstream industry. Taking advantage of family connections is common in the Italian film industry, and the three daughters of Luigi Comencini have all profited from their background, Paola as an editor, Francesca and Cristina directing. Wilma Labate, Francesca Archibugi, and Fiorella Infascelli, have also achieved success, but Archibugi's concentration on the worlds of women and children, while providing consistent material for writers of theses, does not differentiate itself enough for her to achieve a profile different from any of her other European contemporaries. Roberta Torre, on the other hand, aimed to do precisely that by flagrantly subverting the conventions of the Mafia genre (Marcus 2002: 234). In *Tano da morire* (*To Die for Tano*, 1997), she achieves this by combining the musical, the mafia film and neorealist conventions in a delirious pastiche of forms from traditional and popular culture, a particularly Italian form of post-modern hybridity. The action is firmly set in the Vucciria market in Palermo, the stall-holders and local inhabitants performing the songs. Her use of humour and performative and visual excess suggest multiple explanations for the backwardness of Sicily, and therefore debunk much Mafia mythology. Torre won two David di Donatello awards for this film, including Best New Director, repeating this with 1998 Silver Ribbons for her direction, the score, and the entire female cast for their supporting role. Her film achieved the accolade of being described as 'an unusual eruption of energy and vitality into the predominantly flat and boring landscape of current Italian cinema' (Albano 2003: 107). A mixture of Mafia film, love story, *film noir* and political film, *Angela*'s (2002) repetition of the daily routines of taking orders, weighing heroin, delivering shoe boxes, and dressing up in expensive dresses and jewelry for her husband, lays bare not only the repressive gender relationships supporting Mafia society but the extent to which illegal organizations regulate Sicilian life. Its co-production arrangements with the BBC ensured international distribution, but a more conventional style of film-making.

How do you Survive as an *Auteur* Now?

A small number of film-makers moved to take control of their careers in the 1980s by becoming mini-vertically integrated enterprises. Roberto Benigni's popularity is based on the commercial success of the films in which he stars or produces, or both. He won three Oscars for *La vita è bella* (*Life is Beautiful*, 1997), which enabled him to attract the highest budget ever for an Italian film for *Pinocchio*. Nanni Moretti's success as an actor, and actor/director of low-budget television films led to his decision to found his own production company, Sacher Films, which produces his films, and those of Daniele Luchetti. Moretti also owns a cinema, the Sacher in Rome, which showcases independent films and holds its own festivals. Gabriele Salvatores moved into low-budget cinema and established Colorado Films in the 1980s with the producer, Maurizio Totti, the actor Diego Abatantuono, and Paolo Rossi. His commercial success was cemented with *Mediterraneo* (1991), which had a good international distribution and won the 1991 Oscar for Best Foreign Language Film. During the 1990s his budgets progressively increased and his sci-fi film, *Nirvana* (1997), which cost $12 milion, was sold in over thirty-five territories (Bizio 2002: 136). He also founded an independent agency, Moviement, for actors, directors, writers and musicians, in which the members are also shareholders. The generic hybridity of his films, and their spectacular visual flair, enable them to reach an international audience who may not understand all the cultural connotations (for example of the Italian role in the Second

World War in *Mediterraneo*, or the southern poverty behind the spate of kidnappings in the 1970s in *Io non ho paura* (*I'm Not Afraid*, 2002), based on Niccolò Ammaniti's book). Like Benigni and Moretti, Maurizio Nichetti started in television as an actor, forming his own production company to produce films and special effects. His instantly recognizable, clown-like figure, and the verve and originality of his mixing of media, genres and postmodern pastiche make him attuned to a youthful, international audience.

Giuseppe Tornatore shares with Rosi the ability to construct visually spectacular films. His are more grounded in popular Italian cinema, such as the comedy, family drama or coming of age film. He achieved enormous financial success with *Cinema Paradiso* (Italy/France, 1989), after an Oscar for Best Foreign Film led to a further distribution in Italy and abroad. Set in Sicily in the 1940s and 1950s, the film offers pleasures to its international audience at a number of levels. The story of cultural and political change through the life of a small boy, in a cinema, in a small, Sicilian village is told through film clips from the golden age of the *commedia all'italiana*, providing enormous pleasures of recognition for a cinephile audience. Tornatore signals his authorial quality by complex shots of spectacular beauty, containing many extras, such as those within the cinema, and the shots of the open-air screening filling the space of the screen with another screen, its audience on the dock, and the fishing boats in the foreground. By his own admission, Tornatore's favoured style is to bring his characters' feelings to the fore, to use hyperbole to tell his stories (Toffetti 1995: 28). Again, this strategy is useful in communicating with the international audience so that the film's appeal is both in its Italianness, and its emotionality. These characteristics are both present in *Malèna* (US/Italy, 2000), which divided critics but was a great box-office success, due to partnerships with Medusa and Miramax. Another costume drama, set in the 1940s in a Sicilian port, the film combines visually stunning shots of landscape, and of the star, former model Monica Bellucci. The appeals of sex and Italian fashion combine through the fascinated viewpoint of a young adolescent who witnesses the young widow's 'horizontal collaboration' with the enemy after her husband is killed. By selecting this character's point of view, Tornatore is able to ignore feminist views and the wider political context (neither being known as the preoccupations of young boys) and to appeal to a younger audience.

Tornatore also tried filming in English. *La leggenda del pianista sull'oceano* (*The Legend of 1900*, 1998) cashed in on the Titanic boom, Tim Roth's name, and the ability of English-language films to 'reach the parts others don't' (Rosenthal 2004: 6). Although it won a David di Donatello award for best direction, it was a hugely expensive production and, like Bertolucci, he has reverted to less stressful local production since.

Loro di Napoli: Cultural Politics and Naples

There have been attempts to give a collective profile to a group of directors who emerged in Naples in the 1990s. However, Antonio Capuano, Pappi Corsicato, Antonietta de Lillo, Stefano Incerti and Mario Martone are so diverse that, even though they revealed themselves as quite different talents from those discussed above, a manifesto along the lines of Denmark's dogma 95 would be impossible. The vitality of the 'new Neapolitan cinema' was attributed to a collective feeling of confidence and revival in the region (Fofi 1997: 7). To ensure the group's survival, Fofi urged them to choose more radical forms based on local culture, and to establish an autonomous local infrastructure, an unrealistic agenda for contemporary film-makers. Only Martone achieved international distribution, and he moved back into theatre directing after *I Vesuviani* (1996). Although Pappi Corsicato's films *Libera* (1993) and *I buchi neri* (*The Black Holes*, 1995) had limited Italian distribution, they revealed the influence of Almodòvar (for whom Corsicato had worked on *¡Atame!* (*Tie Me Up, Tie Me Down*, 1990) in their exuberant colour palette, concentration on female protagonists and explorations of sexuality. They achieved success on the international festival circuits, but, like his contemporaries, Corsicato has been unable to fulfil Fofi's scenario.

Conclusion

Italian auteurist cinema has had to evolve with the increasing globalization of the media. As a result, contemporary film-makers either use their box-office success to gain larger budgets, which inevitably mean a more mainstream, international style of film-making, or they remain geographically and locally specific. The danger of the international, 'quality' profile lies in the loss of national specificity. For some, the answer has been to take control of part of the production process by combining their directorial with production roles, and by simultaneously building their *auteur* profiles on their own personae as actors. Others follow the regular pattern of authorial stylistic flourishes and serious themes, playing the festival circuits in order to gain recognition, which will lead to international distribution. No contemporary Italian director has achieved the status of Pedro Almodòvar, a film-maker whose production skills, recognizable visual style, controversial subjects and financial success have cemented his worldwide reputation as a cult *auteur*.

6
Making Sense of Changing Reality

We have seen how the epic has been an enduringly popular Italian cinematic genre, allowing film-makers to regularly reappraise and reinvent the peninsula's imperial, Roman past. Italy became a unified nation state in 1860, its territories and city states having been colonized over the centuries by a variety of stronger powers. The south was fought over by successive waves of Normans, Greeks, Arabs from the Maghgreb and Eastern Mediterranean, and then Spain. The north was regarded as fair game by the French and the Austro-Hungarian empire. All left their mark on Italy and the experience of colonization has been marshalled in attempts to explain regional differences, particularly between the north and the *Mezzogiorno*, the south or land of mid-day heat.

In the nineteenth century, colonial conquerors or invaders sought new sources of primary raw materials, and new markets for goods produced, needing to achieve the paradoxical task of examining and mapping conquered territories and peoples in detail in order to establish a right of colonial possession, whilst at the same time categorizing all non-Europeans as different, and inferior in order to justify economic exploitation. Italian scientific expeditions to Libya in the 1930s classified lands and peoples, 'and reinforced the development of "colonial consciousness" among Italians' (Atkinson 2003: 9). The idea of human domination was reinforced, as Ruth Ben-Ghiat's fascinating study has shown, by Italian photographers borrowing techniques of anthropological and criminal photography that had been used by the British in India. However, the photographers' obsession with the black female body was often at odds with overt anti-miscegenation messages (Ben Ghiat 2003: 52–3). This ambivalence or hostility towards outsiders, and the difficulties of conceptualizing a multiracial society will be the focus of this chapter. Examining the plots, images and spectacles chosen to represent particular historical moments permit social, cultural and political concerns to become visible. Similarly, the interest of later generations in particular historical moments, or even the falling out of fashion of a historical period, can be just as interesting for the attitudes they reveal. Exploring some of the ways in which Italian film-makers negotiate ideas of *italianità*, italianness, and what is not Italian, are part and parcel of the process of globalization, which is the logical outcome of the colonial experience. Fears about the penetration and contamination of Italian society, for example, mask the fact that, in the contemporary post-colonial situation, differences between national, social, ethnic groups are being suppressed in the name of a free market in goods and commodities.

Africa and Italy

This process of making sense of contemporary history and of projecting fears and desires onto other peoples is visible in Italian pre-sound cinema in vivid and spectacular form. Italy was a young Republic, only forty to fifty years old and, in this period (the early 1900s), was attempting to construct an empire in the East and North Africa. The Italo-Turkish, and later the Libyan war proved that this imperial ambition was not going to be easily accomplished. Brunetta (1986: 57) suggests that these historical events were a decisive factor in the coalescing of the development of film production, nationalist ideology and imperialist ambitions. Anti-Arab themes are consistently visible both in films based on literary classics, like *Il Cid* (Mario Caserini, 1910), *La Gerusalemme liberata* (*Jerusalem Liberated*, Enrico Guazzone, 1911 and 1918) *I cavalieri di Rodi* (*The Knights of Rhodes*, Mario Caserini, 1912) and in films that celebrated Roman glories, or *Latin* civilization, whether Italian or Spanish (Brunetta 1993a: 171). Costumes and sets were important in connoting the inherent superiority of the Latin – and therefore, by extension, the Italian. Christian and Catholic civilization and values are represented as triumphant.

As Chapter 3 has shown, Giovanni Pastrone's *Cabiria* (1914) provides an interesting template for the depiction of non-Italian populations in this period. The doubling of the hero figure in the noble Roman, Fulvio Axilla, and his companion, the giant Maciste, creates an image of the cerebral and muscular superiority of the Latin peoples. Early in the film they travel to north Africa, their journey taking them to the temple of Moloch, where the enormous sets are designed to impress, and, on an artistic level, indicate the monstrous nature of Carthaginian society (as opposed to the nobility of the Roman). The *mise en scène* encapsulates a number of elements in the Italian understanding of north Africa – the erotic and the exotic are linked to extreme cruelty, and the large crowds milling about give rise to a sense of their unreliability and consequent danger.

Italian films tended to demonize outsiders. The unified Italian state entered the 'scramble for Africa' later than other European powers, suffering a humiliating defeat at Adua by the Abyssians in 1896, which Mussolini was determined to avenge. Mussolini's colonial excusions were not evoked as a glorious episode because Ethiopia and Eritrea, Albania and parts of the Balkans generated no wealth, and failed to absorb Italy's surplus population. Italians, with their 'weak' colonial history and their strong, historical sense of *italianità* or Italianness, have difficulty in moving towards a new sense of national identity that takes into account the ethnic pluralism of Italian society now.

Mira Liehm (1984: 29) has remarked on the prevalence of African stories during the fascist period, attributing this to the fact that the 'government had to find more reasons for its occupation of the African territory than that of Albania'. One of the best known, *Luciano Serra pilota* (*Pilot Luciano Serra*, Goffredo Alessandrini, 1937), co-scripted by Roberto Rossellini, has Amedeo Nazzari and his son sacrificing their lives in the campaign to modernize Italy and colonize Africa. In the enormously popular epic, *Scipione l'Africano* (*Scipio Africanus*, Carmine Gallone, 1937), the Carthaginians are represented as hairy, disorderly and cruel in contrast to the orderly discipline of the Roman troops, and the huge Roman crowds united in their approbation and support of the military leader in his quest to avenge the earlier defeat of Canne. The Carthaginian leader, Hannibal, is larger and hairier than his followers, and his costumes are patterned with flowing, vaguely oriental designs. Hannibal's (presumed) rape of the virtuous Roman matron, Velia (Isa Miranda) is filmed in close-ups emphasizing his bulging eyes and violent gestures, operatic shorthand for his primitive and un-civilized nature. Italian schoolchildren were taken to see the film, and their subsequent reports showed them making links between Scipio's campaign and Mussolini's aim to revenge the earlier defeat of Adua (Carabba 1974: 52–3). Interestingly the national territory has to be defended and unified in fascist films so that differences between north and south are absorbed into the unifying discourse. Although there is a sense that Sicily is vulnerable on account of its riches and geographical proximity to north Africa, there is no suggestion that the south (at this stage) shares characteristics with Africa, ideas which had certainly been rehearsed in the nineteenth century (Moe 2001).

America and Italy

Preoccupations with a very different kind of 'otherness' occur in films produced in the aftermath of the Second World War, that is the presence of Americans on Italian soil, and pervasiveness of American culture. Depiction of this period in later films indicates both popular Italian affinity with American ideals and culture resulting from the experience of the Italian diaspora to North America, and also indicates a sense that not all aspects of American culture are perceived as beneficial and many aspects are seen as threatening or inimical to the traditional Italian way of life. In her essay on Rossellini's *Paisà* (*Paisan*, Roberto Rossellini, 1946), Millicent Marcus (2002: 38) suggests that each of the six episodes making up the film encourages the audience to reflect on Italian affinities with the invaders, and differences from them, 'forcing the viewer to acknowledge the gaps and the conflicts involved in the forging of national identity'. The bonds between Italians and Americans, such as growing up in a rural society (Joe from Jersey and Carmela in the first, Sicilian episode); the consciousness of being poor and marginalized (the unfolding of the conditions of the urchin, Pasquale's life to the black MP, Joe in Naples); Harriet, the American nurse's rejection of distance and her throwing herself into the events of the liberation of Florence; the sharing of ideals of freedom and justice (the final episode of the partisans' fight on the Po delta), all force reflection on the state in which war has left Italy and which will form the terrain of post-war reconstruction. On the other hand, the Rome episode suggests mutual incomprehension in the literal misrecognition of the former lovers, Francesca and Fred, as does the meeting of the American army chaplains and monks in the monastery of Savignano di Romagna.

These moments of cultural exhange enabled American characters to function as convenient stereotypes in Italian films of the 1940s and 1950s, evoking the presence of desires for greater social equality and prosperity, less rigid social conventions, class and gender roles. American culture is a significant element in *Riso amaro* (*Bitter Rice*, Vittorio de Sica, 1948). The rice worker, Silvana, is first encountered as she dances the boogie woogie to a portable record player in front of crowds of her fellow workers waiting for the train. Silvana's dedication to American popular culture can be observed in her choice of cheap magazines for her off-duty rest, music for communal enjoyment as the rice workers meet soldiers from the nearby camp, and in her choice of clothing, motivating her falling for the handsome criminal. American culture is represented as aspirational and exciting, but also shallow and meretricious in contrast to the solid, patriarchal virtues of Silvana's other suitor, the army sergeant, Marco. This dichotomy appears in many other films in this period, suggesting that Italian film is attempting to use representations of American culture as an antonym to Italian virtues in the complex process of constructing a new national image.

This period has also been invoked in Left-wing attempts from the 1970s onwards to explain the origins and workings of Italian organized crime, which also functions as a metaphor for the corrosive power of American-style capitalism and materialism. The presence of America is a constant in the films of Francesco Rosi. In *Lucky Luciano* (1973), the gangster's career is shown to receive enormous impetus from the use by the American armed forces of the organizational skills of the Italian-American Mafia in 1944. The densely organized Naples dance-hall sequence illustrates the exercise of American colonial power. Colonel Charles Poletti (Vincent Gardenia) is shown as energetic but naïve, constantly showering his entourage with soundbites and statements of aims and objectives. Subsequent sequences illustrate how the laudable aims of getting food supplies and military equipment moving, and of winning over the Italian population, melt away in unclear and mysterious chains of actions by the Italian-Americans he employs. In the meantime, in the enormous, Baroque dance hall, Italian girls clutch triangular white bread sandwiches as they dance with GIs, a telling metaphor of the position of the colonized.

America is also a key presence in Rosi's adaptation of Carlo Levi's *Cristo si è fermato a Eboli* (*Christ Stopped at Eboli*, 1979) in which Levi describes his discovery of an archaic, southern Italian world during his spell of internal exile during the fascist period.

In the village to which he is confined he makes friends with a number of *americani*, men who emigrated to the United States to better themselves, and were later lured back to Italy either believing the blandishments of the fascist government, or through home-sickness. The presence of these *americani* serve to highlight Levi's thesis that remote areas of the south were never regarded as

Figure 6.1
Discovering Africa at home, the remote south in *Cristo si è fermato a Eboli* (Francesco Rosi 1979).

worthwhile areas to colonize by the Romans, the Catholic Church, or the Italian state, remaining backward and feudal economically and socially. Levi (Gian Maria Volonté) observes the departure of a young volunteer for the Ethiopian campaign, resplendent in his uniform and helmet adorned with black cocks' feathers. As he waits mutely for the bus, he is accompanied by a litany of imprecations from his black-clad, peasant mother who berates him for leaving them after all the sacrifices they have made to bring him up and educate him, for a war that is not in the peasants' interest. In effect Levi, and Rosi, are making the point that the southern peasantry are as exploited as any African and that the government in Rome is just as much a scourge to its own indigenous populations. Rosi's position of hindsight in 1979 prompts reflection on the subsequent success of the American economic empire in reaching even remote rural areas with media, food and clothing products.

The effects of diaspora are also present in *Dimenticare Palermo* (*To Forget Palermo/The Palermo Connection*, Francesco Rosi, 1990). Carmine Bonavia, a rather shallow, Italian-American politician toys with the idea of taking a stand on the legalization of drugs as a vote-catching exercise. Such a policy is clearly not in the interests of the Sicilian Mafia and, as a result, Carmine receives the attentions of the 'Man of Power' during his honeymoon visit to Palermo to discover his roots. In effect he discovers a parallel universe of the exercise of illegal power, and realizes how thickly entwined it is with his own. New York is shown as polarized, with modern streets and modernist offices and campaign headquarters juxtaposed with run-down school perimeters where drugs are pushed to children. In Palermo, the archaic nature of southern power relationships is repeatedly stressed. A fellow occupant of Carmine's hotel is a reclusive aristocrat (Vittorio Gassman) who upset the Mafia and now never leaves his Baroque hotel surroundings. The world that Carmine discovers outside his hotel door is the classic one of American Express advertisements, crowds, emotional foreigners gesticulating in an incomprehensible language, archaic survivals of past ages in the convent where the nuns dance the minuet, old and dilapidated buildings, arcane rituals such as the killing of the fish in the market, dangerous alleyways and unreliable urchins, prostitutes, drug addicts, drug traffickers who shoot at each other from mopeds. An example of the narrative device of the outsider figure, Carmine is used to examine a familiar world in a new light. Even his hotel room is not inviolable and uncontaminated by the evil from outside as he finds a bunch of jasmine (the 'gift' forced on him by the Mafia) laid upon the matrimonial bed. As in television fiction – 'La piovra' ('Octopus: Power of the Mafia'), 'Il magistrato' ('The Magistrate'), 'Un bambino in fuga' ('A Child on the Run'), for example – the south produces no positive heroes. In *Dimenticare Palermo*, Carmine has to extricate himself from the clutches of the Mafia by his own efforts, by capitulation, but, in doing so, the criminal, capitalist links between America and Italy are brought into sharp focus.

North and South

For much of the last 150 years, the role of the awkward 'Other' in Italian society was fulfilled by the *Mezzogiorno* and its inhabitants, whilst Italians from whatever region of Italy found themselves in that humiliating position in England, France, Germany, Argentina, Australia and North America. The populations of the Italian peninsular have a long experience of diaspora.

The *Mezzogiorno* is an example of the concept of 'dualism' in the economic development of Italy, used in the sense of 'imbalance or disequilibrium', between economically prosperous regions and those that are backward, that is, the north and the agricultural south; industrial dualism between advanced, modern and highly productive sectors of industry, and those that are not; the dualism in the labour market, between those in relatively stable, well-paid jobs and those in marginal occupations (Sassoon 1986: 17). In the 1950s and 1960s the south signified a disruption to the myth of prosperity and post-war boom, and provided a rich repertoire of tropes of backwardness in social organization and relationships. In Pietro Germi's *Divorzio all'italiana* (*Divorce Italian Style*, 1961), the rich Fefé decides to murder his wife in order to marry his younger, and more modern girlfriend; and in *Sedotta e abbandonata* (*Seduced and Abandoned*, 1963), Peppino seduces the schoolgirl sister of his fiancée, but refuses to marry her because she has been dishonoured. The florid colouring, dark eyes and abundant hair of southern actors were used to suggest a hypersexuality, an excess of passion and violence in opposition to northern modernity and restraint. Similarly, the landscapes of Sicily and the south stress climatic excess in harsh contrasts of light and shade, old buildings, stony hills and cactus plants. Any or all of these could be economically used to suggest an archaic world, a problem to a developing, modern economy. Francesco Rosi is one of the few film-makers to interrogate the stereotypes and show the collusion between power blocs, in whose interests this dualism is maintained, in that the north needed the waves of immigrants from the south to work in their factories. In his *Salvatore Giuliano* (1961), we also see how the south fulfils a dual function. It is both the *Africa a casa* (Africa at home), an example of underdevelopment and the primitive that allows exploitation to become visible, the south shorn of its myths of happy peasants and, Rosi claims, a '...key to understanding later Italian politics. The case of Giuliano is typical of all aspects of Italian history' (De Masi: 1980). Rosi shows us the reality of the Third World conditions of the *Mezzogiorno* and suggests various hypotheses as to the causes. Long shots allow the eye to explore the material conditions of life of Sicilian peasants, bandits and townspeople and for symbolic contrasts to be evoked. The fragmented narrative with its juxtapositions of different times and places offers some explanations for the career of the bandit, Giuliano, and suggests collusion between the Mafia and the forces of order.

It is a short step from using the south as a disruption that disturbs the scenario of booming economic prosperity, laying bare the mechanisms of societal oppression, to the use of the south as a metaphor for problems in Italian society as a whole. In Rosi's highly prophetic *Le mani sulla città* (*Hands Over the City*, 1963), the collapse of a slum building constitutes the disruption that allows an investigation into land speculation in Naples, and a delineation of corruption in southern politics. In the film Right-wing members of the Naples Municipal Council may wave their hands in the air and protest their *mani pulite*, their innocence of involvement in corruption, but the investigation of the collapse of a slum building reveals otherwise.[1] What first appears to be a part of the natural, adversarial democratic process is later shown to be a shifting network of alliances between factions, always resulting in advantage to one class.

While many Italian films of the 1960s and 1970s attempted to explore the causes of the Mafia phenomenon, in a significant number the power exercised by criminal organizations like the Mafia was used as a metaphor for legal power relations, where power is exercised by élite groups. Mafia leaders are not elected and are unrepresentative of the lives of ordinary people. In exploring the nature of the 'Other' within Italian society, the link between poverty, social backwardness and conservative institutions (the Church) and the presence of illegal organizations is made. In *A ciascuno il suo* (*To Each His Own*, Elio Petri, 1967), an adaptation of a novel by the Sicilian writer, Leonardo Sciascia, desire for the darkly erotic, but passive female protagonist provokes the murders. Exploration of the social situation of the characters allows the links between the murderer, a lawyer and local dignitary, the Church and the fascist Right to be made. Southern characters are tainted by collusion with the Mafia and female passivity connotes the *omertà*, or conspiracy of silence, by which a population is oppressed.

The south had a brief period of recuperation in the late 1970s and 1980s when depictions of Italy's rural past became popular at the box office. Life in the countryside was represented as somehow more authentic and real. Public scandals and radical politics had emphasized corruption in the institutions asociated with the city in Italy. Changes in cultural values, the break-up of the relationships of the extended family, and women's demands for power-sharing, were reflected in dissatisfaction with the conditions of urban existence. Olmi's *L'albero degli zoccoli* (*The Tree of Wooden Clogs*, 1978) and Rosi's *Cristo si è fermato a Eboli* (*Christ Stopped at Eboli*, 1979)) were in the top twenty Italian box-office hits of the 1978–9 season, having a wide cinema release as well as television exposure by their production partner, RAI. Validation of the rural world and its customs meant that these representations of the south did not escape the nostalgic, diverting attention from the attempt to examine the social context, and often ignoring the fact that rural societies are predominantly ordered in a very hierarchical and conservative way. Peasant characters tend to be individualized, in contrast to earlier films, and the particular oppression of women is glossed over.

From the 1990s reflections on past situations or social relations are used to cue metaphorical associations with contemporary social realities. At the same time, and fighting with the nostalgic impetus towards roots in a slower, less dehumanized world, is a tendency towards the demonization of the south. As Milly Buonanno and Erica Pellegrini (1993: 111) have observed, the image of the *Mezzogiorno di fuoco*, the explosive south, on television is a potent one and is associated with 'crime, illegality, the culture of the conspiracy of silence and violence, an atmosphere of death and darkness, bloodshed and ambush.'

The south of Italy is where social problems are depicted as more visible, where the soil is poorer, domestic comfort less, healthcare and education worse, social relations between the classes more antagonistic. Marco Risi has attempted in his films *Mery per sempre* (*Forever Mary*, 1989) and *Ragazzi fuori* (*Street Boys*, 1990) to draw attention to the dangers for the country of failing to address the underemployment and exploitation of young southerners, but the strangeness and violence of the sub-proletarian world of transvestite prostitutes and demeaning jobs has the effect of reinforcing the south as a site of dangerous abnormality. Similarly, the excessive violence of bandits and mafiosi in *La corsa dell'innocente* (*Flight of the Innocent*, Carlo Carlei, 1992), pursuing a small, Calabrian boy as he attempts to right a wrong and, in *La scorta* (*The Escort*, Ricky Tognazzi, 1993) trying to murder the young policemen protecting an investigating magistrate, signal the south as a crisis point in Italian culture. As Italy's economic situation has become more precarious, there has been a groundswell of support for the populist political leader, Umberto Bossi's Northern League Party, which advocates the drawing of a line across the country just below Rome, and leaving the south to go to the dogs on its own.

The south is constructed as 'Other', the site of problems in society that are displaced from the urban and day to day, to a world where displays of excess are licensed in violence of gesture and situation, finding its ultimate expression in the films of Ciprì and Maresco. The deliberately ugly, black and white visuals, dialogue in Sicilian dialogue, vomit and spitting are designed to shock the middle-class audience and, as Vito Zagarrio (1998: 79–80) suggests, use their vision of Palermo as a metonym for a debased Italy. Once more, by synecdoche, southern abnormality stands for the whole south.

The *Mezzogiorno*, is no longer Italy's *Africa a casa*, and the south has experienced a boom in new technology industries. Nonetheless, it continues to provide tropes of otherness which can be utilized in attempts to depict changing national realities. Gianni Amelio has consistently done this in his films. In *Il ladro di bambini* (*The Stolen Children*, 1992), for example, a Calabrian carabiniere has to deliver two abused Sicilian children to a children's home, but ends up on the road to Sicily. The situations he meets implicate all sections of modern Italy in southern-style corruption (accepting and condoning disability pensions, bribing officials for building permits, but rejecting the victim of child prostitution), but indicate the abiding power of images of children as an indication of what is at stake for the national family.

The Post-colonial World and the Experience of Diaspora

Ginsborg (2001: 61–3) identifies the heart of 1990s problems as the long-term lack of employment for young people in the south, particularly for young women, for whom there is often little alternative to the traditional role of caring for home, children and the elderly. These circumstances impinge on educated and uneducated alike, leading to feelings of apathy or depression, or to the adoption of marginal work, and in extreme cases to crime or drugs. What distinguishes many films from 1990 to the present is the engagement with a post-colonial situation and attempts to come to grips with the realities of postmodern society. Restivo (2002: 164) identifies three main concerns emerging in 1990s cinema

> Questions of uneven development in the context of the centre/periphery divide; questions of the disintegrating urban centres of the great southern cities of Naples and Palermo; questions of the character of Italy as a nation in a period that has seen increasing numbers of immigrants from North Africa, Asia and postcommunist Europe.

The process of making sense of a multiethnic society includes recourse to southern stereotypes outlined earlier, and of mapping these onto other representations of territories and bodies. Italy is one of the most porous countries where immigration is concerned, its miles of coastline being regarded as a weak barrier and a first stepping stone for populations from the Balkans, northern Africa, and the supply chains that stretch from China and Pakistan. From year to year a significant number of contemporary Italian films display a preoccupation with the integration, or not, of non-Italians into Italian society. The whole question of national identity and immigration is currently one of hot debate, fuelled by Cardinal Biffi of Bologna's diatribe against the influx of Muslim populations.[2] Moreover, these *extracomunitari*, or persons from outside the EU (usually a euphemism for Arabs and Africans), are narratively tainted by analogy with another, much earlier, population movement, that of southern Italians. The South, and the Balkans, are regarded as the source of corruption, and site of criminality and petty violence.

Containment within marginal social spaces are features of three very different films. In Bertolucci's *L'assedio* (*Besieged*, 1998), a young African woman takes lodgings with a reclusive English pianist in the heart of Rome, being slowly drawn into his life and the world of Western, classical music. As in the earlier *Io ballo da sola* (*Stealing Beauty*, 1996), the male protagonist gains access to the world of emotion represented by the feminine, his sexual and cultural appropriation of her signalled by compelling her to reveal her story (Wood 2002: 48). This is a potent metaphor for the colonial situation because she remains in the subordinate situation. Roberta Torre's *Sud Side Stori* (*South Side Story*, 2000) claims to be a satirical musical and has been hailed as one of Italy's few attempts to take on the subject of immigration and racial discrimination. The film attacks its themes with a sledgehammer via the romance of street singer, Toni and Nigerian prostitute, Romea. The studio sets contain the couple within narrow alleys and cramped domestic spaces, delineated in garish, primary colours. Significantly, the main vehicle for racist disapproval of the couple is Toni's family, or Romea's 'family' of fellow prostitutes. With heavy-handed metaphor, Romea's profession and situation as colonial, *clandestina* (illegal immigrant), *extracomunitara* (black), exploited and part of the ethnoscape of the African diaspora, is represented as a threat to the Italian family and, by extension, the national family.

Black Africans also pose a threat and are pushed to the margins of society in *Pummarò* (Michele Placido, 1990). Kwaku comes from Ghana to look for his brother, Giobbe, nicknamed Pummarò as he has been working as an illegal tomato picker in the south. This quest narrative allows the progressive discovery of the inhuman conditions of african *clandestini*, exploited as cheap labour and contained within living spaces that resemble those of battery hens. Pummarò's Italian girlfriend is heavily pregnant and Kwaku falls in love with an Italian teacher but the forces which break up these relationships, including the Neapolitan *camorra* or mafia, indicate the difficulties of conceptualizing full racial integration.

What Margins?

In the contemporary world images and information from beyond national borders bombard us, raising the whole question of the effects of globalization of the world economy and particularly media globalization. Ulrich Beck (20034: 14) suggested that 'globalization shakes to its foundations the self-image of a homogeneous, self-contained national space...' and that borders are 'markedly less relevant to everyday behaviour'. Anti-globalization protesters claim that populations will increasingly come to resemble each other as transnational, world-scale corporations dominate world markets. However, the presence of the local is increasingly important, so that the globalizing tendency contains within it the opposing movement and tension of local interests. Appadurai (1990: 299) takes this further in his attempts to explain how the traditional distinction between centre and periphery is called into question by, for example, ethnoscapes or 'landscapes of people', or the cross-border movements of new and old technologies in technoscapes.

The intrusion of events and populations from the Balkans is part of this process of globalization, so that *both* the Balkans *and* Italian national space are experienced contemporaneously, rather than *either/or*. The Balkans are experienced via the presence of that marginal world on mainstream, national television news, and through the physical presence of refugees and immigrants. Globalization theory argues that the transnational flow of media products is associated with the local appropriation of meaning, and this is borne out by studies of how European national media have conceptualized the conflict in the former Yugoslavia (Nohrstedt *et al.* 2000: 400; Pozzato 2000). The Italian press was the most virulent in their name-calling of the Serbs and in foregrounding the criminal elements in Balkan societies. We would expect to see some of these attitudes reflected in fictional works that, consciously or unconsciously, engage with the presence of an ethnic war, and a major population influx, on the margins of Europe, given that the media, and television and the press in particular, actively shape our perception of the world in which we live. In coming to terms with the Balkan situation, Italian film-makers have been able to draw on existing stereotypes and narratives of social tensions. Žižek (2000: 29–30) defines as 'reflexive racism' the construction of images of the multicultural Balkans as a theatre of ethnic horrors. In the hit film, *Pane e tulipani* (*Bread and Tulips*, Silvio Soldini, 2000), this attitude can be observed in the Balkan conmen who rent the bumbling detective a houseboat when he is unable to find a hotel room in Venice, and whose presence draws on southern stereotypes.

L'estate di Davide (*David's Summer*, Carlo Mazzacurati, 1998), made for RAI television, provides another variant on this theme. Davide is a nineteen year old who has done well at school, but who works in a car wash in Turin. Fed up with his relatives, he goes to his uncle's in the country, and makes friends with a young Bosnian, Alem, in hospital. Contact with Alem's world allows the story to become very dramatic, and for sex and drugs and petty criminality to intrude into the rural space. Stealing heroin at the end of the film from the criminal boyfriend of Davide's lover, the boys go south to find Alem's contact (a man who smuggles Albanians into Italy) in order to make a big drug deal. Here the *mise en scène* of place is surplus to narrative requirements. The city and the port are framed to foreground the bright light and pictorial aspects of the southern city, this heightened reality allowing access to Barthes' (1970: 15) *troisième sens*, the third sense which links the south, the Balkans and criminality. Alem is represented as a sympathetic character, blonde and energetic. He works in a bar, a narrative site that enables the protagonist to meet a variety of marginal characters. Interestingly, Alem lives in a church hostel with other *extracomunitari*. Non-Italians are therefore marked out and contained within the rural space, but clearly cannot be controlled altogether. The margins insistently move into public space.

The narrative of Mario Martone's *Teatro di guerra* (1998) follows a group of actors rehearsing Aeschylus' *Seven Against Thebes*, to be performed in Sarajevo. Rehearsals take place in the historic centre of Naples, in the Spagnoli quarter and the action never gets to Sarajevo. Ghezzi (1998: 12–13) compares classical theatre's locating of tragedy 'elsewhere' to Martone's non-depiction of the Bosnian conflict. Both are very forceful absences. Sarajevo, a non-Italian *Mezzogiorno*, becomes a metonym for the disintegration of civic life in danger and moral vacuum as life outside the house where they rehearse become omnipresent. The precarious and chaotic seep into the theatrical space. Some of the actors miss rehearsals as their outside lives impinge. One actor is drug-dependent and has to be watched. Domestic and street noises intrude from outside. For Martone, absence also signifies what he perceives as the almost total absence of outrage and debate about the siege and massacre of Sarajevo. Conflicts in Spain or Vietnam occasioned a collective moral conscoiusness in earlier generations, which is lacking in respect of the Balkans (Montini and Spila, 1997: 12).

An interesting inflection of containment and recourse to images of southern Italy occurs in Carla Apuzzo's *Rose e pistole* (*Roses and Guns*, 1998) featuring two characters called Rosa. The action is set on the edge of Naples, between the run-down, working class, industrial Bagnoli area and the Phlegrean Fields (themselves an unstable part of the earth's crust). The low-life, marginalized characters inhabit a border zone on the outskirts of Naples and 'work' in the telephone sex industry or armed robbery. The younger Rosa and her partner are trying to leave, to start a new life for the baby they are expecting, but her ex-husband sets a hitman on their trail. The interior spaces through which these characters move are constantly coded as transgressive. In dark booths in a dark apartment, male and female 'hotliners' fake intimacy and the erotic, while filing their nails and reading magazines. A strange mathematics teacher stalks them through their habitats, appropriating a black leather mask from a 'dungeon' equipped with life-sized plastic doll, handcuffs, whips. The *mise en scène* quotes the stressed camera angles, high-contrast lighting, darkness and shadows of American *film noir* to suggest that characters are trapped in this marginal milieu. The hitman, Bosnia (who is a Serb), is the ultimate metonym for this chaotic, violent, amoral sector of society, being more excessive in all respects than those for whom he works. By this juxtaposition, a link is made between social breakdown in Italy and the extreme violence of the Balkans, connoting fears present in Italian middle-class society at the Balkanization of the Italian body politic. In the final sequence the camera pans over the beautiful, sunlit, Neapolitan coastline and mediterranean pines as Rosa's voice-over brings her story up to date as she waits, free and pregnant, for the release of her lover from prison. In illustration of what Žižek (1999: 3) terms an 'imaginary cartography, which projects onto the real landscape its own shadowy ideological antagonisms', the outstanding beauty of the quintessentially Italian scene represents the choice of idealized national lifestyle and the narrative expulsion of the non-national regarded as aberrant. In this case, the cinema spectator is put in the subjective space of Rosa's point of view, invited to make an 'inferential journey' outside the text, to connect family, the rule of law and Italian landscape in the establishment of the final narrative equilibrium – the re-establishment of a healthy, conventional *italianità* (Eco, 1979:32). It is striking how many contemporary Italian films feature children, and Chapter 7 will explore this area further.

Although his film *Lamerica* (1994) follows two Italian conmen in their attempts to set up a lucrative scam in Albania, Gianni Amelio's purpose was to make a film about Italy and its past (Amelio, 1994: 4–7). The film is unusual in its linking of Italy's fascist colonialist adventures to the current exodus from Albania. By stripping its

Figure 6.2
The effacement of difference. *Lamerica* (Gianni Amelio, 1994).

Italian protagonist, Gino, of his passport and belongings, and putting the camera in his subjective viewpoint as he becomes one of the hopeful *clandestini* trying to get to Italy, the film forces an identification with the position of the Albanian 'Other'. In effect, Amelio is seeking to remind Italians of their own past as economic migrants and despised immigrants, a fact which has only recently been reiterated by Gian Antonio Stella (2002).

Like English actors in Hollywood, Balkan characters are permitted the dubious honour of portraying villains and monsters whom the texts licence us to loathe. This is one of their functions in *Elvjs e Merilijn* (*Elvis and Marilyn*, Armando Manni, 1998), another RAI co-production. Unusually, this film views Italy from the viewpoint of non-Italians, providing a space for ironic contrasts in the characters constant addition of the words '*la dolce vita*' to '*Italia*'. Elvjs (Nikolai, a Bulgarian motor mechanic) and Merilijn (Ileana, a Romanian from Bucharest who sorts rubbish for a living) win a Bucharest star lookalike competition whose prize is engagement for the summer season 1995 in the Crudité Club in Italy. Their lives in Romania are represented as overwhelmingly exploited, poverty stricken and harsh; their society as consistently corrupt, where they are victims of the vagaries of officials and those in power. They are obliged to go overland to the coast through the former Yugoslavia, encountering danger and brutality the moment they cross the frontier. The soldiers who take them on part of their journey lapse into sudden uneasy silences faced with the unpredictable behaviour of their officers. Ileana, with her pretty face and glamorous blonde hairstyle, is a constant target of male attention. She is abused and spat on, and violently thrown out of the Land Rover at one stage, and Elvjs follows her when he attempts to intervene. However, their treatment at the hands of the Italian entrepreneurs when they finally reach Italy mirrors their physical abuse in Bosnia. Elvjs and Merilijn's act is popular in Romania, but hopelessly outdated in Riccione. The presence of a Hungarian lap dancer and a haggard, drugged Marilyn lookalike in the Crudité Club, and the second club owner's suggestion that Elvjs use a large, rubber penis in his act and that Merilijn entertain the clients, indicate that they are only two of a supply chain of beautiful and hopeful youth from the Balkans. Thus Italy itself is implicated in the brutal sexual traffic from the Balkans to the West, and particularly in the abuse of young women.

More recent films of immigration, such as *Oltre il confine* (*Across the Border*, Rolando Colla, 2002), *Brucio nel vento* (*Burning in the Wind*, Silvio Soldini, 2002), and *Lettere al vento* (*Letters on the Wind*, Edmond Budina, 2002), give more narrative space to the development of character and motivation of Eastern Europeans, Bosnians and Albanians. These recent films continue to have recourse to the visual containment of the 'Other' in restricted spaces, and to the depiction of foreign outsiders as brutal criminals or victims.

Lettere al vento in particular can be considered symptomatic of Italian middle-class concerns that they have lost control of political power, and that the national family is under threat. The main protagonist, an unemployed Albanian teacher, fails in his quest to re-establish normality. The remittances from Italy have dried up and he discovers that his son drowned on the voyage from Albania, and that his identity has been assumed by a brutal gang leader of a vice racket. Criminality threatens not only his own family but also the family of a former friend (significantly a trafficker in *clandestini* who is revealed as responsible for the drowning), whose daughter's tawdry wedding is shown to be the uniting of criminal interests. The breakdown of law and order in Albania is epitomized by the violent abduction of the teacher's daughter from her school classroom by pimps. By the end of the film, he has discovered the truth of his son's disappearance, and why his daughter was inexplicably released from the clutches of her abductors, but he looks on impotently as his son's killer throws a gaudy and hedonistic party aboard his boat. However, unlike Gianni Amelio's film, *Lamerica*, Budina's film does not make overt the connections between the earlier, colonial invasion of Albania, and the contemporary, post-colonial movements of populations, merely hinting at Mafia-like criminal alliances in the wedding sequences.

Colla's *Oltre il confine* has two attractive protagonists but they are unable to form a couple because of the trauma the male protagonist, Reuf, has experienced in losing his wife. Set at the height of violent conflict in the Balkans, exteriors, whether in Bosnia, Italy or the Swiss border are represented as excessively difficult and unfriendly, as are the interiors (the hospital for aged military veterans) which attempt to contain Reuf. The Italian heroine, Agnese (Anna Galiena), does, however, undertake a transformative journey. Early in the film action and *mise en scène* indicate her as a hard, single, selfish career woman, reluctant to care or connect emotionally with her father, and prepared to seek instant sexual gratification with a man she finds attractive. On the one hand, she fits Jordanova's (2001: 56–64) template of the Westerner through whose actions a Balkan situation is delineated and mediated. In her journey Agnese experiences the chaos, unpredictability and dangers of war but, by the end of the film, she has performed the heroic and humanitarian act of going into the Balkan war zone to find Reuf's youngest daughter, who was wounded and left in an orphanage. Agnese also discovers extremes of evil when she finds out that Reuf's wife, a Christian married to a Muslim, was violently abducted by Muslims and taken to a women's camp from which she never returned. Characters refuse to describe what happens to the women in the camp, but we make our own inferences based on newspaper reports of savage abuse and sexual slavery. Todorov (1984: 143–5) suggests that massacre, the extermination of victims without remorse, reveals the weakness of the social fabric whereas sacrifice testifies to the power of the social fabric (1984: 143–5). Agnese's return to Italy successfully reconstitutes Reuf's family and recuperates Italy by one person's goodness, significantly a woman who is instrumental in incorporating the foreign family into the national space. Total integration as represented in the formation of a couple is, however, too much for the narrative to handle.

The protagonist of Soldini's *Brucio nel vento* is the disfunctional, dark and brooding Dalibor, who leads a lonely and self-contained life in Switzerland until he meets his childhood friend, Line. The film ends with the formation of a happy couple but, since we have learned that Dalibor murdered his father, and that Line is in fact his half-sister, it is what might be called a transgressive union. Again, the immigrant (in this case a Hungarian) is depicted in dark and enclosed spaces, or in wooded thickets from where he spies on Line's home. Only at the end, when the lovers have fled from Italian Switzerland, are they represented in the light and open spaces, representing metaphorically the impetus to contain the outsider, and evict him or her from the national space.

Although current films appear to be attempting a more nuanced representation of Balkan elements, very few challenge the stereotypes. One of those is the compilation film, *Intolerance* (1999) which, in short films by several directors, includes conventional documentary, witness and comedy, in order to give faces to stories of violence and abuse, and to debunk the stereotypes.

Borders and Identity

For a narrative space where the attractions of Eastern Europe can be explored, film-makers have to go beyond the Balkans to the eastern edge of Europe. In another narrative juxtaposition, Ferzan Ozpetek has the protagonist of *Il bagno turco, hamman* (*The Turkish Bath: Hamman*, 1997) leave Rome to take possession of and sell the property his aunt has left him in Istanbul. His experience of the warmth of his aunt's friends, and fascination with Turkish culture as represented by the baths, and by the son of his hosts, keeps him in Istanbul. The film does not entirely escape the orientalist tendency in Western culture, which uses spaces outside Western Europe as arenas where sexual and other fantasies can be enacted. Moreover, the tension between Italy and the 'Other' is expressed visually through the choice of architectural paradigms and the *mise en scène* of place. The protagonist's home in Rome is a high-level, modernist apartment (he is an architect), all straight lines, plate glass and open spaces. By contrast, the house and bath he inherits lie in the old quarters of Istanbul, and are characterized by dark, closed, mysterious spaces, jumbled streets, labyrinthine passages, spyholes and sexual ambivalence. Movement within these spaces reinforces the contrast. The relationship of the architect and his wife is shown as strained and non-communicative, whereas the closed spaces of Istanbul provoke a change in him, from reserved, time-conscious business man, to a lover and activist. This oscillation between order and disorder, the rational and the excessive has been defined by Calabrese (1992: 12–15) as neo-Baroque, a particularly Italian inflection of postmodernism. The narrative is structured in terms of a search for personal authenticity expressed both as licence to enjoy a homosexual relationship, and campaigning to prevent the destruction of national heritage by greedy and wholesale development of modernist flats and office blocks. Both architectural paradigms coexist as signifying systems, inviting the conclusion that personal truth and authenticity do not necessarily reside in what seems regular, functional and ordered. Modernism's claim to honesty and rationality is represented, at a metaphorical level, both as insufficient to explain the complexity of contemporary life, and unattractive in its cutting off of the possibilities of other ways of being.

The sense of the regenerative possibilities of chaos and the picaresque are also present in *La tregua* (*The Truce*, Francesco Rosi, 1996) as the main protagonist, Primo Levi (John Turturro) journeys from Auschwitz, across Eastern Europe to Turin. The film raises complex, metaphysical issues about identity, history and responsibility. By making Primo's companions on his journey representative of different Italian regions, Rosi indicates a hope, a faith in the pluralism of Italian post-war society. There is no demonizing of Eastern Europe, but in clear indications of the responsibility of the West for the holocaust lie indications of contemporary Western complicity in the 'madness' that has returned in the form of ethnic violence in the Balkans (Wood, 1998: 279–80).

Conclusion

In contemporary, postmodern Italy, the *Mezzogiorno* provides a potent repertoire of tropes through which film-makers attempt to comprehend the effects of globalization and the post-colonial movement of populations. Southern Italy is a boundary zone where tensions in society are made visible. In the 1980s, the south was rehabilitated as part of the rural world represented as more natural and a repository of healthy, human values. However, it has been unable to sustain this representation, except perhaps in advertisements. Unable to support a positive representation in the 1990s, given the lack of social structures with which modern women (especially) and men could identify, it has succumbed to a scapegoat scenario. The revelations of corruption and the networks of the *tangentopoli* were too similar to stereotypical representations of southern power systems for the *Mezzogiorno* to escape being demonized as the place where the evil part of modern society becomes visible.

The interpenetration of ethnic 'Others' into the Italian national space, and the spectre of social breakdown raised by media reports of the Balkan situation, are clearly represented as a source of anxiety and threat. Recent films incorporating the presence of people or events from the former Yugoslavia are dominated by representations of violence, social and personal evil, monstrous characters and unbearable situations, incompetence and petty criminality. The texts use two strategies to attempt to make sense of these excessive elements; firstly through recourse to earlier stereotypical images of the south of Italy and to southern architecture, and secondly by attempting to contain the threatening disorder, enclosing the outsider characters in emprisoning spaces and dark interiors. Examination of the complex narratives in which Italian film-makers incorporate characters and events associated with the Balkans and how social space in constructed in these postmodern texts allows deep social tensions to be identified. Balkan characters are ranked low in hierarchies of positive values and, with few exceptions, the films display a conservative ideological position in that narrative resolutions hark back to earlier templates of an ideal of Italianness in which the family, and the self-sacrificing role of women are key elements. Recourse to this conservative template in narratives involving the Balkans signals that this construction is still attractive and desired, but the violence and disruption are indicative of changes in gender and political power relationships in Italian society. For the moment threats to the national self-image are displaced onto the Balkans and Eastern Europe, reminding Italians of the precariousness of life and the fragility of their constructed image of the nation.

The threatening 'Others' in Italian cinema, whether specifically or metaphorically southern Italian, must be regarded as constructions, to be deconstructed, demystified and put into their historical and cultural context. In the current political situation in Italy, it is likely that the south will continue to function as a boundary zone in film and television narratives where it cannot quite be assimilated into the realms of unproblematic discourse. When the 'Other' is represented as demonized, as ultimately and essentially evil, or as a threatening, hidden force, then dominant ideology cloaks the reasons for the situation and swerves away from critical examination.

7

Gender Representations and Gender Politics

Giorgio Olmoti's (1998) book in the series devoted to the photographic history of Italy shows the seismic social changes which took place in the 1950s and 1960s. Photographs of peasant women bent double under huge loads, of lavish provincial weddings and the pervasive presence of priests and Church festivals give way to scenes of factory life, of industrial strikes, immigrants, scooters and working women. Italian cinema was but one arena in which the battle of the sexes was played out at this time, that is the impetus of women to escape traditional restrictions on their movements and daily choices of action, and the desires on the part of men to re-establish male authority and control at a time of historical change.

Although many women are active in Italian politics and institutions, fashion and the cultural industries, fictional female bodies do not seem to be able to represent political or social power. This characteristic goes some way towards explaining the lack of many *femmes fatales* in Italian *film noir*, for example. Between 1948 and 1968 the Censorship Commission and the Catholic Church caused problems for films that projected a pessimistic view of the Italian family, and therefore women's traditional role. Female power became a sign that something was amiss, resulting in characters who formed the disruption that started an investigation, or transgressive models of femininity (the prostitute or hyper-sexual woman) which bore the blame for social malaise. Angela dalle Vacche (1992: 15) suggests

that Italian patriarchal culture conceptualizes the past as the father
and the body politic as male, Italian cinema employing 'homosocial'
narratives to represent fathers and sons in history and public life,
while pushing mothers toward biology and the private sphere. In
fact, the 'battle of the sexes' has many complex functions in Italian
cinema – as satire on traditional society, commentary on the present,
and rehearsal of new social habits amongst others. Historical films
are often conveniently set prior to the feminist debates of the 1970s
in order to evoke comforting images of societies in which not only
women, but the lower classes, know their place. Italian comedies
and 'women's films' reflect the needs of their production era for
the rehearsal of new roles, and the violence of male melodramas
indicates the presence of interesting tensions in Italian society. This
chapter will therefore explore the forms in which some of these
tensions have surfaced.

Hyperfemininity and the *Diva* of Silent Cinema

As Chapter 1 has shown, Italian silent cinema provided examples
of a range of representations of the feminine, reflecting the increasing involvement of women outside the home in the period of
rapid industrialization. However, it is the figure of the *diva*, the un-
attainable goddess of the silver screen, who is best remembered.
In teasing out the meaning of star charisma, Richard Dyer (1991:
58–9) suggests that they should be studied in their entire context,
and usually occur at times of political and social instability and
transition. The most famous of these actors, Francesca Bertini, Italia
Almirante Manzini, Lyda Borelli, Leda Gys, and Pina Menichelli,
encapsulated a combination of feminine models from the previous
century and the energetic impulses of the new one. What they have in
common is their physicality, their imposing body shape and gestures
connoting a range of emotions, and their hyper-femininity, an excess
of sexuality necessary in a less sexually explicit age. In *Cabiria* the
figure of Sofonisba (Italia Almirante Manzini), daughter of King
Hasdrubal, is a fascinating tragic heroine, her image featuring
on much of the film's publicity material. Sofonisba is first encountered lounging in a chair, stroking a leopard, wearing a crown-like
head dress and a gorgeous costume. Although clearly signalled as
someone important, she is contained by her surroundings. Whereas
the rest of Hasdrubal's palace is constructed on a monumental scale,
Sofinisba's quarters are smaller, and the ornate ceiling, and window
wall imprison her. She is not in charge of her own fate as her father
first promises her to his ally Massinissa, with whom she falls in love,
but he is defeated in battle and her father promises her to another
ally, the elderly General Siphax.

Cabiria contains numerous examples of the exotic, but Sofonisba
is the exotic focus of the story, and in her the exotic and the erotic

Figure 7.1
Sofonisba *Cabiria* (Giovanni Pastrone, 1914).

fuse. The leopards and doves that surround her are metaphors for her wild, passionate, yet gentle nature. Her costumes must have given immense pleasure to sections of the audience, and are designed to accentuate her femininity and foreground her sexual nature. Her bodices are draped with strands of pearls, with tassels from her breasts, her hips accentuated by net-like, or swagged over-skirts, which graphically indicate her large behind. Sofonisba's gestures are of strong emotion, and are made more visible by her bare, soft, arms, and her servants functioning as a chorus to amplify her emotion by their own expressions and gestures. Whereas, in narrative terms, the character of Sofonisba has a protective role, making sure that Cabiria survives to adulthood, and providing a contrast to the restraint of the Roman girl, the amount of screen space devoted to Sofinisba's story and to her spectacular body is indicative of other concerns. Her sexual allure promises to deliver actions unrestrained by Italian social conventions, while her transgressive behaviour in falling in love with Massinissa suggests the dangers represented by female autonomy. She is a complex and larger-than-life character who succeeds in becoming more than the sum of her narrative functions.

There have been many attempts to understand the power and role of the *diva* of silent cinema. Vittorio Martinelli (1998: 353) speculates that the male audience went to admire and experience the *diva*'s body and dangerous unpredictability, while the female audience went to observe her dresses, vitality, and to envy her impossible love affairs. All of these aspects are present in *Gli ultimi giorni di Pompei* (*The Last Days of Pompeii*, Amleto Palermi and Carmine Gallone, 1926). In its claim to 'authenticity' in its portrayal of Roman life, the film combines lingering shots of the naked breasts of Roman women in the baths, half-naked dancing girls and the coy girl presented to the heroine's brother by the Egyptian High Priest, smothered in flowers, on a tray, for his consumption. The film also clothes its main female characters in sumptuous drapery patterned with *art* nouveau designs (the *stile Liberty*), whose silken sheen is emphasized by colour tinting. Whilst the heroine, Ione (Rina De Liguoro), is a model of Roman modesty, beauty and rejection of decadence, her rivals for Glauco's (Victor Varconyil) love permit rebellion, spite, revenge to be rehearsed.

The *diva*'s challenge to traditional notions of femininity is still the focus of male erotic drives (Torriglia 2002: 40–1). Angela dalle Vacche (1992: 30), on the other hand, gives prominence to the classical notion that only spectacle 'can adequately represent historic events' and that 'the injection of an historical dimension into a private realm requires the space of a spectacle where individual characters may allegorize the national body'. These critical paradigms seek to explain power relationships. Thus the *mise en scène* of *Cabiria* and Sofonisba's hypersexuality represent the subjugation and containment of women and, the same time, the dangerous, alluring softness of the Eastern population, standing for Italy's enemies of the time. Whereas the male protagonist is split into two figures (representing the positive intellectual and the physical attributes of the Roman), the balance of the two female protagonists is skewed in favour of Sofonisba, as Cabiria is a youthful and helpless figure.

In the 1920s the gentle giant Maciste, played by the former docker Bartolomeo Pagano, achieved his own *filone*, starring in several spectacular adventures. *Maciste all'inferno* (*Maciste in Hell*, Guido Brignone, 1925), is inspired by the engravings of Gustave Doré, Dante's *Inferno*, and popular drama. As an expensive film, it was destined to international distribution and is therefore clearly structured through the intertitles and the language of spatial and gestural organization. It was also marketed with the titillating promise of sex (female nudity) and violence (fights galore). A sentimental love story was intercut with the adventures of Maciste in hell, and is particularly interesting on two counts. First, Maciste is completely supportive of his beloved's pregnancy by another man and, second, his adventures in hell include a range of feminine temptations. The over-arching moral framework cannot compete with the gusto with which Maciste succumbs to the temptations of hell.

The hyper-emotionality of female and male actors marks them out as extraordinary beings, but also as subjects who have escaped social control and the 'normal' regulations of behaviour. They choose their own love objects and act in their own, rather than family interests. However, the melancholy that is also present in so many performances signals the consciousness that escape is only temporary and fate will end the behaviour in which the audience revels.

Representing the Modern, Progressive State in the Fascist Period

The personae of the *dive* or seducers of silent historical films were too extraordinary to be integrated into narratives depicting a modern world in which all sections of society worked to build a strong country, and fascist ideology encouraged women to serve through their roles as wives and mothers, subservient to men. As Marcia Landy (1989: 116) suggests, this subservient role is pervasive, but 'the presence of disguises, doubling, and secrecy provides the way to read these films against the grain' in that they expose the strategies necessary to keep women in their place. Thus, in *Maddalena, zero in condotta* (*Maddalena, Zero in Conduct*, 1940) the two heroines, Maddalena (Carla del Poggio) and her teacher, Signorina Malgari, represent youthful disruption and mature acceptance. Maddalena's attempts to find her teacher a husband are successful and, in the process, she finds a husband herself. Both poles of behaviour indicate the difficulties of resolution in the marriage scenario. The containment of Maddalena's youthful ebulliance is insufficiently prepared for in narrative terms, and the hard work she has to undertake to match her teacher is a sign that acceptance of 'female destiny' connotes a passivity that actually militates against the female character achieving her desires.

The symbolic trials that male protagonists have to undergo, and disguises they have to adopt are similarly indicative of the difficulties of constructing the image of the modern man (Landy 1986: 141). The changes that the heroes played by Amedeo Nazzari go through in films such as *Cavalleria* (*Cavalry*, Goffredo Alessandrini, 1936) and *Un pilota ritorna* (*A Pilot Returns*, Roberto Rossellini, 1942) in this period, and the sacrifices they make embody this process. His large, upright figure, his rejection of the temptations of feminine beauty, overcoming of many vicissitudes, and final sacrifices for his country set him up as a model of the traditional Italian male. By contrast, Vittorio de Sica's comedy roles revolved around narratives in which he was either restored to the straight and narrow by a determined woman, or disguised himself (*Il signor Max* (*Mister Max*, Mario Camerini, 1937) as a member of another class but reverted to his former place in life at the end. Both behavioural templates allowed social mobility and new manners to be rehearsed whilst showing the class ideology behind masculine behaviour.

Stereotypes of the Traditional Italian Hero

As writers about other national cinemas have explored, representations of masculinity in popular fictions are never unitary but provide a range of dynamic and competing cultural types, which come to the forefront and recede in relation to changes in film production, audience taste and social change (Dyer 1987; Vincendeau 2000; Spicer 2001). Thus the split personae of the male protagonist in the silent era indicates the difficulties of forming the 'imagined community' of Italian nationhood (Anderson 1991). In crucial periods, such as the 1910s, the Fascist period, and the beginning of the First Republic, the personae of male actors embodied characteristics and representations of power necessary to support ideologies of cohesion in the national family. Gino Cervi, for example, played medieval heroes in the 1930s whose exploits consolidated a version of male combatitiveness in the service of the city (and nation) State. A plump, classical actor, his expressiveness usually connoted the acceptable face of authority for the later post-war period. His role as the communist mayor in the Don Camillo films in the 1950s allowed communist rhetoric to be rehearsed and contained and made fun of. Although the Left had been excluded from power since the war, the early 1950s saw an opening up to Centre-Left politics and the vigorous presence of the PCI. Cervi's roles constitute a more modern rehearsal of social change and a more complex interaction with cultural currents of the time than Nazzari's rather stiff landowners and engineers. An early example of the actor-director, Vittorio De Sica's matinee idol looks and established place in Left-wing intellectual circles ensured his survival in the post-war period, and his partnership with the screenwriter and theorist, Cesare Zavattini, resulted in some of the classics of neorealism. From the 1950s his greatest box-office triumphs were in the *Bread, Love and . . .* comedies in which he played Carabiniere Marshall Carotenuto, locked in an erotic battle of wills with a peasant Gina Lollobrigida. Thus De Sica's comedy roles rehearse in a light vein stories of male authority in conflict with female resistance to containment within traditional social structures.

Amedeo Nazzari was an actor who resembled Errol Flynn and made 113 films between 1935 and 1978. Nazzari was more than usually obsessive about maintaining a relationship with his public, only accepting roles as positive, moral characters through which he could represent the best aspects of Italianness (Gubitosi 1998: 11). When one considers the social, political and economic changes through which his career passed, the success of that career achieves an emblematic status and the star becomes a cultural icon. Gubitosi (1998: 1) claims that Nazzari represented a concentration of the qualities felt to be typical of the Italian male – handsome, brave, honest, a good worker, father, husband, lover – so that he was the focus of female fantasies and the nexus of acceptable propaganda for Mussolini's 'new' Italy and at the same time a representation of positive qualities of bygone ages. Nazzari's persona was that of a handsome but ordinary man, and carefully unassociated with any particular region. As a result, he had a prolific career acting out positive Italian male attributes associated with a mythic past rather than only one region. He consistently played fathers, or if he wasn't a father, he stood in that relationship to groups without his far-sightedness or moral qualities – women and children, workers, soldiers. Nazzari's gestural range was not large, but his movements were decisive. Physically he was imposing, tall, broad shouldered, with delicate hands and facial features, and fair, curly hair. He could therefore embody power and sensitivity. Many close ups also foregrounded his ability to suggest strong emotion through his expressive eyes and the direction of his gaze. However, the fact that his second bout of popularity occurred in melodramas from 1949 to 1956, and that, at the turn of a new millennium, videos of his films still circulate in countries of the Italian diaspora, such as Australia, is evidence of the response his persona engenders in immigrant communities having to negotiate the integration of their own Italian identity within 'modern', Anglo-Saxon social hierarchies.

Rehearsing New Masculinities

Raf Vallone, Vittorio Gassman, Renato Salvatori, Walter Chiari, Marcello Mastroianni and Alberto Sordi were very different from their predecessors. They established themselves in *neorealismo rosa*, enabling a variety of youthful masculine responses to social change to be rehearsed. In reviews of Raf Vallone's work, there is much mention of his robust physical presence, the connotational possibilities of his gestural range, and particularly the rich, warm tones of his voice. Renato Salvatori (from central Italy) and Marcello Mastroianni (like De Sica from Naples) both established their careers in this period in comedies set in urban, working class milieux. The persona of both actors at this time was of strength, energy, sexual vigour, and charm, allied to a marked unawareness of the meaning of events, the trope of irony providing a space for audience involvement. Mastroianni's theatrical training and contacts in Italian intellectual circles allowed him to move across a greater generic range than Salvatori and to interpret roles of more complex masculinity in art cinema. Mastroianni's character type was evolving from the proletarian to the middle class, a process that was in itself a reflection of the evolution of post-war Italian society.

Salvatori, a former merchant seaman had a considerable physical presence, beautiful body, and a gift for expressing sincerity. He was launched in a series of sentimental comedies structured around the physical attributes of the main actors. Throughout *Poveri ma belli* (*Poor but Handsome*, Dino Risi, Italy, 1956), Salvatore (Salvatori) and Romolo (Maurizio Arena) erupt into the public spaces of Rome. These are bodies at ease with their own physicality, and their own surroundings. Salvatore is a lifeguard, Romolo works in his uncle's record shop; they like clothes, pop music, dancing and girls, and themselves. Salvatore's constant prop is a comb and it is in frequent use. Significantly, many of this younger generation had a sporting background. Raf Vallone played for Torino first team, Gassman played basket ball. Their physicality marked them out as different from the non-professional actors who played peasants, fishermen, the unemployed. Their size, athleticism, vigorous gestures indicate their force, their virility and their health. Similarly, their objects of desire are the plump, well-endowed starlets who were spotted in Miss Italia contests, and who personify the desire for wellbeing and prosperity of the period of reconstruction.

Vittorio Gassman's career is interesting in the 1950s because he regularly played as many villains as heroes. Physically he was tall and extremely handsome, with very dark, expressive eyes. He embodies that very Italian trait of *fare bella figura*, the art of showing oneself to best advantage, an important personal asset in the years leading up to the economic boom. Gassman appeared in at least two films with Nazzari, one of which, *Il lupo della Sila* (*The Wolf of the Sila*, Duilio Coletti, Italy, 1949) illustrates their generational differences. Pietro (Gassman), a poor Calabrian farmer and the mainstay of his mother and little sister, Rosaria (Laura Cortese), wants to marry his lover, Orsola (Luisa Rossi), the sister of the local landowner, Don Rocco Barra (Nazzari). Falsely accused of murder, Pietro will not compromise Orsola, with whom he has spent the night, by using her as his alibi. In spite of Pietro's mother's entreaties, the landowner refuses to let Orsola give evidence and Pietro is killed in a shootout with the carabinieri. Years later, Rosaria (Silvana Mangano) plots revenge and goes to work for Don Rocco, leading him on to propose marriage to her, although she has fallen in love with his son, Salvatore (Jacques Sernas). Don Rocco pursues the lovers with murderous intent but is shot by his sister, Orsola. This convoluted melodrama, set in the rural south, sets two forms of masculinity in opposition. Positive attributes cohere around the figures of Pietro (darkly handsome, large, physically and sexually active, noble, emotional) and Don Rocco's son, Salvatore (fair and handsome, passionate, sexually active, educated, sensitive, modern). Don Rocco, on the other hand, embodies the many contradictions of the traditional Italian patriarch. As represented by Nazzari, he is handsome and shown actively working and employing others, clearly respected in his community, and addressed with deference. However, his pipe, rural breeches and fur-trimmed cloaks contrast with his son's sports jackets and check shirts, and it is Don Rocco's patriarchal and class attitudes that precipitate the tragedy. He refuses to allow his sister to marry a peasant, and his injunction that 'the women of this house never go out alone' backfires when Rosaria and Salvatore fall in love within the household. Although Rosaria, the desired object of both father and son, is represented as a traditional passionate woman, the physicality and performance of Mangano mark her out as modern. Her wide lips, full breasts and hips connote health and fecundity, while the deep timbre of her voice and her contemporary clothing (patterned blouse and spotted skirt with a frilly hem) indicate a certain independence and interest in fashion. This film is typical in representing youth as trying to rebel against rigid patriarchal attitudes. Although intellectuals deplored consumerism as a 'negative process', John Foot (2001: 33) has suggested that it could also liberate, 'creating a space for rebellion in the face of staid and conservative social rules'. Moreover, it is possible to see in popular Italian films, as Brunetta (1999: 192–3) has observed, a socio-economic journey as the protagonists of these films gradually acquire clothes which express their own individuality, their own transport, and then their own free time.

Gassman's characters were often described as 'monsters', their excessiveness forming part of the 'instructions' of the audience of how to react to new situations . In *Anna* (Alberto Lattuada, 1951) he teams with Mangano and Vallone. The poles of male sexuality are represented by the openness and honesty of Vallone and the perversity of Gassman. A life free of bourgeois constraints and allowing full rein to male sexual appetites is depicted in *Kean: genio e sregolatezza* (*Kean: wild genius*, co-directed by Gassman and Francesco Rosi, 1956). The theatrical milieu is designed and shot with saturated colour complementing the excessiveness and hypersexuality of Gassman's performance. His villains allow the audience to experience extremes and rehearse weakness and shame, failure and incompetence, and to make judgements about unacceptable behaviour in the struggle for survival and a bigger slice of the postwar cake.

In the new comedy vehicles the working-class origins and speech patterns of these hyper-masculine boys and plump, sensual girls were emphasized as if this class environment provided a space in which new, freer social interactions could safely be rehearsed. The performances of the younger generation of sex bombs of 1950s comedy emphasized both their physical attributes and their class origins. These stars epitomize the class that has left poverty behind, can enjoy the fat of the land (as long as it knows its place) and, as Spinazzola (1974: 131) suggests, can look forward to a future 'rich in electrical appliances, furniture on the never never, and a lovely Fiat 600'. The physical expressivity of both groups of actors mentioned, through body shape, gesture, the importance of eyes and voice, is extremely important, functioning as markers of agency and possibility. The film-maker, Ettore Scola, claimed that Italian comedy was 'the slightly degenerate offspring of neorealism . . . born to pacify . . . prosperous, provincial Italy, without much reference to reality', but this view of realism is very limited (Aprà and Pistagnesi 1986: 51). As Gianni Canova (1999: 1) suggests, by focusing on problematic attempts to resolve emotional and sexual conflicts, these popular films become 'realist' in spite of themselves because they thereby have to engage with questions and situations ignored by more 'serious' drama. In effect, what we see in Italian films between 1946 and 1955 is the construction of a what Bourdieu (1993: 161–175) defines as a *habitus*. Profound economic and social changes in Italian society at this time meant that gender hierarchies and models of masculine behaviour had to be renegotiated because they became less easy to reconcile with models associated with modernization, American capitalism and culture. At the same time, and this is a worldwide phenomenon, a new generation of young men and a new class are making their bid for cultural power. The roles of younger actors in particular function to differentiate their generation or their social group from their elders. Performances of masculinity in 1950s films reveal an increasing use of new competences, such as how to function as a successful male away from the traditional family unit, how to be successful emotionally with women in new economic and social conditions, how to use popular culture to bond with other people in your *habitus*, how to be a consumer, how to get by in society and put yourself at the best advantage. Social dispositions and attitudes are learned over time and cinema is but one arena where changes in attitude may be rehearsed. In this respect, it can be argued that popular neorealist cinema is important in that it provided a forum for the performance of a far richer range of types of masculine behaviour than 'classical' neorealism, making visible not only the constructedness of patriarchal beliefs but also what was at stake in their maintenance – prosperity and sexual gratification.

Flesh and Abundance

Some of Italy's best known female stars achieved fame and fortune in the post-war period and their range is just as interesting as their male counterparts. Gina Lollobrigida and Sophia Loren are the best known of the many young women whose most memorable attributes were their fleshy and well-endowed bodies. Economic prosperity came gradually to Italy after the Second World War, with wages held down tightly until the mid-1950s (Duggan and Wagstaff 1995: 14). As a result, Italians had little disposable income for consumer goods until wages took off after 1956, forcing the pace of the economic boom. Visits to the cinema represented a cheap way of accessing consumption. Cinema ticket sales and audience figures were huge in these years. As a result, the Italian film industry was concerned to develop the careers of a raft of younger stars who would find popularity with international as well as national audiences. The Miss Italia contests of the late 1940s provided a happy hunting ground for film producers and started the careers of Silvana Mangano, Gina Lollobrigida, Sophia Loren, Lucia Bosè, Silvana Pampanini, and Marisa Allasio.

The narratives developed for these spirited, younger women stress their youth and innocence, and their physical attributes. Known as

Figure 7.2

Prosperity written on the female body; Giovanna (Marisa Allasio in hat) and friends (*Poveri ma belli*, Dino Risi, 1956).

the *maggiorate fisiche* (the physically well endowed), they literally embody prosperity. The desire to forget wartime hardships, and the collision with the materialism of American culture resulted in a deeply held and widespread aspiration of the majority of the Italian population to achieve a measure of prosperity. The curvaceous, fleshy bodies of the new stars, their little tummies, full lips and expressive eyes are metonyms for a society that could go beyond the basic preoccupation of obtaining enough to eat, and had the energy to conquer a place in society, nice clothes, a fridge and material possessions. However, whereas Silvana Mangano's role in *Riso amaro* (1948) was indicative of the tensions between traditional culture and the desire for material goods, as the 1950s progressed, this conflict rapidly became superceded by more traditional comedy love stories where new dresses, records, cars, jobs for girls, were not signalled narratively as significant.

In films such as *Poveri, ma belli* (*Poor but Handsome*, Dino Risi, Italy, 1956) and *Belle, ma povere* (*Beautiful but Poor*, Dino Risi, 1957), desires for material comfort are represented by record shops, clothes, leisure activities, and even continuing education classes. But unease with the upward mobility of women is embodied in the shape of the ambitious Giovanna (Marisa Allasio), who is more beautiful, better endowed, more enigmatic, than the sisters of the male characters, and therefore represents the level of effort, of material wealth, necessary to win her.

Sophia Loren's role in *La bella mugnaia* (*The Beautiful Miller's Wife*, Mario Camerini, 1955) is also indicative of the social changes and tensions of the time, and of what was at stake for women. As Carmela, the wife of the miller, Luca (Marcello Mastroianni) she uses her beauty and wit to avoid paying the taxes that oppress the rest of the population, by teasing and suggestiveness towards men in power. However, at a local festival, the spectacle of her flying backwards and forwards on a swing causes a riot in which Luca is arrested, and the Governor of Campania takes the opportunity to try to call in favours given to Carmela. In this role, Loren's 'to be looked at-ness' (Mulvey 1975) is motivated narratively by her centrality within the frame as the object of male desire (the tax gatherers and Governor) or male control (Luca) and by her performance of herself as erotic spectacle on the swing as her flying skirts bare her legs. However, the female stars who came from beauty pageants or who play characters ambitious for a modelling career are the equivalent of the sporty male protagonists in their embodiment of self-discipline and control in their grooming of their bodies. In effect they represent the acceptance of social norms and templates of masculinity and femininity, which are then played out in brief rebellions or courtship rituals in closed narratives, concluding with their integration or reintegration into a community. This explains the presence of crowds of other actors, children, families or villagers, around the main characters because,

Figure 7.3
Recognition of limits,
Marina the *bersagliera*
(Gina Lollobrigida). *Pane,
amore e fantasia* (Luigi
Comencini, 1954).

as Foucault (1977: 202–3) observed in his study of the panopticon, force is unnecessary when the subject is aware of his/her visibility. The disciplined body interiorizes the power relation, watching itself and disciplining itself and thereby becoming 'the principle of his own subjection'.

Loren's southern physicality (she was from Naples), dark hair and eyes, voluptuous mouth and figure, tapped into mythic Mediterranean earth-mother stereotypes, so that she was able to suggest both the desirability of plenitude and prosperity, and the promise of sexual fulfilment. Setting *La bella mugnaia* in the Italy of 1860, under Spanish rule, allows Camerini to present Carmela's trouncing of men of power without incurring the wrath of the censors for lack of respect for institutions, while still doing exactly that. Loren's astute management of her career gave her unusual longevity in the film industry, mainly by sticking to comedy genres, by moving into dramas by acclaimed writers or directors, or international comedies in which either her earthiness, or her motherhood, or both, were emphasized. She therefore avoided having to move into popular genres such as the *peplum*, Mafia film or the western to which many southern types were marginalized. Over time she gradually achieved iconic status, helped by her pairing with that other icon, Marcello Mastroianni, particularly during the 'Golden Age' of Italian comedy of the 1960s. However, another slightly older actress with an earthy, mediterranean persona, Anna Magnani, had problems sustaining a career in the 1950s and 1960s although the huge public mourning at her death and the name by which she was known by her public, Nanarella, indicate her hold on public consciousness.

Magnani was a successful star of the theatrical review, with a strong, combative persona that made the closure of her 1950s social dramas and comedies difficult to achieve. Narratively, therefore, she has to be tricked into situations in which her unruly nature is punished, usually by being cheated by the upper classes – *Abbasso la ricchezza!* (*Down With Riches*, Gennaro Righelli, 1946) or a conman (*Risate di Gioia*, Mario Monicelli, 1960). Significantly, Magnani often played prostitutes. In this period there are a notable number of films featuring prostitutes (or sexually active unmarried women) as protagonists. In this, desire, and desire for prosperity is inscribed on the body of the female protagonists, prostitution being a metaphor for capitalist consumption and exploitation when the materialism of American society represented a worryingly attractive alternative to the serious republican virtues that were being proposed. Prostitution narratives make plain the mechanisms of the exploitation of women and provide a metaphor for women's marriage bargain.

The 'fallen-woman' narratives, made by men, also responded to market imperatives, creating a space for male fantasies of desire and possession, which had been unleashed by access to films from other countries. Contemporary reviews of these 1950s films stress the 'typical Italian nature' of the actresses. Lollobrigida, for example, is referred to as warm, southern, passionate, as if these were essential characteristics of Italian womanhood, rather than a female stereotype that embodied the projection of male preoccupations and desires.

Narratives of sparky peasant girls, such as those featuring Gina Lollobrigida, are matched by a significant number of films centred on the lives and aspirations of servant girls, such as *Cronache di poveri amanti* (*Tales of Poor Lovers*, Carlo Lizzani, 1953). Servants become protagonists, rather than being extras in stories of glamourous middle-class women and, in stories of social mobility, focalize desires for material comfort, a home of one's own, even if provided predominantly by that familiar *deus ex machina*, the handsome hero. Significantly, the object of hatred in the plot is the Signora, who manipulates the youthful inmates of the street from her room as a money lender, the ultimate negative image of the capitalist economy.

Female characters in popular Italian genre films of the late 1940s and 1950s rehearse female stereotypes already present in Italian culture, but bear the imprint of the tensions between traditional social arrangements and the realities of a modern world moving towards the economic boom. By focusing on the notion of prosperity as causing a disruption and constituting an opposition to traditional narrative norms of female self-sacrifice, the extent of tensions in Italian culture becomes visible. These tensions are explored in more sophisticated ways in both art and popular cinema in the 1960s. Women too are developing a new *habitus*, exploring how to combine work and family, enjoying narratives of rebellion, riches, social mobility and the conquest of status men. That the increased confidence and demands of women were experienced as profoundly disorienting can be guaged from narrative tensions in these films, and the transference of desires for greater sexual and social freedom onto the bodies of the female protagonists. The preponderance of excessive representations of the female body and material prosperity indicates the level of male unease at a new and more modern way of making relationships with women, and dealing with female autonomy.

The Lure of Sexual Freedom

The influence of the Catholic Church succeeded in delaying the sexual revolution in Italy but the growth of tourism from Northern Europe, and media interest, meant that Italians were well aware of it. The battle of the sexes was played out with increasingly erotic content in the 1960s, under the guise of the social problem film, or the drama of social class where sexual allure and freedom was usually embodied in the lower class woman, rehearsing social change at a distance from the middle-class *milieu*. Popular genre cinema especially used its codes and conventions to cloak erotic content, giving rise to the *filone* of the summer holiday and beach party films of the 1950s and the torrid temptresses of the *peplum*. With the relaxation of censorship, the *filone erotico* has been a constant financially successful strand in Italian cinema. In the last thirty years the ultimate metaphor for male domination and control has been repeatedly played out in the severely codified forms of the soft and hard versions of the pornofilm. Angela Prudenzi (1997: 336) defines the 'golden rule' of soft porn as 'giving the spectator what it wants. That is, a good dose of tits and bums, possibly not exhibited, but "stolen" from under the shower or climbing the stairs, of chaste couplings . . . More or less clear *doubles entendres*, pretty but accessible female protagonists, and male actors whose physicality was so ordinary as to suggest "this could happen to me".' 'Pretty but accessible' is the most common template for female actors in erotic cinema, so that fiery Mediterranean voluptuousness, combined with a certain passivity, allows narratives to combine enormous sexual temptation for male characters, and their control of female characters in the sexual act. There are of course a range of female stereotypes available to correspond to particular male desires, from the childish to the more mature, from innocence to the degraded. The number of films produced enabled the launch of many acting careers, such as those of Ornella Muti and Laura Antonelli, and the sustaining of others. Ornella Muti's physical type is fairly typical in suggesting youthful passivity and availability at the same time. This passivity also explains the transition of many Italian models to a film career, masking their lack of acting training.

Comedies and art cinema alike have both tried to take advantage of the popularity of erotic cinema, and subvert its rigid codes. However, the consumption of film in a private rather than public setting via video or DVD has consolidated its codes along with its investment potential. International erotic cinema, such as that of Tinto Brass, is now 'harder' and more explicit in what it will show, but its conventions are still the familiar ones. *Senso '45* (*Black Angel*, Tinto Brass, 2002) contains a high level of redundancy, Livia's (Anna Galiena) swooning face being accompanied by her voice over declaring her feelings of submission, helplessness, or only achieving identity through her relationship with the Nazi, Helmut Schultz (Gabriel Garko). Adapted from the same book by Camillo Boito as Visconti's *Senso*, the film uses the icononography of the Nazi-porn *filone* (violent sex, the naked female body in borrowed black uniforms, perversion and sadism), fetishizes the female body by fragmenting it into scarlet lips, and parts reflected in mirrors, and also manages an erotic *pastiche* of Pina's shooting in Rossellini's *Roma città aperta* with a totally unmotivated crotch shot of the dead woman in her black stockings. The presence of the grotesque, fragmentation and narrative excess all indicate the fragility of this fantasy of sexual mastery, which teeters, and occasionally plunges into parody, revealing the instability of the patriarchal regime upon which it rests.

Representations of Male Violence

As American films featuring Italo-Americans show, there is an obverse side to the coin of representation of Italian masculinity in which violence connotes a struggle for male supremacy. Sensitivity is replaced by aggression, individualism, physical energy and what Jane Caputi (1999: 150) defines as 'eroticized domination (over the "feminine", which can be embodied in females or males).' Western culture has engendered a large number of male myths, powerful masculine figures whose purpose is to impose order on disorder,

and make sense of events, thus enabling an understanding of the
unknown, or the irrational, making it less terrifying. Stereotypes
of male dominance are ideological in their revealing 'the channels
by which power replicates itself, the means by which behaviour
is prescribed' (Chapman 1988: 227). As the bandit films of
neorealismo nero, and the convoluted melodramatic narratives of
neorealismo rosa show, violence is also the outward manifestation
of the difficulties of maintaining an image of patriarchal masculinity
which dominates Italian culture at a time of national defeat and
enormous social change. The popular genres of the latter half of
the twentieth century indicate the arenas where male conflicts can
be played out at a distance from contemporary life, the 'sword and
sandal' epic, the western, and the horror film. Political struggles
are also played out in the form of violent male conflicts in 'serious'
social and art cinema, the assassinations and murders that recur in
contemporary history supplying a range of possible characters and
scenarios.

In Francesco Rosi's *Il caso Mattei* (*The Mattei Affair*, 1972)
the conflict between Italian and American power systems, which
may have led to Mattei's death, is dramatized in the confrontation
between Mattei, representing Italian interests and the Italian State,
and the American oil man, representing the powerful colonial
interests of capitalist big business on the American model.
Mattei's bargaining with the American oilman is a representation
of institutionalized and ritualized male conflict. The film illustrates
the fact that, in the latter half of the twentieth century, the exercise
of power is not simply a matter of physical constraint, limiting
the freedom of others. It is about language, who controls it and
who constructs definitions and meanings. Mattei is depicted as at a
disadvantage because he does not have access to the language of his
opponent. His performance indicates a style of power characterized
by force – of gesture and personality – and charm. The mere listing
of dialogue in the published script suppresses the impact of what
Fairclough calls the visuals (gesture, facial expression, movement,
posture) which accompany the verbal part of discourse (Rosi and
Scalfari 1972: 118–21; Fairclough 1989: 27). Placed in an ornate
dining room, the positioning of the characters expresses conflict
metaphorically. Low-angle camera positions emphasize the visual
richness of the environment, the repetition of columns supporting
interlacing vaulting on the ceiling. At a connotative level, the *mise en
scène* evokes 'a cultural lifestyle which distinguishes a status group
with a special identity in society', that of the wealthy aristocratic
or industrialist classes which could afford a leisure lifestyle, and
counterposes to it the white collar functionaries who embody the
new power orders (Turner 1988: 11). In the late twentieth century
wealth and power combine not in inheritance but in multinational
corporations.

Since Rosi's films are concerned to show how legal and illegal power is exercised, the rituals by which men cement their power are illustrated, such as the trappings of the office and boardroom with large lamps and statuettes, and particularly the all-male mealtime gathering, a scene that recurs in Italian crime fiction, particularly the Mafia film. Placing characters around a table allows a community to be illustrated, and shots and answering reverse shots to delineate conflict visually. Social or political conflict was often embodied in the violent male protagonist, representing one class, group or idea, and an equally violent male antagonist, representing an opposite viewpoint. This template has also been useful in exploring the social realities of violent and marginalized male groups, such as *Ultrà – Ultras (Some Lose, Some Die ... Some Win)* Ricky Tognazzi, 1991 – set amongst violent football gangs, *Mery per sempre (Forever Mary*, Marco Risi, 1989) and *Ragazzi fuori (Street Boys*, Marco Risi, 1990) showing how the cycle of deprivation leads young southern males to lives of crime and violence. From the 1980s, figures representing law and order are rehabilitated and male power takes another form.

New Male Roles in Contemporary Italian Cinema

In the early 1990s, and again in the early twenty-first century, the violent conflicts between extreme political factions, such as the Red Brigades, and the State, or between the Mafia and the State have been delineated on film through representative characters, based on historical fact. In these films, mainly with magistrate, journalist or policeman heroes, male power derives from the protagonist's moral authority rather than the ability to wreak excessive violence. In Vittorio Sindoni's *Una fredda mattina di maggio (A Cold May Morning*, 1990), the moral qualities of the journalist, Ruggero (Sergio Castellitto), are set against the extreme violence of the youthful terrorists. Set in 1976, and based on the character of the journalist Walter Tobagi, Ruggero is shown campaigning in his union branch for political moderation and training in new technology, and in a happy, warm domestic environment with his wife and child. The terrorists, on the other hand, are shown as ultra-violent, upper middle class, unprincipled, sexist and ambitious for power. Ruggero's assassination by the terrorist group represents a victory for an ideal of civic responsibility and domestic virtues in that the narrative uncovers the selfishness and amorality of his violent opponents. Sindoni stresses the importance of this struggle by a *mise en scène* of spectacular, asymmetric compositions, *film noir* lighting contrasts, and titles alluding to real events.

Upright and positive male protagonists are regularly played by Michele Placido, a popular television actor who has made the transition to cinema on the back of performances exploring the moral dilemmas of society at the end of the twentieth century. As he has both matured as an actor, and aged physically, his assumption of roles of masculine authority have been matched by his development of a directorial and production role. His central role in RAI television's series, 'La piovra' ('Octopus: Power of the Mafia') in the 1980s lent gravitas to his persona as upholder of traditional virtues of the Italian republic. This role carries over intertextually to the films he has produced and directed subsequently, such as *Un eroe borghese* (*Middle-Class Hero*, Michele Placido, 1994), in which he plays the lower middle-class, and middle-aged, policeman assigned to assist the investigating magistrate, Giorgio Ambrosoli (Fabrizio Bentivoglio) investigate the corruption case of the Banca Ambrosiana. The positive virtues of loyalty, integrity, honesty, adherence to republican ideals and dogged persistence are set against the secrecy and corruption of Michele Sindona and his associates. Ambrosoli's movements and social interactions are shown as stiff and formal, a literal correlative for his moral integrity, except where he is depicted relaxing amongst his attractive and supportive family.

This masculine template of the victim of violence who is also morally victorious is found in many films. In *Il partigiano Johnny* (*Johnny the Partisan*, Guido Chiesa, 2000), the idealistic hero (Stefano Dionisi) joins the resistance but finds cold, hunger, confusion and death. Peppino Impastato (Luigi Lo Cascio) fights the web of Mafia interests in his local town, Cinisi, in Sicily, in *I cento passi* (*The 100 Steps*, Marco Tullio Giordana, 2000) through denunciations and savage humour over the radio, but is killed in an explosion. However, defeats send conflicting messages. The feminized, sensitive, intelligent, moral model of masculinity is depicted in healthy family relationships, but its defeat by violent means signals the difficulty of adopting the 'new man' role, which also finds expression in unbalanced visual composition, visual excess and *noir* elements. Moreover, this protagonist's female companions generally remain in supportive and subordinate roles, maintaining the traditional female stereotype. Margarethe von Trotta is one of the few film-makers to show a proactive heroine in *Il lungo silenzio* (*The Long Silence*, 1993). The wife (Carla Gravina) of the murdered magistrate, Marco Canova (Jacques Perrin) is a doctor who takes up the fight against those in government who, implicated in mafia corruption, killed her husband. She too is killed, but the film concludes with a mosaic of female faces naming names in a television programme.

Excess (in the form of the grotesque), defeat (in the sense of acknowledging the inability to change or modify events), and a sense of ethical integrity are also characteristics of the protagonists created by Nanni Moretti. As Chapter 2 has explored, these are also characteristics of the *commedia all'italiana*, but Roberto de Gaetano (2002: 12) has also identified Moretti's neorealist inheritance in his ethical desire to engage with the contemporary world, even when he cannot change it. Although critics often succumb to the temptation to see Moretti's films, in which he is also the main protagonist, as purely autobiographical, De Gaetano (1999: 116) suggests that Moretti never totally performs himself in his roles as Michele Apicella but transforms himself into a grotesque mask, under which he collects all the clichés and commonplaces of a psycho-social identity. According to Millicent Marcus (2002: 286), this positions him within a tradition of the social body in Italian cinema, whereby his body on screen offers an image of identification through which the male spectator can imagine their role in the historical process. In fact, from *Io sono un autarchico* (*I am Self-sufficient*, 1976) and *Ecce Bombo* (1978), through *Sogni d'oro* (*Sweet Dreams*, 1981), *La messa è finita* (*The Mass is Over*, 1985) and *Palombella rossa* (*Red Lob*, 1989) onwards, Moretti demonstrates the process of evolving a *habitus* for the generation formed in the events of 1968. Thus, his characters show how they differentiate themselves by chanting slogans from their political passions as committed Left-wingers, their commitment to utopian change, their attempts to come to terms with what the Communist Party has become. Moretti's obsession with sloppy, cliché-ridden language and diatribes against meaningless distortions of communication is reiterated from film to film, reflecting his concerns that the imprecision and slippage of contemporary media language is implicated in the mediocrity of the Italian political process, represented by Berlusconi's rise to power. Linguistic precision is therefore one of Moretti's arms in his ethical fight against the postmodern infantilization of the electorate. As Marcus (2002: 292) has pointed out, *Caro diario* (*Dear Diary*, 1993) marks 'a radical turn away from exemplarity' and 'a will to speak for no one but himself'. Moretti also cuts through to the quick of issues such as the complicity of doctors in the unprincipled product exploitation of drug barons, Berlusconi's manipulation of the media, and the reluctance of people to take personal responsibility for life events. He does this by evoking the raw power of the human trajectory from life to death. *Caro diario* contains Super 8 footage of Moretti's chemotherapy, *Aprile* (1998) the birth of his son, and *La stanza del figlio* (*The Son's Room*, 2001) the grief-filled personal stock-taking of the fictional psychiatrist.

Nanni Moretti therefore embodies attempts to move towards a modern template for masculinity when traditional models still have a force, but where his forceful rejection of coercive mediocrity endows him with authorial weight.

Problematic Masculinity

The masculinity stereotype of violent domination and control, and the difficulty of conceiving a masculine role in which sensitivity and

Figure 7.4
A feminized male face;
Marcello Mastroianni in
Il bell'Antonio (Mauro
Bolognini, 1960).

moral superiority do not entail damage to the patriarchal model, both indicate the negotiation of responses to modernity, and the fear that loss of power entails. It is not surprising therefore, that, in its obsession with masculinity, Italian cinema should abound with representations of impotence. Impotence is present in Italian cinema not only in its sexual form but in narratives that somehow fail to reach successful closure in the re-establishment of the *status quo*, that is male dominance.

   In spite of his construction as icon of the 'Latin lover' by Anglo-Saxon critics, Marcello Mastroianni built his long career on portrayals of male attempts to negotiate a successful modern template of masculinity. His representations were often of problematic masculinities, such as that in Fellini's *La dolce vita* (1960) and *8½* (1963) in which the doubts and uncertainties of his characters drive the narrative forward. In *Il bell'Antoniono* (*The Beautiful Antonio*, Mauro Bolognini, 1960), he plays a sexually impotent character, whose wife (Claudia Cardinale) has to admit to being a virgin a year after the wedding. The camera feminizes Mastroianni, focusing on his beautiful eyes, long eyelashes and soft mouth and, in stressing his passivity and ease in male company, hints at homosexuality. And in Ettore Scola's *Una giornata particolare* (*A Special Day*, 1977), Mastroianni plays opposite Sophia Loren's downtrodden housewife as a homosexual clerk. The background of collective hysteria at Hitler's triumphal visit to Rome in 1938 provides a metaphor for the excessive reaction against any form of sexual difference. The glorification of male power, fascism (and therefore coercive patriarchal control) is also implicated in the marginalization and psychological alienation of women.

Sexual impotence is an effective representation of the extreme loss of patriarchal power, which is more often explored in narratives in which male power is problematic or cannot be exercised effectively. Set in the late 1950s, the hero (Rutger Hauer) of Olmi's *La leggenda del santo bevitore* (*Legend of the Holy Drinker*, 1988) is a vagabond, enclosed in dark drinking dens. The film documents his failure to bring any enterprise to a successful conclusion, although he has been given money to help him rejoin society. In the Taviani brothers' *Il sole anche di notte* (*Night Sun*, 1990), Baron Sergio Giuramondo (Julian Sands) becomes a monk after discovering that his bride (Nastassia Kinski) was the mistress of the King of Naples. Rejecting class, wealth, honours, he retreats to a desolate Sicilian hillside to become a hermit in a ruined tower. The trajectory of renunciation allows power structures to be examined, the rituals by which aristocratic power displays and maintains itself, the hypocrisy of the Catholic Church and its use of show and miracles to maintain its hold on the population, and the threat represented by the power of female sexuality. The film is also an invitation to ponder on how to achieve self-knowledge and an equilibrium with nature and one's fellows.

Sex has a strange effect on Trompetto (Maurizio Nichetti) in his *Volere volare* (1991). Trompetto is a sound recordist who becomes romantically involved with Martina (Angela Finocchiaro), who makes a living by satisfying the sexual fantasies of her bizarre range of clients. Both are lonely, he because his obsession for collecting perfect sounds, that is, *mastery* in his profession, isolates him, and she because in a marginalized profession, where she controls scenarios of fetishism and subjection which ignore her own desires. He finds himself turning into a completely cartoon figure, but this loss of control attracts and satisfies Martina.

Loss of control also underlies Mimmo Calopresti's *La seconda volta* (*The Second Time*, 1996) and *La felicità costa niente* (*Happiness Costs Nothing*, 2003). In the former, Professor Alberto Sajevo (Nanni Moretti) recognizes a woman in the street as the terrorist who shot him twelve years before, leaving a bullet still lodged in his head. His obsessive following of Lisa (Valeria Bruni Tedeschi), and eventual contact, represent his desire to know the cause of her attack, to re-establish a control over his life that was brutally removed when he was objectified as a terrorist target. In the latter film, the life of a successful architect, Sergio (Calopresti), suddenly seems meaningless and he starts to neglect his career and leaves his wife (Valeria Bruni Tedeschi) for a young woman, whom he mistreats along with all his friends. Sergio combines argumentativeness and lack of self-knowledge. His diatribes against money are met with laughter by his construction workers, his lectures to his downstairs neighbour against wife abuse are rewarded with a beating, and he fails to recognize that the woman to whom he offers shelter (Francesca Neri) must, and in fact does, have a past that includes mental illness. Divesting himself of the power of agency over his life, Sergio goes downhill and is finally rescued by his friend, Francesco (Vincent Perez), who finds him disoriented and suffering from liver damage, presumably from another beating. The colour tones become very black and white as Sergio's abdication of power becomes literally inscribed on his body, ending with him inert on the operating table as doctors attempt to save his life.

The impossibility of achieving equality or equilibrium between the sexes is also explored in *Un viaggio chiamato amore* (*A Journey Called Love*, Michele Placido, 2002), which charts the tempestuous and destructive affair between two well-known Italian writers, Dino Campana (Stefano Accorsi) and Sibilla Aleramo (Laura Morante). Sibilla rejected victimhood when she left her violent husband who raped her and whom she was forced to marry when pregnant at the age of sixteen. An early feminist icon, she published poetry and books and lived a life of sexual freedom. Sibilla is represented as unrestrained and excessive in her desire for love and self-expression. Dino is mentally unstable, and is eventually committed to an asylum. The desire for control has led to his withdrawing to a remote provincial area in order to write and Sibilla's demanding intensity is matched by his own, and escalating violence towards her. The graphic violence of his beating of Sibilla is the performative counterpart of the excess of the wild landscapes through which they walk, connoting the dysfunctional nature of their relationship.

Children

Representations of children are important in Italian cinema either as a commentary on the battle of the sexes, as symbols of the possibility of national regeneration as in neorealist cinema, or as a reminder of what is at stake for the national family (Landy 2000: 234). Thus the accusing stares of the child, Pricò, in *I bambini ci guardano* (*The Children Are Watching Us*, Vittorio De Sica, 1942) condemn his mother's actions in breaking the family and preferring her lover. Child figures are rarely sexualized, their sexual neutrality investing them with the ability to comment, implicitly or explicitly, on the state of their world. Neorealist films are full of children. Bruno's comforting of his father after his humiliatingly failed attempt to steal a bicycle indicates the power of actual or metaphorical family solidarity in *Ladri di biciclette* (*Bicycle Thieves*, Vittorio de Sica, 1948). So too does the routing of Ricci by the mob of neighbours and the mother of the only other son we see, the thief from the Via del Panico. Loyalty to the metaphorical family by the two

Figure 7.5
The ideal world of innocent children. *Io non ho paura* (Gabriele Salvatores, 2003).

boys in *Sciuscià* (*Shoeshine*, Vittorio De Sica, 1946), and by the street urchin, Pasquale, in the Neapolitan episode of *Paisà* (*Paisan*, Roberto Rossellini, 1946) allow ideological connections to be made between the actual family and its power relationship to society in showing the consequences of the breakdown of the conventional couple.

Although eleven-year-old Rosetta (Valentina Scalici) has been prostituted by her mother in *Il ladro di bambini* (*The Stolen Children*, Gianni Amelio, 1992), Amelio is careful not to sexualize the character. Millicent Marcus's (2002: 154–77) subtle analysis of the interplay of glances between the children and the carabiniere, Antonio (Enrico lo Verso) identifies a process of healthy parenting, teaching how to give support to each other and achieve a positive self-image. Nine-year-old Michele's (Giuseppe Cristiano) observation of adults uncovers other realities in Gabriele Salvatores' *Io non ho paura* (*I'm Not Scared*, 2003). The opening shots of the black crow poised over the dark hole in the sunlit cornfield presages Michele's discovery of the boy hidden in a dark pit outside a ruined farmhouse, and the dark side of the adults in his life. He sees the vanity of his father who is tempted by the financial rewards of kidnapping, and the powerlessness of his mother, who will not intervene. In the material deprivation of the home, there is a suggestion that the unequal relationship of the couple is mirrored by that of the south and north of Italy.

Knowledge, Power and Women's Worlds

Male characters who observe and investigate their surroundings provide another interesting inflection of the power/powerlessness equation. Male figures in this template are seen observing and analysing a context; point of view shots, cued by gaze direction proliferate. If knowledge is power, then the desire to know motivates the middle-class, educated male characters, seeking to gain access to knowledge. The investigating characters in these films seem to indicate, by their performance and by the areas in which they seek knowledge, that other, perhaps equally valid, social relationships exist.

The far-reaching changes in the position of women in Italy after 1968 and the increased numbers of articulate, well-educated women and the women's movement had cultural effects in mainstream as well as sub-cultural areas of publishing and the media, which have made monolithic depictions of power structures more problematic. As Lumley (1990: 119) has suggested, the most coherent attempts to 'criticise the dominant institutions and "ways of life", and to propose alternatives have come from counter-cultures in the last twenty years'. Significant of the shift in emphasis is that peasants, and especially women, act as 'gateways' to an understanding of the magical, the irrational, and the emotional side of the psyche, elements not assigned value in traditional, masculine, culture. In *Cristo si è fermato a Eboli* (*Christ Stopped at Eboli*, Francesco Rosi, 1979), Carlo Levi (Gian Maria Volonté) is sent into internal exile in a remote rural area by the fascist government but uses his imprisonment, and his earthy servant, Giulia (Irene Papas), to gain knowledge of peasant society. Marta in *Tre fratelli* (*Three Brothers*, Francesco Rosi, 1981) functions as a bridge between her warring parents, between north and south, the ancient lore of the rural world represented by her grandfather, and the urban world that has lost contact with its roots.

The Italian dramatic tradition of the ensemble film, such as Monicelli's *Speriamo che sia femmina* (*Let's Hope It's a Girl*, 1986), in which many characters interact, is a healthy alternative to the searching male protagonist, while still giving opportunities to explore a social situation. Alternative families reflect the fact that Italy has one of the lowest birthrates in Europe and the large extended family, so often supported by women's sacrifices, has given way to more flexible and unconventional networks. Moreover, the stress on working relationships (which is coded as a feminine skill), rather than power conflicts, mirror the attributes perceived as necessary for success in post-industrial society. Ferzan Ozpetek's films all concern the search for happiness and fulfilment of a range of diverse characters, bound together for mutual support. The protagonist (Alessandro Gassman) of *Il bagno turco – Hamman* (*Hamman: The*

Figure 7.6

The narrative device of the child who observes, without understanding, the adult world of her parents (Marco Baliani and Sandra Ceccarelli) and grandmother (Virna Lisi). *Il più bel giorno della mia vita* (Cristina Comencini, 2002).

Turkish Bath, 1997) discovers community, a purpose in opposing the greed of developers, and a new love in Istanbul, through his ability to connect with other people which has been suppressed in Italy. In *Harem suare* (1999) the occupants of the Sultan's harem escape the iron control of their bodies through intellectual and physical flight. Telling stories, dangerous love affairs and different sexualities allow them to create communities and escape the rule that would have them only relate to their master. *Le fate ignoranti* (*Ignorant Fairies*, 2001) counterposes the inward-looking life of widow Antonia (Margherita Buy) to that of Michele (Stefano Accorsi), her husband's gay lover. Her involvement with Michele's life and friends exposes her to a more pluralistic and emotionally interesting lifestyle. Giovanna's (Giovanna Mezzogiorno) involvement with the elderly man found on the Ponte Sisto (Massimo Girotti) and her neighbour Lorenzo (Raoul Bova) in *La finestra di fronte* (*Facing Window*, 2003) opens up new relationships and new skills as she sublimates her desires in the production of fantastic cakes.

Cristina Comencini's films are also concerned with the transformative power of relationships, rather than individual power struggles. Like Ozpetek's *Le fate ignoranti*, *Il più bel giorno della mia vita* (*The Best Day of My Life*, 2002) is typical in exploring the attitudes of women towards themselves, their sexuality and their families.

The widowed mother, Irene (Virna Lisi), comes to some understanding of her daughter Rita's (Sandra Ceccarelli) obsession with a new man when she catches some soft porn films on her television and realizes what she missed in the perfunctory lovemaking of her late husband. Her widowed daughter, Sara's (Margherita Buy) emotional isolation is pierced by the wisdom of her teenage son, and by the man she 'meets' via her mobile phone. The male lover of Irene's son, Claudio (Luigi lo Cascio) insinuates himself into the family space, inaugurating a new phase of acceptance of his homosexuality. Like *Matrimoni* (*Marriages*, 1998) Cristina Comencini's films share with soap opera a more fluid and contemporary display of the myriad ways of being a woman or man in contemporary Italian society. Soap opera, the socially sanctioned form of contemporary melodrama, rehearses responses to social change, resisting the closure of fixed representations.

Conclusion

Italian cinema has been described as obsessed with the concerns of men and marginalizing the female, yet Paolo Pillitteri (1992: 100) claims that women have been the true centres of Italian comedy since the 1950s. The films discussed here are but a fraction of the examples of Italian cinema's preoccupation with gender power and sexual relationships. The tensions of reconciling traditional patriarchal structures and values and the moral power of the mother in Italian culture with new roles for men and women are visible in countless social-crisis films. Films since the mid-1950s explore, directly or indirectly, the trauma represented by any threat of loss of patriarchal control. An interest in alternatives to the patriarchal family can be seen in films in which social fragmentation into groupings for the mutual support of members is not marked by coercion. Whereas there are large number of films set in male working arenas, Italian cinema tends to place its female characters predominantly in the domestic sphere, representing the lack of access to knowledge through which male dominance has been maintained (Spain 1992: 197). As this chapter has hinted, in the ebb and flow of these battles over acceptable gender roles, excessive elements are often expressed visually and performatively through spatial configurations. The next chapter will explore further visual style and the use of space.

8

Visual Style and the Use of Cinematic Space

The study of filmic space is especially fruitful in the case of Italian cinema as it raises questions of class and gender representations, authorial intent, artistic conventions, technology and meaning construction. As Marcia Landy (1998) has illustrated, the growth of cinema in the last century provided another medium through which 'common sense' assumptions about the nature of society could be ordered, rehearsed and modified through narratives and representations that drew on earlier examples and traditions, and proposed new ones. Screen narratives, characters and actions become part of the repertoire of everyday references used in social contact. Film was therefore only one way in which a hegemony – that is, generally accepted notions of how different sectors of society were supposed to act – was established. The construction of any cinematic world on the screen is therefore ideological, because it represents assumptions about the nature of that world – for example, who should exercise power, and how – within it. The complex interaction between the process of film-making, which uses and appropriates fragments of geographic sites (actual or constructed), and the activity of viewing, in which the viewer 'reads' and consumes onscreen space as bodies move through it prompts Giuliana Bruno (2002: 15–16) to argue that the emotion of viewing space requires a 'spatio-corporeal' approach to analysing cinema. She defines this as a 'haptic' approach, which

means 'able to come into contact with.' As a function of
the skin ... the haptic ... constitutes the reciprocal con*tact*
between us and the environment... But the haptic is also
related to kinesthesis, the ability of our bodies to sense their
own movement in space. (Bruno 2002: 6)

The approach of analysing the construction of space, and movement
within space, as well as the direction of character or camera point
of view is particularly appropriate in the case of Italian cinema's
deployment of spectacular images and the mobile camera.

Italy has a history of hundreds of years of artistic endeavour.
Any street or church or public building in the country will provide
familiar solutions to problems of visual communication, and models
for meaning production that can be applied to another visual art,
film. This chapter will therefore explore some of the stylistic tropes of
Italian cinema and the use of the potential of *mise en scène* and cinematography to model cinematic space. Cinematic space can function
as a correlative of the dramas enacted within it by suggesting similar
or contrary meanings. The former strategy is that of homology,
whereby meanings are suggested in different forms (dialogue can
make a statement, which is then illustrated visually), reinforcing an
impression of the reality of the story world. The latter strategy is that
of irony, whereby there is a mismatch. Space can become spectacle,
'a signifier of the film's subject, a metaphor for the state of mind of
the protagonist' (Aitken and Zonn 1994: 17). As previous chapters
have explored, Italian cinema's constant engagement with history,
identity, its constant recourse to realist conventions to anchor the
film's diegetic world firmly to the spaces of contemporary Italy, and
the equally pervasive use of visual spectacle and excess, signal that
economic, political, social and gender power relations are still in a
state of traumatic flux.

Of the many realist conventions aiming to create authenticity
of place, André Bazin (1967: 39) considered the European style of
film-making with the mobile camera moving through space, rather
than American-style continuity editing, to be superior because of its
temporal realism. The long take's time coincided with the scene's
action. The European long take is, however, much more complex in its
construction, and is also used primarily for its expressive possibilities
(Henderson 1976: 316). Contemporary Italian film-makers move
freely between the fast editing of American cinema and the mobile
camera of the European style. Sound is also important, being used
to model space in the sense that noises and voices reverberating off
their surroundings indicate volume. As the elderly Donato Giuranna
(Charles Vanel) gets off the bus and walks to the post office to send
telegrams to his three sons to tell them their mother is dead in *Tre
fratelli* (*Three Brothers*, Francesco Rosi, 1981), the calls of jackdaws
echo off the walls of buildings surrounding the piazza. The sound,

and the tracking shot following Giuranna's walk, indicates that this is a large and empty space, economically adding another detail to the accumulated sense of southern depopulation. A detailed study of how music invests space with meaning is beyond the scope of this chapter but the slightly oriental trills of Luis Enrique Bacalov's music in *Una storia semplice* (*A Simple Story*, Emidio Greco, 1991) hint that there may be a Mafia dimension to the supposed suicide being investigated by a Sicilian carabiniere.

The social struggles identified in earlier chapters are played out in in cinematic spaces that make disruption visible. Harvey (1990: 239) suggests that disruption is a feature of postmodern, late capitalist societies, betraying an 'instability in the spatial and temporal bases for the reproduction of the social order'. We will return to the idea of disruption which, as previous chapters have touched on, is a key to understanding Italian cinema of the last half of the twentieth century, and was particularly important at the crisis point in the 1970s when film was dislodged from its primary role in the construction of representations of the social world by the explosion of television, and from the 1990s onwards by political and global developments.

The Pictorial Heritage

The shape and appearance of public spaces in cities and towns are profoundly emblematic of ideas of community, society and civiliza-tion which organized the lives of those who used them. The *mise en scène* of Italian films exploits the possibilities of environment and artistic heritage. John White's (1987) analyses of architectural structures in hundreds of paintings and frescoes from antiquity to the Renaissance in Italy show that artists delighted in the artistic possibilities of the recreation of space, but then had difficulties in harmonizing the depiction of realistic space with the demands of the visual plane of the story. Strongly stressed orthogonals lead the eye into Renaissance compositions, creating a strong impression of spatial depth. White (1987: 158) suggests that one of the techniques developed to arrest the apparent movement through the surface into depth was asymmetry, another the repetition of diagonals because both are 'more likely to destroy the spontaneous and complete acceptance of illusion'. Similarly, diagonal cinematic compositions can therefore simultaneously indicate the presence of a real world constituted in deep space – and through the movement of the eye to the vanishing point, of the presence of offscreen space – and at the same time, put a brake on the realism effect. Cinema can draw on additional, subtle brakes on realism, such as figure movement and camera movement. In their walk across Rome in *Ladri di biciclette*, for example, Antonio and his son, Bruno, are at one point situated in a street, in which their movement forwards towards the camera is at odds with the strongly diagonal movement of the eye, pedestrians and vehicles away from camera. The emotional effect is to convey the difficulty of their task. Manipulation of the perspectival systems is, therefore, one way of controlling both the impression of realism and the attention of the spectator.

The use of intense light contrasts, that is, *chiaroscuro*, is a feature particularly of Italian Baroque painting, which combined the use of illusionistic detail (such as the dirty feet of the drowned Madonna in Caravaggio's *The Death of the Virgin*, 1605–6, Louvre), with figural construction designed to lead the eye to significant elements and enhance the dramatic and emotional impact. The development of still photography and electric light encouraged early twentieth-century Italian artists to experiment again with the depiction of light in order to express the modern world. Strong shadows on faces and buildings are features of the paintings of the Futurist artists Umberto Boccioni, Gino Severini, Giacomo Balla and Mario Sironi, and the metaphysical paintings of Giorgio De Chirico. Sironi's paintings of the late teens and 1920s are particularly interesting for their stark depiction of city peripheries – factories, railway lines, stark modern buildings – and for his use of insistent diagonal compositions to express feelings of solitude and urban alienation.

In the context of thinking about the interaction of social processes and cultural texts, the rich visual heritage of Italy must be kept in mind as part of Italian film-makers' use, and enjoyment of the possibilities of complexity of visual and kinetic composition.

Dramas of Space and Dramas within Space

Dramatic visual compositions in Italian cinema find their counterpart in the use of melodrama in the sense of heightened and hyperbolic drama where personal issues are made to stand for social uncertainty and the incapacity to resolve some of the conflicts of the fraught modern world. Peter Brooks' (1976: 13–22) contention that melodrama comes into being 'in a world where the traditional imperatives of truth and ethics have been violently thrown into question, yet where the promulgation of truth and ethics, their instauration as a way of life, is of immediate, daily, political concern' offers an immediate insight into the usefulness of this form for a mainstream cinema which seeks to engage with political and social reality. Brooks (1976: 2) describes the narrator figure of melodrama as 'pressuring the surface of reality in order to make it yield the full, true terms of his story', which both accords with the display of doubts and the use of the investigative form in *film noir*, and with the use of spectacular *mise en scène*. Italian social and political films have frequent recourse to the codes and conventions of melodrama, within the framework of realism, because of the need to symbolize and make references to an actual world, and an emotional response is necessary in order that the audience is fully persuaded of the truth of the world depicted. Discontent with the present, in the form of excavation of the past, through the interplay of communicativeness and ambiguity, evocations of symbolic spaces where ritualized action takes place, the use of space to communicate 'third meanings' in the texts (Barthes 1970), and visual excess are all indications of attempts to fix a meaning that remains fluid and resists closure. The idea of film's 'sensory spatiality' being a 'haptic emotive terrain' (Bruno 2002: 16) invests films' *mise en scène* with both richness and ambiguity. The drive towards the establishment of a context represents a forceful assertion of time, of history, of complexity working against the tendency, particularly in recent mass culture, to render everything as present and without roots.

Italian Design Traditions

The impression of reality described above masks a film's production of the clues as to how we are to read it, that is, the work of the creative team of director, set designer, director of photography, costume designer, editor. Keith Reader (2000: 37) points to the lack of any serious consideration of 'how the rôle of set designer as part-auteur of a film might be articulated or conceptualised' and suggests that notions of realism and space might provide ways in which to theorize it in future. Bruno, however, reminds us that the work of cinematic scenography is to construct a *habitus* in which clothes, architecture, interiors, cosmetics, the gestures and morphology of bodies 'define our way of living space' (Bruno 2002: 322). Scenographic space is the construction of a team whose work bears the imprint of their own societal structures, practices and ideologies. Francesco Rosi, for example, described working on the southern Italian square where the detective interrogates the tramp (*Cadaveri eccellenti*, 1975) to cover up the green of the area around the monument in order not to disturb the 'rarefied atmosphere of a De Chirico painting'.[1] History films regularly cover up signs of the modern city, for example when the partisans enter Padua in Daniele Luchetti's *I piccoli maestri* (*The Little Teachers*, 1998) (Canova 2000: 74–5). Lina Nerli Taviani describes washing the costumes for *Kaos* (Paolo and Vittorio Taviani, 1984), and laying them out in the sun for a month in order to achieve a worn and bleached look (Masi 1990: 88). In this way, clothing became an indicator of geography, of the effects of the hot sun and the economic deprivation of Sicily.

Creative teams are put together on the basis of particular expertise and professional links. Costume designers, for example, when talking about their careers, might mention their links to Piero

Gherardi (who won Oscars for his designs for Fellini) or Piero Tosi (who won prizes for his work for Visconti). As Jill Forbes (1997: 21) observed, designers are generally conservative but professional practices depend on the fresh approach of outsiders to disturb the tendency towards stereotyping. As Chapter 1 has shown, Italian film production has become polarized between big-budget, international production, and low- to mid-budget film-making, which still maintains some of the earlier craft ethos. For every designer such as Andrea Crisanti, who could command the construction of the main square of a Colombian town (in Rosi's *Cronaca di una morte annunciata* (*Chronicle of a Death Foretold*, 1987) or a Sicilian fort (in his *Dimenticare Palermo* (*To Forget Palermo*, 1990), there are others who reuse existing studio sets, or costumes. Lina Nerli Taviani, for example, describes how Italian designer costumes end up in the wardrobes of actors after the end of filming, but that historical costumes survive and have a long career from film to film (Masi 1990: 86). Since most Italian cinema is 'poor cinema' in that the collective creative talents far exceed the budgets, the recycling of old clothing from market stalls is inscribed in an aspect of professional practice that privileges the impression of realism. Besides keeping costume budgets low, the use and reuse of designs from film to film gives the impression of quality, often in excess of any individual budget, and a distinctive and characteristic look to Italian cinema. The other words which recur in describing the work of set and costume designers are 'stylization' and 'grotesque', for example in the work of Enrico Job for his wife, Lina Wertmüller (Masi 1990: 47). The interplay of the grotesque, violence and the excessive with order and the modern are aspects which we will explore next in how one sector of Italian cinema attempts to assert the primacy of masculine concerns.

Spaces of Masculine Action

The *mise en scène* of institutional space in exterior and interior sets and locations, and how figures act and exercise power within those spaces make social relationships visible. The very European use of the mobile camera and intra-sequence long take is also used as a tool to link diegetic events firmly to the world of contemporary Italy. Italy is exceptionally rich architecturally so that the range of architectural paradigms chosen as expressive of institutional practices or values is particularly significant. Francesco Maselli's *Il sospetto* (*Suspicion*, 1975), set between Paris and Turin, provides one paradigm in its use of classical architecture. The protagonist, Emilio (Gian Maria Volonté), is an expatriate communist militant who is sent to Turin in 1934 in order to identify a spy. The film repeatedly makes use of long shots of classical pedimented windows, arches in cloister-like galleries and high angle long shots in grey, black and muted tones. The overall impression is of impenetrability. The protagonist constantly looks around, monitoring his environment, trying to penetrate his surroundings to find information. He fails in his quest, becoming one of the sacrificial activists of the Communist Party when he is arrested and interrogated by OVRA, the fascist Security Police. The interrogator reveals that Emilio was himself 'penetrated', brainwashed and planted as a spy so that he would identify communist contacts in Turin. The *mise en scène* thus connects the two metaregimes of communism and fascism in their denial of the importance of the freedom of the individual. This architectural paradigm is re-evoked in *Così ridevano* (*The Way We Laughed*, Gianni Amelio, 1998) in which the ordered proportions of the Piazza San Carlo in Turin contrast to ragged groups of southern immigrants.

Although classical architecture provides a recurring metaphor for an ordered, stable, coercive system of values, by far the most commonly evoked architectural style in 1970s conspiracy thrillers is that of the 1960s. *Indagine su un cittadino al di sopra di ogni sospetto* (*Investigation of a Citizen Above Suspicion*, Elio Petri, 1970) is one of the most interesting films of the 1970s *giallo politico*, and is almost entirely set in Rome, but chooses to ignore the better known or parliamentary monuments of the city, preferring instead long shots of grey, concrete or stone-faced modernist office blocks in the 1960s 'brutalist' style. Buildings are differentiated from one another by their institutional names above the main doors, but exteriors are uncommunicative of their function and it is movement by the protagonist, a high-ranking policeman, il Dottore (Gian Maria Volonté), into the interiors that conveys information. In this film we know from the very beginning that the policeman has murdered his mistress on the day of his promotion from Head of the Homicide section to Head of the Political section of the police force. The film's investigates the nature of the institution through the actions of this emblematic character, and is a metaphysical exploration of the nature of justice and power. The forceful, violent gestures and speech of il Dottore coerce his subordinates so that the kinetic elements add another level of meaning, suggesting how male power provides a model for the activity of political power, and that 'truth' does not necessarily reside in what seems regular, functional and open to explanation.

In *Il caso Mattei* (*The Mattei Affair*, 1972), *Lucky Luciano* (1973), *Cadaveri eccellenti* (*Illustrious Corpses*, 1975) Rosi employs the investigative mode in order to explore the nature of power relationships in Italian society. The disruptions that provoke the investigations are exceptional events, violence or death, which disturb the carefully constructed and maintained impression of normality preferred by those in power. They contain many set pieces of showy and spectacular *mise en scène*, and the foregrounding of architectural space in wide-angle long shots. Grey and uncommunicative modernist architecture and institutional spaces contrast to the excesses (stressed camera angles and strongly diagonal spatial compositions) and decorative aspects of Baroque buildings (Wood 1998: 285). A Baroque visual excess represents the tension between power and order, and revolt and disorder. Internal conflicts are externalized. Omar Calabrese (1992: 25) provides a persuasive explanation of the conflict of visual styles, defining as neo-Baroque the rejection of stability and the presence of turbulence. In this respect the neo-Baroque in Italy is an expression of the postmodern undermining of the grand metanarratives.

Colour texture is used as a thematic correlative in *Il caso Mattei* to suggest a dichotomy between modernity and backwardness (Ryan and Kellner 1988: 68). Two different visual regimes structure the film. Cool colours and the ordered lines of modernist architecture are associated with Enrico Mattei (the Head of ENI, Italy's State Hydrocarbon Corporation), connoting modernity. His stress on order, cleanliness, modern business practices, contrasts with the environment of his opponents, characterized by disorder, or the excessive decoration of the Baroque to represent the backwardness of the 'old' Italy of clientelistic and corrupt business and political practices. This film features large numbers of television monitors within the frame, which play an important part in generating the film's 'reality effect' and illustrating the constructing of hegemony. The professional practice of media institutions tends to construct representations of the famous as powerful individuals, rather than as examples of institutional practices themselves. However, analysis of the workings of the hegemonic process implies that a brake has to be put on the 'reality effect'. Thus, media sequences are invariably marked by excess; one television monitor, one photograph, one journalist is rarely used. Banks of television monitors in darkened rooms, sheaves of photographs that then fade into or dissolve into re-enactments, direct address to camera by journalists and experts, all disturb the illusion of reality. In effect, what is being made visual is the tension between two versions of politics or ideology. Fluidity, ambiguity, doubts, excess expressed visually or in monstrous characters or in the performance of violence, are techniques used by political film-makers to visualize the tension between one system which aims to present itself as simple, natural and uncontrovertible, and another which seeks to discredit it and reveal its inner workings and true nature. In effect, Italian political thrillers are male melodramas rehearsing shifting power relationships in Italian society, cloaking themselves in the *giallo* format in order to reach the mass audience, and using *noir* conventions to suggest disfunctional elements in Italian life.

A feature of all these films is the striking visual beauty of representations of the interiors and exteriors of buildings. The framing of the
buildings and the lens used emphasize their monumentality, volumes
and architectural planes. Thus, in *Cadaveri eccellenti*, shafts of light
illuminate Judge Varga (Charles Vanel) as he walks towards camera
in the crypt of the Baroque church, so that he appears to be walking
through progressively larger frames, a visual representation of *mise
en abîme* and the layering of versions of the truth. Varga's murder is
the disruption that starts the investigation, whose ramifications are
immediately indicated in the funeral sequence. The eulogy and the
representation of the powerful hierarchies (legal and illegal) massed
within the enormous Baroque cathedral make links to other men
of power who commissioned such showy and flamboyant art to
celebrate the power of the Church.

Architectural shots have different functions within the narrative
of Rosi's films. In one way they form part of the cultural or reference
code of the film and relate to the audience's historical and artistic
knowledge of Italy. In another way, Rosi's intention is to liberate
the text from being too narrowly realist through this access to the
poetic and excessive possibilities of film (Ciment 1976: 168–9). What
Rosi calls a metaphysical dimension, and elsewhere heightened
realism, has more in common with early twentieth-century *pittura
metafisica*.[2] In tracing the origins of De Chirico's metaphysical
painting, Robert Hughes (1991: 215) defines it as 'a question of
mood, the sense of a reality drenched in human emotion, almost
pulpy with memory'. These instances of heightened reality, linked
to architectural space, function as memory signs, 'where the link
between past, present and future is expressed in the materiality of
objects (Rowlands 1997: 9). Calabrese (1992: 194) suggests that,
in postmodern, neo-Baroque works, order and disorder, classical
and Baroque, coexist as signifying systems. In these thrillers, there is
an oscillation between simplicity and complexity as the disruptions
disturb the equilibrium, the simple explanation. We move towards
understanding in small steps, hypotactically, until the big picture is
visible.

One of the most powerful tropes, for making the big picture
visible, and one that occurs centrally in Rosi's *Cadaveri eccellenti*
and Petri's *Indagine su un cittadino al di sopra di ogni sospetto* is
that of the panopticon. Foucault (1997: 206–7) writes about prisons
being designed so that the prison population (the prison heterotopia)
can be under surveillance at every moment. In these two films we
have visual representations of the panopticon suggesting a hidden
and all-powerful control of society.

Rosi's panopticon is the laboratory of the head of the political
police, to which the honest detective, Rogas (Lino Ventura) is
assigned. Rogas's looks and questioning glances motivate the
camera's illustration of how the panopticon works. The scale of

Figure 8.1
The panopticon. *Cadaveri eccellenti* (Francesco Rosi, 1976).

surveillance is indicated via repetition of television screens and the burble of tape recordings, evoking other diegetic spaces. In Petri's film, the political police also operate a panopticon, with banks of tape recorders, conducting a surveillance of the unwitting citizens of Rome. The figure of the panopticon represents the intrusion into the text of the ultimate, metadiscursive, level of meaning, making plain how power is exercised, and the ideology of those who use it.

Politics and Space in Contemporary Italian Films

The 1980s provided further events to persuade Italian writers, film-makers, journalists and critics that they were living in a *film noir*. Prime Minister Aldo Moro was kidnapped and murdered by the Red Brigades in 1978 at a time when he was seeking closer relations between Christian Democrats and communists. Ginsborg (2001) describes how the webs of corruption gradually unravelled, culminating in the arrests of a whole raft of the political and business classes in 1992–3. Investigation of the disgraced banker, Michele Sindona in March 1981 revealed the membership of the P2 masonic lodge, which included officers of the secret services, heads of the Carabinieri and Guardia di Finanza, the armed services, police, bankers, businessmen and politicians. Subsequently, the banker Roberto Calvi was found hanging under Blackfriars Bridge in London. Investigations of murders during the 'strategy of tension' years uncovered the existence of a hidden armed network called 'Gladio', part of the Italian secret services and linked to the CIA. Italian politicians were widely considered to be corrupt so that the magistrates investigating the *tangentopoli* scandals and links between mafia and politicians had wide support. A whole new institutional class, that of the magistrature, became available for hero roles.

Films of the late 1990s and early 2000s that revisit this period use the same spatial paradigms as films of the 1970s to indicate oppositions, but with a subtle difference. Whereas the political films of the 1970s could not name names, they were concerned to make absolutely clear the opposition between a traditional, clientelistic and undemocratic exercise of power, and the needs of the modern State. The spate of films that rework that historical period are not so much concerned to promote a Left-wing version of events, although they usually do, as to indicate that the problem (corruption or criminality) which is being investigated is to be assigned to traditional forms of masculinity which are at odds with those necessary for success in the world of the new millennium. The diegetic worlds of the films of the 1990s and 2000s therefore include representations of domestic *milieux*, feminized spaces within which the protagonists act with confidence and competence. Because this figure who performs competently in the masculine world of investigation, and the feminine, domestic world recurs so frequently, there is more than a suggestion that the traditional fragmentation of male endeavour into specialized activities is to be resisted (Lefebvre 1991). Doreen Massey (1996) raises the possibility of the eastern, holistic and participatory approach to knowledge as potentially more progressive, and certainly the moral authority of these judicial investigator figures in Italian cinema derives from the fact that their competence in the spheres of both reason and emotion enables them to represent the national as well as the local community.

I banchieri di Dio (*God's Bankers*, Giuseppe Ferrara, 2002) has an enormously complex amount of information to give in its exploration of the ramifications of Roberto Calvi's direction of the Banco Ambrosiano, his relationship with Archbishop Marcinkus, president of the Vatican bank, with the Catholic Church, with Italian criminal elements, and his mysterious death. Ferrara uses black and white flashbacks to repeat information about the identity of key players, but also uses colour codings in very interesting ways. The conventions of *film noir* and the *giallo*, high contrast lighting, shadows, and intrusive yellow tones, are used to indicate the presence of mysteries and doubts about the official version of events. Ferrara also uses saturated red colour to indicate the presence of events whose origin lies in the Vatican or Christian Democrat party. The scarlet skull cap and sashes of Marcinkus (Rutger Hauer) rhyme with the scarlet carpets of the Vatican interiors and the carpet of the seedy London hotel in which Calvi (Omero Antonutti) spends his last days. The presence of scarlet in the bank's boardroom signals corrupt links, and the clothing of girls and a boy at a party indicate the source of instructions to give sexual favours. After the court appearance, which establishes a large hole in the bank's finances, Calvi and Party Secretary, Francesco Pazienza (Alessandro Gassman), are depicted descending an extremely ornate, scarlet-carpeted staircase,

Figure 8.2
Spatial representation
of the impossibility of
knowing the truth. *I
banchieri di dio* (Giuseppe
Ferrara, 2002).

whose white balustrades are shot to give the impression of a circular Escher puzzle.

The traditional spaces in which male power is exercised are permeated with the violence that indicates the retrograde nature of this behaviour in the context of modern society.

Men Wandering to New Spaces

Earlier chapters have discussed some of the outward manifestations of the seismic social changes in Italy from the 1940s onwards. Neorealist films, in particular, feature characters moving across space in order to convey information on hitherto ignored social groups. In Antonio's hunt for the bicycle across Rome, *Ladri di biciclette* often fills the frame with uncomprehending and uncaring witnesses to Antonio's journey. In moving towards its young protagonist's suicide, tracking shots in *Germania anno* zero (*Germany Year Zero*, Roberto Rossellini, 1948) journey through desolate and ruined cityscapes, whose other occupants are similarly uncaring, expressing the isolation of the individual and the breakdown of the sense of community. In Rossellini's *Paisà* (1947), individual episodes enact events in archetypically representative areas of Italy, while embedding commentary upon those events. In the Neapolitan episode, the Black soldier comes to consciousness of the social deprivation of his child guide by journeying into the space that he calls home, the cave occupied by hundreds of people. The accumulation of apparently random details of other lives and actions (such as the man surveying events from his roof top) presents a haptic mosaic of community of purpose against the enemy. The *mise en scène* of neorealist films forces the viewer to participate emotionally in the discovery of truths by following the movement of characters within space.

Moving from a very stratified society in which the urban pro-letariat, the provincial bourgeoisie and rural inhabitants had almost insurmountable obstacles to moving out of their class of origin, Italian males had to construct a new *habitus*, in which they could define themselves in opposition to other social groupings around them. Cinematic space is also a forum for this process. The grotesque characters played by Alberto Sordi embodied the position of the lower middle class, shedding principles in the struggle for survival, faced with the ambitions of the working class and southerners. His figure is constantly active, moving through and seeking to dominate space, his own limited education putting him one step ahead (for the moment) of his lower-class competitors. In Fellini's *I vitelloni* (1953), Sordi's character acts with confidence in his environment, but Fellini uses the excesses (hyperactivity, mugging to camera) of his performance to show that his unadventurous and infantile nature is not conducive to success.

Marcello Mastroianni's characters perform the same function for the middle classes. Far from the 'Latin Lover' stereotypes, his roles in *La dolce vita* (1960) and *8½* (1963) as a journalist and film-maker (both representative of new additions to the *habitus*) in fact enact incompetence. He literally errs as he wanders (in Italian, *errare*) through the city-centre streets and outskirts of Rome. His movements through space signify him as unsuccessful in his relationships with women (a suicidal fiancée is left crying in a stark, modern corridor which is the opposite of a homely, family space), and, in his acquired cynicism, to have left religious certainty behind him (from his helicopter carrying the Christ statue, he and the pilot flirt with the bikini-clad girls below). He projects his own desires onto the figure of the star (Anita Ekberg) as he traverses the dark spaces of Rome, and mis-reads the actions of his mentor (Alain Cuny), interpreting Steiner's thunderous renditions on the organ as superlative creativity whereas it presages traumatic suicide and murder. Fashion shoots in the modernist exteriors of Mussolini's EUR area of Rome comment both on Mussolini's construction of modernity and on the spurious nature of the construction of a modern self-image by the media industries.

After the orgy scene in *la dolce vita*, Marcello ends up on the beach outside Ostia, where a sea monster has washed up. Anec-dotally, it was suggested that the monster represented the Montesi scandal (Pinkus 2003: 21). Wilma Montesi was found dead on a beach in the area and, although reconstructions of events and witness testimonies implicated upper-class parties, sex and drugs in her death, no one has ever been brought to account for her death. In effect, Marcello's presence on the beach, and the fish, represent the evolution of a modern masculinity which, in its financial reliance on the *habitus* it has conquered (its knowledges of how to act in a variety of social situations, its access to the large spaces of middle-class dwellings, to designer clothes, fashionable hairstyles, leisure pursuits), has deliberately lost contact with ethical issues. Marcello in *La dolce vita* is essentially an observer, rather than an initiator, of action, reinforced by the picaresque character of Fellini's narrative construction. Each scenographic space through which the protagonist wanders provokes a new reflection on the grotesque re-ordering of human experience. The children who claim to have witnessed a manifestation of the madonna, for example, are depicted in a bare wasteland, surrounded by crowds, scattered with useless scaffolding structures, suggesting failing attempts to *construct* modern faith.

Road Movies of the Psyche

By the 1970s other visualizations of appropriate social action are being rehearsed, in which intelligent and aware, but powerless, male individuals watch events and attempt to order experience to their advantage. Liliana Cavani's interest in the figure of Saint Francis is an example of attempts to render male supremacy as needing to evolve. In *Francesco* (1989), the saint (Mickey Rourke) gives up his upper middle-class inheritance and ambitions for poverty and a more holistic view of the universe. The spaces within which he chooses to act become increasingly wild, dark and painful, acting as metaphors of the trauma of the loss of male control, and the potential damage of unregulated exploitation of the environment. Pain and trauma are, however, transcended by the images of Saint Clare (Helena Bonham Carter) and Francesco's disciples commenting on their spiritual journey within the flapping linen blinds of the tent on the hillside.

The wanderings of Saint Francis through the Italian landscape could be called a road movie of the soul. Road movies, and all sorts of journeys, occur frequently in Italian cinema, either as the central narrative trajectory, or alluded to as part of the experience of characters. Mirco Melanco's study of the journey theme identifies three motivations; the opportunity the journey creates for showing similarities and differences within contemporary constructions of the notion of Italy; to work through meanings around leaving home; and, through study of how characters behave in these spatial pellegrinations, to develop a sense of Italian national identity (Melanco 1996: 217). The importance of the road theme undoubtedly derives from the Italian experience of internal and external diaspora. Films whose central premise is the journey often use the crossing of disparate geographies to construct a sense of Italy as a set of differences bound together in a positive way by common concerns. More often, journeys are alluded to from a position of stasis. Visconti's *Rocco e i suoi fratelli* (*Rocco and his Brothers*,

1960) starts from the end of the journey, as the Parondi family reach Milan, where the cultural 'baggage' which they have brought with them will affect the new home they have to construct. The factory workers of Antonioni's *Il deserto rosso* (*The Red Desert*, 1964) discuss the possibility of emigration to South America in a closed room covered with maps. In their questions about family arrangements, they reveal a more grounded sense of what 'home' is made of than does Giuliana (Monica Vitti), represented as psychically adrift in her modernist house and polluted surroundings. The elderly men whose homesickness, and Mussolini's call, have drawn back to the remote rural town in Rosi's *Cristo si è fermato a Eboli* (*Christ Stopped at Eboli*, 1979) are depicted in the closed spaces of the bar or barber's shop as they reminisce about America. The travels, which have come round full circle, emphasize the static nature of southern society, from which they fled in the first place.

The interplay of stasis and movement is interesting in Cristina Comencini's *La fine è nota* (*The End is Known*, 1993). The magistrate leaves home to investigate the identity of the man who fell from his window. By the end of the film the magistrate has discovered not only the reality of southern poverty and underdevelopment, but also the falseness of his relationship with his wife. His home has featured in a glossy style magazine of interior design. His beautiful, immaculate, designer-clad wife (Valerie Kaprisky) reigns over the stylish and ordered interior. The clues to the sham of this image of home lie in the labyrinthine coils of the *art deco* banisters of the staircase, the lighting that assumes sulphurous yellow tones at night, and the small, spiky metal statuette, which seems out of place in the apartment's perfection. The journey links two targets, suggesting that the selfishness and materialism of one is implicated in the reduced circumstances of the other.

In *La mia generazione* (*My Generation*, Wilma Labate, 1996) a carabiniere captain's (Silvio Orlando) ostensible purpose is to persuade Red Brigades prisoner, Braccio (Claudio Amendola) to collaborate with the authorities, but their journey across Italy reveals ugly, desolate urban peripheries, truck stops and rubbish-strewn no man's lands, lack of care for the 'homeland' rhyming with Braccio's lack of care in his relationship with Giulia (Francesca Neri). The ugliness of the liminal spaces of urban Italy recurs in the 1990s in films too numerous to mention. Metal fences, too-narrow pavements, vandalized bus stops the length of the peninsular occur in *Il ladro di bambini* (*The Stolen Children*, Gianni Amelio, 1992), apt clothings for the hostile world in which the children find themselves. The textualizing and exploration of urban peripheries have a political function in Pasolini's films as he depicts worlds outside capitalism and its power structures (Konstantarakos 2000: 112–14).

Rural Landscapes and Identity

Rural landscapes are treated with ambivalence in Italian cinema, particularly those of the south. Attempts to understand and control the southern, rural world have undergone an evolution in representation since the 1960s. The scenario of *Africa a casa*, Africa at home, a Third World area at odds with the developmental ethos of the industrial north, is present in Rosi's *Salvatore Giuliano* (1962), in which the disruptive event initiating the investigation is that of the death of the bandit, Salvatore Giuliano, whose body was discovered in a courtyard in Castelvetrano, Sicily, on 5 July 1950. Juxtaposing re-enactments from different points in Giuliano's life allow the interlacing of Rosi's three main narrative concerns – the establishment of the truth and destruction of myths about Giuliano's career; the establishment of the socio-economic and the affective context which provided the fertile ground for the formation of myths of the bandit; and the representation of the means by which those in power used Giuliano for their own ends. Space and landscape structure a range of contrasts and oppositions at a symbolic level. A voice-off introduces the bandit and his home territory, authoritatively delineating the context in which Giuliano operates, its geography, politics and methods. The *mise en scène* illustrates the soundtrack in a long take, which establishes in long shot the physical environment. Camera movements emphasize points made in the voiceover. The first half of the sequence ends with a visual transfer to the figure of Giuliano, his face obscured by binoculars, thus establishing the metaphor of control. Noise and camera movements then signal transfers to the soldiers who are arriving in Montelepre, and to the villagers who are reacting to their arrival. The accelerated editing rhythm gives the impression of panic, while also delivering further shots of flight and concealment, reinforced by the dark tones and incomplete viewpoints. The second half of the sequence is constructed to illustrate the truth of the statements made in the initial voiceover, that Giuliano's supremacy over the military lies in his control of the mountain heights, by superior weapons and communications and by his hold over the populace, a visual expression of what *omertà* means. The expressions of panic on the part of the villagers and the impassivity of the soldiers, give rise to a symbolic contrast between oppressors and oppressed, power and powerlessness. Throughout the film the oppression of ordinary people is emphasized – by Rome, by the police and *carabinieri* who represent the State, by the bandits and by the Mafia.

The focus of the investigation in Rosi's *Lucky Luciano* (1973) is on how the mafioso achieved and maintained power, and its effects. The film does not choose to investigate the causes of the Mafia phenomenon but, through quite complex organization of the visual and narrative material, suggests the link between poverty, social backwardness and conservative institutions (the Church) and the presence of illegal organizations. The short but effective sequence, for example, where Luciano visits the cemetery of Lercara Friddi in Sicily shows him surrounded by local dignitaries and on familiar terms with the priest. Their conversation is interrupted by the sound of keening, whose source is explained in a beautifully framed, wide-angle long shot. Perspectival lines draw the eye from the group of gangsters and dignitaries in the foreground, to rows of tombs and wailing women, dressed in black. In a succession of medium shots, the camera pans over the tomb inscriptions that testify to lives cut short by the Mafia. As the gangsters leave, a donkey passes the row of their mercedes cars, neatly implicating their wealth in the maintenance of rural poverty, demonstrating how figures endow space with symbolic meaning.

The situation of the south of Italy is also examined in Rosi's *Tre fratelli* (*Three Brothers*, 1981) with the death of a mother providing the disruption which brings the brothers back to the family farmhouse in Apulia. Their presence there for twenty-four hours prior to the funeral allows memories and dreams to be evoked, and an exploration of the lives of representatives of different social realities. The tone of the film is overtly lyrical and emotional, yet the film manages to address issues such as juvenile delinquency, the family, marriage, work, exploitation, pollution, corruption, terrorism, the power of the media, the nature of democracy, greed, humanism, the Third World, rural marginalization, emigration, violent protest, unemployment and sexual relationships. The urban, modern world is a constant presence in a narrative set in the archaic, rural world, so as to suggest that events in both are interlinked. This is achieved by the familiar means of cross-cutting between locations, by flashbacks and dream sequences and, more subtly and interestingly, by the presence of news reports on television screens in rural bars.

Evocation of rural Italy is undoubtedly one of the pleasures generated by films such as Ermanno Olmi's *L'albero degli zoccoli* (*The Tree of Wooden Clogs*, 1978) in which visual beauty is juxtaposed with sequences illustrating the hardship and exploitation of rural life, while alluding to lost skills and a sense of community. In the late 1970s, changes in cultural values, the break-up of the extended family, and women's demands for power-sharing, were reflected in dissatisfaction with the conditions of urban existence. *Cristo si è fermato a Eboli* and *Tre fratelli* are concerned to validate practices and beliefs in rural society, which is evoked metonymically in images that owe as much to the iconography of advertising, tourism and the heritage industry, as to the inheritance of neorealism. Whereas the interiors and exteriors of peasant houses in *Salvatore Giuliano* are framed in long shot in order to suggest the extreme poverty and rigid social divisions of rural Italy, later films display the graphic properties of buildings in long shots of often striking visual beauty.

The wide-angle lens and low-angle shot are used to great effect to display the satisfying volumes and planes of farmhouses, streets, rural churches and houses.

In the 1990s, rural Italy, particularly the south, became demonized in its media representations by association with the corruption revealed by the *tangentopoli* scandals. Current media representations of the south rarely delineate the economic and ideological reasons behind cultural manifestations. One exception is Gabriele Salvatores' *Io non ho paura* (*I'm Not Afraid*, 2003) in which the surroundings and actions of the group of families living in the middle of the countryside convey the sense of how economic poverty impacts on people without educational or work opportunities. There is little evidence that they have a moral framework from church or community, resulting in a certain ethical shortfall and casual brutality towards the boy the adults kidnap. Salvatores introduces shots of birds of prey, owls, ravens, crows into the high-angle long shots of the golden beauty of the cornfields to suggest the dark and predatory side of rural life.

The Female Body and Space

In 1950s cinema, watching figures represent the panoptic surveillance and control of the female protagonists. This trope recurs frequently in Italian cinema. In the 1960s, art films contested the legitimacy of this conservative control. Visconti's *Vaghe stelle dell'orsa* (*Sandra*, 1965) has a female protagonist (Claudia Cardinale) whose attempt to come to terms on her own with her father's Jewish identity and betrayal, and her brother's attempts at sexual annexation, are expressed spatially. The dark, lowering atmosphere of the streets of provincial Viterbo, and of her home, the noise of the wind in the garden containing the memorial to her father, and the dark, huge cistern into which she descends to meet her brother (Jean Sorel) express the difficulties, for a woman, of negotiating identity, and public expression of private traumas. This process is rendered more overt in horror cinema of the period, whose spaces often contain intimidatory and massive architectural features (tombs and vaults) within which the feminine is entrapped and annihilated.

The difficulties in establishing female identity are explored in Delia's (Anna Bonaiuto) visit to Naples for her mother's funeral and to investigate her mother's death in *L'amore molesto* (Mario Martone, 1998). Áine O'Healy (1999: 249) locates this difficulty in the association of historic Naples with the female body and, in patriarchal societies the construction of women as abject. In its modern construction Naples is part of the inferior south.

In Delia's journeys through the central areas of the city, she loses control of her constructed, northern persona of professional woman

Figure 8.3
Delia (Anna Bonaiuto) reduced to elemental woman. *L'amore molesto* (Mario Martone, 1998).

when she loses her grey suit. The red slip-dress which she wears emphasizes her female identity, parallelled by her mother's wearing of the red bra and panties on the beach with Caserta. The panoptic function of crowds to regulate female behaviour is evoked as Delia's red dress exposes her to the gaze of crowds in the streets, and her mother's semi-naked body is exposed on the beach. Delia's recovery of her own memories of her mother (Licia Maglietta) as victim of her father's violence are interspersed with encounters with her uncle, her father and Caserta, all of whom attempt to reinscribe her under patriarchal control. The stripping away of layers of memory, and her asexual, northern carapace, culminates in the derelict basement pastry shop as the camera moves through the vaulted arches. In the final frame of this structure *en abîme*, Delia sits on the bed, wearing her mother's dark blue jacket, finally recalling her sexual violation as a child, understanding the mechanism by which her trauma was distorted as sexual transgression on her mother's part. Martone's film evokes the space of Naples with great complexity to illuminate the position of women and his city.

The beauty of sky, sea and parched landscapes are associated with Grazia (Valeria Golino) in *Respiro* (*Grazia's Island*, Emanuele Crialese, 2002). She is the only character seen to escape the drudgery of the fishing industry, amusing her children, singing and dancing, riding her vespa across the island and swimming naked in the sea. Here the panoptic, the watching activities of the entire community, is unable to curb Grazia's unconventional activities, so provoking the brutal suggested solution of sending her away to a mainland hospital. Grazia's son hides her in a cave overlooking the sea, which removes her from the threat, but also contains the unruly feminine principle, and robs it of its transgressive power.

Conclusion

The writer on the subject of the use of space in Italian cinema is spoilt for choice of examples and indeed, a whole chapter could have engaged with Fellini's inventive and hyperbolic use of space in his films. The art historical, cinematic (and televisual) heritage of Italian visual culture provides an actively used repertoire of spatial cues to the construction of meanings, and these are also accessible to the educated, international audience, able to appreciate and enjoy the Taviani brothers' recourse to fifteenth-century art, Pasolini's playing with religious painting in *La ricotta* (1963), or Amelio's and Nichetti's engagement with neorealist classics. Italy's strong craft traditions of scenographic construction result in professional expertise which is recognized by employment on big-budget international productions. Directors also regularly work on television commercials, honing their skills in communicating economically by visual sign language. Above all the importance of performance in Italian social life lends added complexity to cinematic spatial constructions as figures, and the camera moves through them.

In many cases, the characteristics of place are used as signifiers of character or class. Ritualized male conflict is often expressed as attempts to dominate space by moving through it in a violent or purposive way, the desire for control represented by a *mise en scène*, which contains elements perceived as possible threats. The figures of subordinate men, immigrants and women are contained in enclosed spaces, and thereby robbed of agency. Female characters are generally assigned less freedom of movement within space and, as we have shown, are often accompanied by groups or crowds of people monitoring and observing their movements, a visual representation of patriarchal control in traditional Italian society. As this and previous chapters have demonstrated, the spatial paradigms selected as cinematic sets or locations are never neutral, and are always expressive of power relations, and the instability of ideologies of gender, class and value.

Conclusion

This book has attempted to celebrate the richness of an incredibly productive national cinema. Conventional film criticism ignores the often very interesting work that art film directors had to accomplish to make films. All too frequently Italian films are discussed as if they existed outside any context of production or reception, nationally or internationally. In this study, the 'ghosts at the feast', are the American films, which have influenced the subjects and style of Italian films since the 1930s but have beset the Italian film industry through their competitiveness and, since the 1960s, by their dominance of the distribution networks. This book rejects the idea that the popular culture, and the industrial realities of film-making in Italy are unworthy of study.

Italian producers, film-makers and creative personnel have always had to be pragmatic in their navigating of an often Byzantine industry. For the English academic, the discovery of enormously creative solutions to problems such as how to get one's money out of Italy when blocked by national legislation, how to amortize the costs of building sets for expensive art films that would never, in a million years, make their money back, how to overcome the limitations of one's budget by filming 'back to back' on sets constructed for another film, and using costumes designed for another, more expensive production, how to play the grants and subventions game and still produce something interesting, all these aspects have been part of the pleasure I have gained from studying the combination of sheer anarchy, and discipline, involved in film-making in Italy. These two characteristics are reflected in Italian cinema's production of voluminous statistics on sectors of the market in order to assess the risk involved in making a film, and the often wonderfully exuberant result on the silver screen. No student of cinema can afford to ignore the industrial realities of film-making, least of all in the Italian context.

The interesting and creative nature of the production context of Italian cinema has been explored in Chapter 1 via the career of Francesco Rosi. Rosi has usually been considered to be the inheritor of Visconti in his visual flair and career adherence to serious themes, but his skills have also included his navigation of the structures of the Italian, and global film industries. Critics seeking a consistent directorial profile have often had problems with directors who produce work which appears either frivolous, such as Rosi's *C'era una volta* (1967), which starred Sophia Loren and Omar Sharif in a Neapolitan fairy story, or populist, such as his bullfighting biopic, *Il momento della verità* (*The Moment of Truth*, 1964). Looked at in the context of the Italian film industry as a whole, such films become explicable, as does the inscription of directorial flourishes in Italian film genres.

The notion that Italian film genres are in fact more flexible structures than appear in American cinema has also been explored. There is enormous pleasure in unravelling frenetic activity in Italian film-making in order to take advantage of American blockbusters with million dollar publicity budgets. Once an American epic was announced, Italian production would swing into action in order to release the national film at the same time as the mega-budget American version started to mount its huge publicity campaign. International developments in the film industries have made the distinction between mainstream and art cinema less clear cut. The art cinema institution in the 1950s and 1960s was dominated by auteurist films, but developed to encompass the exhibition of mainstream films from other countries in their original language. Cross-fertilization also took place, with American film-makers experimenting with art and avant garde cinematic techniques, and European film-makers reworking Hollywood genre conventions. More importantly, from the 1990s onwards, all European films have had problems in finding exhibition space in their home as well as foreign markets. The dominance of American distribution and exhibition chains has been reinforced by the building of multi-plexes so that Italian films (like their counterparts all over Europe) become art films in their own markets. Co-production with television ensures a mass audience if broadcast at favourable times of day and year, but militates against diffusion on video or DVD unless the film was previously well-received critically or at the cinema box office

– or achieved an Oscar nomination. Emidio Greco is a case in point here. He makes thoughtful, interesting films for television but they do not display the cinematic authorial flourishes that will ensure that they are noticed at international festivals and, in the case of *Milonga* (1999), an incomprehensible title hampered success. To be designated a successful *auteur* today, a director needs to conquer an international reputation in order to secure a budget that will enable him or her to express a personal view without being constrained too much by genre expectations. However, Jean Gili (2000: 427) has shown that, even in the traditionally important French market, Italian films are generally confined to independent or art cinema circuits and are unsuccessful. Italian films are usually only purchased by British broadcasters, video and DVD distributors if they have had some sort of cinema exhibition in Britain (Wagstaff 2000: 441). An enthusiastic and well-connected production company that can make good deals is therefore key. Inevitably, the early work of Italian directors is not exported so that knowledge of work by, say, Gianni Amelio, Gabriele Salvatores or Nanni Moretti will be incomplete and usually only represented by one or two isolated films.

State subventions continue to be important in the survival of the Italian film industry in the current context of globalized media interests. Effectively they enable Italian productions to cover their costs in case they are unable to secure international distribution deals. An element of reality was injected into previous legislation by the requirement that Italian films in receipt of grants repay their initial subvention when economically successful, or forfeit any right to access future grants. This proviso was successful in concentrating the minds of film-makers who, in the past, would have taken the money and not bothered about the audience or reception of their film.

The Berlusconi government's new film law of 2003 made arrangements for the support of Italian cinema from 2004 to 2006, bringing all legislative arrangements for cinema under the Ministero per i beni e le attività culturale (the Ministry of Cultural Properties and Activities). Support is available for films defined as 'of significant cultural or artistic interest or exceptional visual quality'. To be eligible, a film must have an Italian director, treatment and script-writer (or majority Italian writing team), sound recording in Italian, an Italian technical troupe, and the spending of at least 30 per cent of the budget in Italy. Feature films that are recognized as of cultural interest can apply for Article 13 subventions of up to 50 per cent of the cost of the film. For first or second films, this is increased to 90 per cent, less any pre-sales. Subventions have to be paid back within three years, and those that have not achieved a minimum of box-office receipts set by the Ministry will not receive any subventions based on their cinema release. There are important contributions for the distribution in Italy of Italian films recognized as of cultural interest, and similar contributions to export agencies, based on box-office receipts outside Italy. Tax breaks for updating and modernizing cinemas, and for investing in new technology are also provided for. Funds are available for prizes at film festivals, for the conservation and restoration of classic Italian films, for festivals, trade events, publications, journals and cultural organizations devoted to film. Production companies in receipt of subventions have to deposit a negative copy of the film in the Cineteca Nazionale (the national film archive).

The new law therefore continues to attempt practical measures for the survival of Italian cinema. Although the majority of films are made with television co-production finance, a cinema release is essential in order to access additional funds based on quality and box-office receipts. In common with other European countries, Italian films have difficulty in obtaining distribution in a sector controlled by American interests, but this factor is recognized in incentives for American-controlled chains to programme Italian films. Of course, distributors will make financial calculations of the returns of American films without subventions and Italian films with, but the new law at least provides the possibility of developing an arena in which Italian films can be seen. Above all, the new law continues to inscribe within professional practice the notions of quality, and especially visual quality, and the quality of the creative team. The director, writing and technical team are particularly singled out, but the troupe must also contain a majority of Italian directors of photography, editors, actors, composers, set designers, costume designers, studios and technical companies. The craft traditions of Italian cinema continue to be important and, given the emphasis of this particular book it is clear that visual virtuosity is rewarded as being culturally significant.

Co-productions with other countries of the European Union, usually including one or more television investors, are the norm in the contemporary production context. This has the advantage of ensuring that production costs are covered, as in Daniele Lucchetti's *Dillo con parole mie* (*Ginger and Cinnamon*, 2003).[1] Lucchetti's film is an entertaining, low-budget holiday film and, although he was apologetic about the films's lack of political 'bite' in critical terms, it is perfectly realized as a televisual representation of changing sexual *mores*, particularly in the contrast between the older female protagonist who retains the compulsion to achieve a traditional ideal of domestic perfection, and the fourteen-year old Meggy, for whom this ideal matters not a jot in her desire to lose her virginity and start her journey of self-discovery. Television contracts have been particularly important in ensuring international visibility for Italian films. Berlusconi's satellite television interests cover Latin America so that the interests of the communities of the Italian diaspora can be catered for. The Australian channel, SBS, receives government assistance to devise programming that reflects the cultural diversity of the country, and Italian cinema is able to achieve sales in this area, usually based on box-office success in Italy or on critical success on the festival circuit. Globalized media interests represent some small advantage for Italian cinema.

The new law makes some recognition of the necessity of dubbing or subtitling Italian cinema (Article 12, 3b), and here a heartfelt plea to production companies is in order. DVDs are cheap to produce. How expensive is it to provide subtitles in other languages so that Italian films can become known and appreciated outside Italy? Those of us who try to teach Italian cinema at every opportunity are constantly thwarted by the unavailability of subtitled prints.

Popular cinema has traditionally not sought an international release, aiming to amortize its costs on the home market. Although the sheer numbers of films produced in the heyday of the 1950s and 1960s gave space for the development of creative careers, the development of star profiles and skills training for technical personnel, opportunities are more limited in the contemporary film industry. Chapter 2 has explored how Italian film genres take advantage of the low-budget realities of popular cinema in the *filone* phenomenon, whereby the box-office potential of interesting themes is rapidly identified and exploited, until tastes change or the cinema-going public tires. Popular cinema not only draws on Italy's rich cultural heritage, but has also provided opportunities for the rehearsal of social change and concerns about gender power, albeit often unconsciously. The carnevalesque and the rude have been constant elements of Italian comedies, for example, debunking the pretensions of classes with social or economic power, and exacting revenge, in the form of savage satire, on the political classes who cling on to power in Italy. That this attachment to power has resulted in illegal power structures (the Mafia and the *camorra*), assassinations, massacres and violent events, for which no responsibility has usually been found, is reflected in the constant presence of the grotesque in Italian cinema.

The co-existence in Italian cinema of grotesque and excessive elements with the conventions of cinematic realism were explored in Chapter 3. The epic and the historical film are constants of popular and auteurist cinema, providing frequent opportunities to make sense of the world. Threats to a successful image of a modern, pluralistic Italy have taken the form of frequent atrocities, shootings, assassinations and other violent events, providing cinema with fertile sources of stories. Key historical moments provide cinematic opportunities to examine the complex context of an event, and contemporary attitudes to it. Excess indicates the traumatic nature of the modernization of Italy in the First and Second Republics, and realist modes of film-making are used to lend authority to rejection of simple interpretations of events.

Cinematic realism has always had more prestige amongst Italian film critics and Chapter 4 argued that it takes many different forms. The realist cinematic conventions of authenticity of place in location shooting, use of non-professional actors and narratives of marginalized sections of the population were rapidly perceived as insufficient to explain the complexity of events. The affective charge of melodrama was useful in restoring complexity, and the convoluted melodramas of the 1950s could explore both the effects of family breakdown, emigration, social change of all kinds, and different attitudes to them. Self-sacrifice on the part of the good character might close the narrative, but how moral dilemmas were worked out, and bad characters acted, allowed social values to be tested, accepted, negotiated or rejected.

Directors aspiring to the status of *auteur* had to consider the cultural prestige of realism, and how to represent their films as their own personal vision. Chapter 5 compares the careers of some of the 'Great Men' of Italian cinema to those of male and female film-makers in the very different circumstances of the contemporary film industry. Situating *auteur* film-making in the wider context of Italian and international cinema and the media allows its connections to, and continuities with, popular cinema to become visible. Authorial or art cinema is still rewarded if it achieves criteria of quality and, as such, is more likely to get foreign distribution. However, due to American domination of global media networks, Italian cinema is a minority in its own market. The alternative is to move into an international style of film-making, which either plays heavily on stereotypes of Italianness, or uses non-Italian actors, and globally successful books to adapt. As Bernardo Bertolucci has shown, once a film-maker has achieved an international reputation, it is possible to return to smaller budgets.

At the end of the twentieth century and beginning of the twenty-first, the notion of clear distinctions between Italian and non-Italian cannot be maintained in a situation in which the non-Italian is visible both within the national territory and on television screens. The process of constructing a national identity, and of coming to terms with social and global change assume interesting forms in Italian cinema. In characterizing enemies, occupying forces or immigrants, films have recourse to earlier stereotypes, particularly those associated with southern Italy. Chapter 6 identified violence and hyperbole in representations of the 'Other' in Italian cinematic discourse and, in the case of contemporary cinema, a *mise en scène*, which locates immigrants in dark, difficult and enclosed spaces. Both of these strategies reveal anxieties about the effects of the porosity of national borders, and desires to push non-Italians to the margins where they can be observed and controlled.

Another aspect of power relations in Italian society was explored in Chapter 7. Although many female stars achieved international reputations, the narrative spaces that they occupy usually allow rebellion and independence to be acted out, while reintegrating them within traditional patriarchal power structures at the film's conclusion. Male violence and conflict in films set in the worlds of business and politics also act as an index of social crisis and anxieties about loss of power. The latter finds expression in a significant number of films concerning male impotence, either sexual or in the form of ineffective control of events. The evolution of representations of masculinity is marked not only by grotesque or excessive elements that betray the difficulties of the work of patriarchal control, but also by the rehearsal of more emotional ways of being.

The rehearsal of stereotypes and new gender models is played out spatially as characters control their environment, or rebel against that control. Complexity can be expressed through the interplay of opposing visual regimes, most notably those of Classical and Baroque architectural forms. The representation of space in Italian cinema has always been interesting, and Italian cinema has a rich cultural heritage on which to draw. The strong professional and craft traditions of the creative teams of Italian cinema are recognized by prestigious prizes nationally and internationally. Overcoming budget limitations is inscribed in the professional practices of re-using sets and costumes, so that low-budget films often display an unexpected flair and visual quality. The European style of the long take and the use of the mobile camera within sequences, lends itself to an additional level of meaning construction in which movement of characters invests space with emotion and ideas. As this and previous chapters have demonstrated, the virtuosity of Italian film-makers is expressed through spectacle, and the visual beauty of the *mise en scène* of place. Spectacle as surplus to narrative requirements indicates both the existence of instability of meaning in the story world and the controlling presence of the director.

Italian legislation governing the film industry shows the import-ance for national prestige of a film's whole creative team in achieving visual quality and serious purpose. New technologies and delivery systems are subverting previously held explanations of what film is, how it is made and consumed. Directors of photography, rather than directors, are beginning to stress their own centrality to the production, and their right to oversee the colour and framing of their film when transferred to other media formats (Gelato 2004: 20). Moreover, although cinema lost its prime position as a social experience for the first time when commercial television channels proliferated in the mid-1970s, the more recent development of niche channels, and pay television have further displaced visits to the cinema (like football) from central importance in social life (Barlozzetti 2004: 5). However, filmed fiction in the form of mini-series, soaps, television films, occupies a cardinal, prime-time position on the wide-ranging terrestrial television channels in Italy. Since the media and publishing industries are now so interlinked, proliferation of modes for the consumption of film represent opportunities for the discovery of new talents coming from documentary, or the critically despised genres of horror and erotic drama.

The pleasurable spectacularity and theatricality of Italian cinema is symptomatic of preoccupations with national, regional and personal identity, and continues to find an audience response. The violent events and major social transformations in Italian history are matched by disruption and instability in filmic representations of the modern world, characteristics of postmodernity that are also encouraged by commercial film practices favouring hybrid *filoni*. Since the Second World War, explorations of identity take place against the background of a palimpsest of past and present representations of stasis and disruption. This is unlikely to change for some time yet.

Filmography

Abbasso la miseria! (*Down with Poverty!* Gennaro Righelli, 1945)

Abbasso la ricchezza! (*Down With Riches!* Gennaro Righelli, 1946)

Accatone (Pier Paolo Pasolini, 1961)

Achtung banditi! (Carlo Lizzani, 1949)

A ciascuno il suo (*We Still Kill the Old Way*, Elio Petri, 1967)

L'albero degli zoccoli (*The Tree of Wooden Clogs*, Ermanno Olmi, 1978)

Les amants (*The Lovers*, Louis Malle, 1958)

Amarcord (Federico Fellini, 1973)

L'amore (*Love: Two Love Stories*, Roberto Rossellini, 1948)

L'amore molesto (Mario Martone, 1998)

Angela (Roberta Torre, 2002)

Anna (Alberto Lattuada, Italy, 1951

Anni difficili (*Difficult Years*, Luigi Zampa, 1948)

Anno uno (*Year One*, Roberto Rossellini, 1974)

Aprile (Nanni Moretti, 1998)

L'armata Brancaleone (*For Love and Gold*, Mario Monicelli, 1966)

Arrivano i titani (*The Titans are Coming*, Duccio Tessari, 1961)

L'assassino (*The Assassin*, Elio Petri, 1961)

L'assedio (*Besieged*, Bernardo Bertolucci, 1998)

Assunta Spina (Gustavo Serena, 1915)

¡Atame! (*Tie Me Up, Tie Me Down*, Pedro Almodòvar, 1990)

Avanti, c'è posto (*There's room at the front*, Mario Bonnard, 1942)

L'avventura (Michelangelo Antonioni, 1960)

Un'avventura di Salvator Rosa (*An Adventure of Salvator Rosa*, Alessandro Blasetti, 1940)

Le avventure di Pinocchio (*The Adventures of Pinocchio*, Luigi Comencini, 1972)

Il bagno turco – Hamman (*Hamman: The Turkish Bath*, Ferzan Ozpetek, 1997)

I bambini ci guardano (*The Children Are Watching Us*, Vittorio De Sica, 1942)

I banchieri di Dio (*God's Bankers*, Giuseppe Ferrara, 2002)

Il bandito (*The Bandit*, Alberto Lattuada, 1946)

Il barbiere di Siviglia (*The Barber of Seville*, Mario Costa, 1946)

Batticuore (*Heartbeat*, Mario Camerini, 1939)

La bella mugnaia (*The Beautiful Miller's Wife*, Mario Camerini, 1955)

Il bell'Antonio (*The Beautiful Antonio*, Mauro Bolognini, 1960)

Belle, ma povere (*Beautiful But Poor*, Dino Risi, 1957)

Bellissima (Luchino Visconti, 1951)

Il bidone (*The Swindler*, Federico Fellini, 1955)

Il bigamo (*The Bigamist*, Luciano Emmer, 1956)

Blaise Pascal (Roberto Rossellini, ORTF, 1971–2)

Blow-up (Michelangelo Antonioni, 1966)

Brucio nel vento (*Burning in the Wind*, Silvio Soldini, 2001)

I buchi neri (*The Black Holes*, Pappi Corsicato, 1995)

Buongiorno notte (Marco Bellocchio, 2003)

Il buono, il brutto, il cattivo (*The Good, the Bad, and the Ugly*, Sergio Leone, 1966)

Cabiria (Giovanni Pastrone, 1914)

Caccia tragica (*Tragic Pursuit*, Giuseppe De Santis, 1947)

Cadaveri eccellenti (*Illustrious Corpses*, Francesco Rosi, 1975)

La caduta degli dei (*The Damned*, Luchino Visconti, 1969)

La caduta di Troia (*The Fall of Troy*, Giovanni Pastrone, Enrico Guazzone, 1911)

Callas Forever (Franco Zeffirelli, 2002)

Camicia nera (*Black Shirt*, Giovacchino Forzano, 1933)

Camicie rosse (*Red Shirts*, Goffredo Alessandrini, 1952)

Campo de' fiori (Mario Bonnard, 1943)

Cannibal Holocaust (Ruggero Deodato, 1979)

Carmen (Francesco Rosi, 1984)

Caro diario (*Dear Diary*, Nanni Moretti, 1993)

Carosello Napoletano (*Neapolitan Roundabout*, Ettore Giannini, 1953)

Il cartaio (*The Card Player*, Dario Argento, 2003)

Casa Ricordi (*The House of Ricordi*, Carmine Gallone, 1954)

Il caso Mattei (*The Mattei Affair*, Francesco Rosi, 1972)

Catene (*Chains*, Raffaello Matarazzo, 1950)

Cavalleria (*Cavalry*, Goffredo Alessandrini, 1936)

I cavalieri di Rodi (*The Knights of Rhodes*, Mario Caserini, 1912)

I cento passi (*The Hundred Steps*, Marco Tullio Giordano, 2000)

C'era una volta (*Cinderella – Italian Style*, Francesco Rosi, 1967)

Le chiavi di casa (*The Keys of the House*, Gianni Amelio, 2004)

Il ciclone (*The Cyclone*, Leonardo Pieraccioni, 1997)

Il Cid (Mario Caserini, 1910)

Cinema Paradiso (Giuseppe Tornatore, 1989)

La città delle donne (*City of Women*, Federico Fellini, 1980)

Cleopatra (Joseph Mankiewicz, 1963)

I clowns (Federico Fellini, 1970)

La commare secca (*The Grim Reaper*, Bernardo Bertolucci, 1962)

Il conformista (*The Conformist*, Bernardo Bertolucci, 1970)

La corsa dell'innocente (*Flight of the Innocent*, Carlo Carlei, 1992)

Così ridevano (*The Way We Laughed*, Gianni Amelio, 1998)

Cristo si è fermato a Eboli (*Christ Stopped at Eboli*, Francesco Rosi, 1979)

Cronaca di un amore (*Story of a Love Affair*, Michelangelo Antonioni, 1950)

Cronaca di una morte annunciata (*Chronicle of a Death Foretold*, Francesco Rosi, 1987)

Cronache di poveri amanti (*Tales of Poor Lovers*, Carlo Lizzani, 1953)

I dannati della terra (*The Damned of the Earth*, Valentino Orsini, 1969)

Danza macabra (Antonio Margheriti, 1963)

Daunbailò (*Down By Law*, Jim Jarmusch, 1986)

Il Decamerone (*Decameron*, Pier Paolo Pasolini, 1971)

Il deserto rosso (*The Red Desert*, Michelangelo Antonioni, 1964)

Dillo con parole mie (*Ginger and Cinnamon*, Daniele Luchetti, 2003)

Dimenticare Palermo (*To Forget Palermo*, Francesco Rosi, 1990)

Divorzio all'italiana (*Divorce Italian Style*, Pietro Germi, 1961)

La dolce vita (Federico Fellini, 1960)

Don Camillo e l'Onorevole Peppone (*Don Camillo and Peppone*, Carmine Gallone, 1953)

La donna della Domenica (*Sunday Woman*, Luigi Comencini, 1975)

Ecce Bombo (Nanni Moretti, 1978)

Edipo re (*Edipus Rex*, Pier Paolo Pasolini, 1967)

Elvjs e Merilijn (*Elvis and Marilyn*, Armando Manni, 1998)

Enrico IV (Amleto Palermi, 1926)

Ercole contro Moloch (*Hercules versus Moloch*, Giorgio Ferroni, 1964)

Un eroe borghese (*Middle-Class hero*, Michele Placido, 1994)

L'Eroe di Babilonia (*The Beast of Babylon Against the Son of Hercules*, Siro Marcellini, 1963)

Eros (Third episode, Michelangelo Antonioni, 2004)

L'eruzione dell'Etna (*The Eruption of Mt Etna*, Ambrosio Productions, 1910)

L'estate di Davide (*David's Summer*, Carlo Mazzacurati, 1998)

Europa '51 (Roberto Rossellini, 1952)

Fabiola (Alessandro Blasetti, 1948)

La famiglia (*The Family*, Ettore Scola, 1987)

Il Fantasma dell'opera (*The Phantom of the Opera*, Dario Argento, 1998)

Le fate ignoranti (*Ignorant Fairies*, Ferzan Ozpetek, 2001)

La felicità non costa niente (*Happiness Costs Nothing*, Mimmo Calopresti, 2003)

Fellini Casanova (Federico Fellini, 1976)

Fellini Roma (Federico Fellini, 1972)

Fellini Satyricon (Federico Fellini, 1969)

I figli di nessuno (*Nobody's Children*, Rafaello Matarazzo, 1951)

La fine è nota (*The End is Known*, Cristina Comencini, 1993)

La finestra di fronte (*Facing Window*, Ferzan Ozpetek, 2003)

Il fiore delle mille e una notte (*The Arabian Nights*, Pier Paolo Pasolini, 1974)

Francesco (Liliana Cavani, 1989)

Francesco giullare di Dio (*Francis God's Jester*, Roberto Rossellini, 1950)

Una fredda mattina di maggio (*A Cold May Morning*, Vittorio Sindoni, 1990)

La frusta e il corpo (*The Whip and the Body*, Mario Bava, 1963)

Fuori del mondo (*Out of this World*, Giuseppe Piccione, 1999)

Il gattopardo (*The Leopard*, Luchino Visconti, 1963)

Germania anno zero (*Germany Year Zero*, Roberto Rossellini, 1948)

La Gerusalemme liberata (*Jerusalem Liberated*, Enrico Guazzone, 1911 and 1918)

Ginger e Fred (*Ginger and Fred*, Federico Fellini, 1985)

Il gioco di Ripley (*Ripley's Game*, Liliana Cavani, 2002)

Una giornata particolare (*A Special Day*, Ettore Scola, 1977)

Giorno per giorno disperatamente (*Desperately, Day By Day*, Ettore Giannelli, 1961)

Gioventù perduta (*Lost Youth*, Pietro Germi, 1948)

Giulietta degli spiriti (*Juliet of the Spirits*, Federico Fellini, 1965)

Grazia zia (*Thank You, Aunt*, Salvatore Samperi, 1968)

Gruppo di famiglia in un interno (*Conversation Piece*, Luchino Visconti, 1974)

Harem suare (Ferzan Ozpetek, 1999)

The Hunchback of Notre Dame (Gary Trousdale/Kirk Wise, 1996)

Indagine su un cittadino al di sopra di ogni sospetto (*Investigation of a Citizen Above Suspicion*, Elio Petri, 1970)

Identificazione di una donna (*Identification of a Woman*, Michelangelo Antonioni, 1982)

Independence Day (Roland Emmerich, 1996)

India Matri Bhumi (*India*, Roberto Rossellini, 1959)

L'iniziaziazione (*The Initiation*, Gianfranco Mingozzi, 1986)

L'innocente (*The Intruder*, Luchino Visconti, 1976)

In nome della legge (*In the Name of the Law*, Pietro Germi, 1949)

In nome del popolo italiano (*In the Name of the Italian People*, Dino Risi, 1971)

Intervista (Federico Fellini, 1987)

Intolerance (Compilation film, various film-makers, 1999)

Io ballo da sola (*Stealing Beauty*, Bernardo Bertolucci, 1996)

Io non ho paura (*I'm Not Afraid*, Gabriele Salvatores, 2002)

Io sono un autarchico (*I am Self-sufficient*, Nanni Moretti, 1976)

Jaws (Steven Spielberg, 1975)

Johnny Stecchino (Roberto Benigni, 1991)

Kean: genio e sregolatezza (*Kean: wild genius*, Vittorio Gassman and Francesco Rosi, 1956)

Ladri di biciclette (*Bicycle Thieves*, Vittorio De Sica, 1948)

Ladri di Saponette (*The Icycle Thief*, Maurizio Nichetti, 1989)

Il ladro di bambini (*The Stolen Children*, Gianni Amelio, 1992)

Lamerica (Gianni Amelio, 1994)

The Last Emperor (Bernardo Bertolucci, 1987)

La leggenda del pianista sull'oceano (*The Legend of 1900*, Giuseppe Tornatore, 1998)

La leggenda del santo bevitore (*Legend of the Holy Drinker*, Ermanno Olmi, 1988)

Lettere al vento (*Letters on the Wind*, Edmond Budina, 2002)

Libera (Pappi Corsicato, 1993)

Little Buddha (Bernardo Bertolucci, 1993)

La lotta dell'uomo per la sua sopravvivenza (Roberto Rossellini, RAI, 1967–9)

Luciano Serra pilota (*Pilot Luciano Serra*, Goffredo Alessandrini, 1937)

Luci di varietà (*Variety Lights*, Federico Fellini with Alberto Lattuada, 1950)

Lucky Luciano (Francesco Rosi, 1973)

Ludwig (Luchino Visconti, 1973)

La luna (Bernardo Bertolucci, 1979)

Il lungo silenzio (*The Long Silence*, Margarethe von Trotta, 1993)

Il lupo della Sila (*The Wolf of the Sila*, Duilio Coletti, Italy, 1949

Maciste alla corte del Gran Khan (*Maciste at the Court of the Great Khan*, Riccardo Freda, 1964)

Maciste all'inferno (*Maciste in Hell*, Guido Brignone, 1925)

Maddalena, zero in condotta (*Maddalena, Zero in Conduct*, Vittorio De Sica, 1940

I magliari (Francesco Rosi, 1959)

Malèna (Giuseppe Tornatore, 2000)

Mamma Roma (Pier Paolo Pasolini, 1962)

Mangiati vivi! (*Eaten Alive*, Umberto Lenzi, 1980)

Le mani sulla città (*Hands Over the City*, Francesco Rosi, 1964)

Marcantonio e Cleopatra (*Mark Anthony and Cleopatra*, Enrico Guazzoni, 1913)

Marianna Ucrìa (Roberto Faenza, 1997)

La maschera del demonio (*Mask of the Demon*, Mario Bava, 1960)

Matrimoni (*Marriages*, Cristina Comencini, 1998)

Medea (Pier Paolo Pasolini, 1969)

Mediterraneo (Gabriele Salvatores, 1991)

La meglio gioventù (*The Best of Youth*, Marco Tullio Giordana, 2003

Mery per sempre (*Forever Mary*, Marco Risi, 1988)

La messa è finita (*The Mass is Over*, Nanni Moretti, 1985)

Metello (Mauro Bolognini, 1970)

La mia generazione (*My Generation*, Wilma Labate, 1996)

Milano violenta (Mario Caiano, 1975–6)

Milonga (Emidio Greco, 1999)

Miracolo a Milano (*Miracle in Milan*, Vittorio De Sica, 1950)

Il momento della verità (*The Moment of Truth*, Francesco Rosi, 1964)

Morte a Venezia (*Death in Venice*, Luchino Visconti, 1971)

Napoli violenta (*Death Dealers*, Umberto Lenzi, 1976)

Nel segno di Roma (*Sign of the Gladiator*, Guido Brignone, 1959)

Nerone (*Nero*, Luigi Maggi, 1909)

Nirvana (Gabriele Salvatores, 1997)

Non ho sonno (*Sleepless*, Dario Argento, 2000)

Non si sevizia un paperino (*Don't Torture a Duck*, Lucio Fulci, 1976)

La notte (*The Night*, Michelangelo Antonioni, 1961)

Le notti bianche (*White Nights*, Luchino Visconti, 1957)

Le notti di Cabiria (*Nights of Cabiria*, Federico Fellini, 1957)

Novecento (*1900*, Bernardo Bertolucci, 1976)

Oltre il confine (*Across the Border*, Rolando Colla, 2002)

L'Onorevole Angelina (*Angelina*, Luigi Zampa, 1947)

L'ora di religione (*My Mother's Smile*, Marco Bellocchio, 2002)

L'oro di Napoli (*The Gold of Naples*, Vittorio De Sica, 1954)

Ossessione (Luchino Visconti, 1943)

8½ (Federico Fellini, 1963)

Padre Padrone (*Father and Master*, Paolo and Vittorio Taviani, 1977)

Pagliacci (Mario Costa, 1949)

Paisà (*Paisan*, Roberto Rossellini, 1946)

Palombella rossa (*Red Lob*, Nanni Moretti, 1989)

Pane, amore e fantasia (*Bread, Love and Fantasy*, Luigi Comencini, 1954)

Pane e tulipani (*Bread and Tulips*, Silvio Soldini, 2000)

Par-delà des nuages (*Beyond the Clouds*, Michelangelo Antonioni, 1996)

Parigi è sempre Parigi (*Paris is Always Paris*, Luciano Emmer, 1951)

Une partie de campagne (Jean Renoir, 1936)

Il partigiano Johnny (*Johnny the Partisan*, Guido Chiesa, 2000)

Partner (Bernardo Bertolucci, 1968)

Pasqualino Settebellezze (*Seven Beauties*, Lina Wertmüller, 1976)

Patrizia e schiava (*Afra, Patrician Slave*, Cines, 1910)

Per un pugno di dollari (*For a Fistful of Dollars*, Sergio Leone, 1964)

Piccolo Buddha (*Little Buddha*, Bernardo Bertolucci, 1993)

I piccoli maestri (*The Little Teachers*, Daniele Luchetti, 1998)

Un pilota ritorna (*A Pilot Returns*, Roberto Rossellini, 1942)

Pinocchio (Roberto Benigni, 2002)

Il più bel giorno della mia vita (*The Best Day of My Life*, Cristina Comencini, 2002)

Porcile (*Pig Pen*, Pier Paolo Pasolini, 1969)

Il portiere di notte (*The Night Porter*, Liliana Cavani, 1974)

Il postino (Michael Radford, 1994)

Poveri ma belli (*Poor but Handsome*, Dino Risi, Italy, 1956)

Il Principe di Homberg di Heinrich von Kleist (*The Prince of Homberg*, Marco Bellocchio, 1997)

Professione: reporter (*The Passenger*, Michelangelo Antonioni, 1975)

Profondo rosso (*Deep Red*, Dario Argento, 1975)

Proibito (*Forbidden*, Mario Monicelli, 1954)

I pugni in tasca (*Fists in the Pocket*, Marco Bellocchio, 1965)

Pummarò (Michele Placido, 1990)

Quattro mosche di veluto grigio (*Four Flies on Grey Velvet*, Dario Argento, 1971)

Quattro passi fra le nuvole (*Four Steps in the Clouds*, Alessandro Blasetti, 1942)

Quo vadis? (Enrico Guazzoni, 1913)

I racconti di Canterbury (*The Canterbury Tales*, Pier Paolo Pasolini, 1972)

Racconti romani (*Roman Tales*, Gianni Franciolini, 1955)

Radiofreccia (Luciano Ligabue, 1998)

Ragazzi fuori (*Street Boys*, Marco Risi, 1990)

Respiro (*Grazia's Island*, Emanuele Crialese, 2002)

La ricotta (Pier Paolo Pasolini; third episode of *Rogopag*, 1963)

Rigoletto (Carmine Gallone, 1947)

Risate di Gioia (*The Passionate Thief*, Mario Monicelli, 1960)

Riso amaro (*Bitter Rice*, Giuseppe De Santis, 1948)

Il ritorno di Cagliostro (*The Return of Cagliostro*, Daniele Ciprì and Franco Maresco, 2002)

Rocco e i suoi fratelli (*Rocco and his Brothers*, Luchino Visconti, 1960)

Roma bene (Carlo Lizzani, 1971)

Roma città aperta (*Rome Open City*, Roberto Rossellini, 1945)

Roma drogata: la polizia non può intervenire (*Drugged Rome: The Police are Powerless*, Lucio Manaccino, 1975–6)

Rose e pistole (*Roses and Guns*, Carla Apuzzo, 1998)

Sacco e Vanzetti (Giuliano Montaldo, 1971)

Salò e le 120 giornate di Sodoma (*Salò: or the 120 Days of Sodom*, Pier Paolo Pasolini, 1975)

Salon Kitty (Tinto Brass, 1976)

Salvatore Giuliano (Francesco Rosi, 1961)

Scandalosa Gilda (Gabriele Lavia, 1985)

Lo sceicco bianco (*The White Sheik*, Federico Fellini, 1952)

Scipione l'africano (*Scipio Africanus*, Carmine Gallone, 1937)

Sciuscià (*Shoeshine*, Vittorio De Sica, 1946)

La scorta (*The Escort*, Ricky Tognazzi, 1993)

La seconda volta (*The Second Time*, Mimmo Calopresti, 1996)

Sedotta e abbandonata (*Seduced and Abandoned*, Pietro Germi, 1962)

Senso (Luchino Visconti, 1954)

Senso '45 (*Black Angel*, Tinto Brass, 2002)

Senza pietà (Without Pity, Alberto Lattuada, 1948)

La sfida (*The Challenge*, Francesco Rosi, 1958)

The Sheltering Sky (Bernardo Bertolucci, 1990)

La signora senza camelie (*Lady Without Camelias*, Michelangelo Antonioni, 1952)

Il signor Max (*Mister Max*, Mario Camerini, 1937)

The Silence of the Lambs (Jonathan Demme, 1991)

La sindrome di Stendhal (*The Stendhal Syndrome*, Dario Argento, 1996)

Sogni d'oro (*Sweet Dreams*, Nanni Moretti, 1981)

Il sole anche di notte (*Night Sun*, Paolo and Vittorio Taviani, 1990)

Il sole sorge ancora (*The Sun Rises Again*, Aldo Vergano, 1946)

I soliti ignoti (*Big Deal on Madonna Street*, Mario Monicelli, 1958)

Il sorpasso (*Easy Life*, Dino Risi, 1962)

Il sospetto (*Suspicion*, Francesco Maselli, 1975)

Sotto il segno dello scorpione (*Under the Sign of the Scorpion*, Paolo and Vittorio Taviani, 1969)

Sovversivi (*Subversives*, Paolo and Vittorio Taviani, 1967)

Spartaco or *Il gladiatore della Tracia* (*The Thracian Gladiator*, Giovanni Enrico Vidali, 1913)

Spartacus (Stanley Kubrick, 1960)

Speriamo che sia femmina (*Let's Hope It's a Girl*, Mario Monicelli, 1986)

La stanza del figlio (*The Son's Room*, Nanni Moretti, 2001)

Star Wars (George Lucas, USA, 1977)

Una storia semplice (*A Simple Story*, Emidio Greco, 1991)

La strada (Federico Fellini, 1954)

La strategia del ragno (*The Spider's Stratagem*, Bernardo Bertolucci, 1970)

Stromboli (Roberto Rossellini, 1950)

Sud Side Stori (*South Side Story*, Roberta Torre, 2000)

Tano da morire (*To Die for Tano*, Roberta Torre, 1997)

Teatro di guerra (Mario Martone, 1998)

Un tè con Mussolini (*Tea With Mussolini*, Franco Zeffirelli, 2000)

Tenebre (*Tenebrae*, Dario Argento, 1982)

Il tè nel deserto (*The Sheltering Sky*, Bernardo Bertolucci, 1990)

Teorema (*Theorem*, Pier Paolo Pasolini, 1968)

La terra trema (Luchino Visconti, 1948)

Tombolo paradiso nero (*Tombolo, Black Paradise*, Giorgio Ferroni, 1947)

Torino nera (Carlo Lizzani, 1972)

Tormento (*Torment*, Rafaello Matarazzo, 1950)

Totò al giro d'Italia (*Totò's Tour of Italy*, Mario Mattoli, 1948)

Totò che visse due volte (*Totò who Lived Twice*, Daniele Ciprì and Franco Maresco, 1998)

Totò contro Maciste (*Totò versus Maciste*, Fernando Cerchio, 1962)

Totò e Cleopatra (*Totò and Cleopatra*, Fernando Cerchio, 1963)

Trauma (Dario Argento, 1993)

Tre fratelli (*Three Brothers*, Francesco Rosi, 1981)

La tregua (*The Truce*, Francesco Rosi, 1996)

Uccellacci e uccellini (*Hawks and Sparrows*, Pier Paolo Pasolini, 1966)

L'uccello dalle piume di cristallo (*The Bird with the Crystal Plumage*, Dario Argento, 1970)

Gli ultimi giorni di Pompei (*The Last Days of Pompeii*, Amleto Palermi and Carmine Gallone, 1926)

Ultimo Tango a Parigi (*Last Tango in Paris*, Bernardo Bertolucci, 1972)

Ultrà (*Ultras, Some Lose, Some Die… Some Win*, Ricky Tognazzi, 1991)

Uomini contro (*Just Another War*, Francesco Rosi, 1969)

Uomini sul fondo (*SOS Submarine*, Francesco De Robertis, 1941)

Vaghe stelle dell'orsa (*Sandra*, Luchino Visconti, 1965)

Il vangelo secondo Matteo (*The Gospel According to Saint Matthew*, Pier Paolo Pasolini, 1964)

I Vesuviani (Antonio Capuano, Pappi Corsicato, Antonietta De Lillo, Mario Martone, 1996)

Viaggi di nozze (*Honeymoons*, Carlo Verdone, 1992)

Un viaggio chiamato amore (*A Journey Called Love*, Michele Placido, 2002)

Viaggio in Italia (*Voyage to Italy*, Roberto Rossellini, 1954)

I vinti (*The Vanquished*, Michelangelo Antonioni, 1952)

Una vita difficile (*A Difficult Life*, Dino Risi, 1961)

La vita è bella (*Life is Beautiful*, Ludovico Bragaglia, 1943)

La vita è bella (*Life is Beautiful*, Roberto Benigni, 1997)

I vitelloni (Federico Fellini, 1953)

Viva l'Italia (*Long Live Italy*, Roberto Rossellini, 1960)

Vivere in pace (*To Live in Peace*, Luigi Zampa, 1946)

La voce della luna (Federico Fellini, 1990)

Vogliamo i colonelli (*We Want the Colonels*, Mario Monicelli, 1974)

Volere volare (Maurizio Nichetti, 1991)

Zabriskie Point (Michelangelo Antonioni, 1969)

Lo zio di Brooklyn (*The Uncle from Brooklyn*, Daniele Ciprì and Franco Maresco, 1995)

Notes

Chapter 1 What is Italian Cinema?

1. Statistics are compiled by the Associazione Generale dello Spettacolo (AGIS) and published in the weekly trade paper, *Giornale dello Spettacolo*; by the Associazione Nazionale Industrie Cinematografiche e Audiovisive (ANICA) published in the fortnightly trade paper, *Cinema d'oggi*; and by the Società Italiana Autori Editori (SIAE) yearly statistical volume, *Lo Spettacolo in Italia*. The latter provides detailed statistics on all forms of entertainment in Italy, from opera to sport and circuses. From the early 1970s Nazional Controlcine provided an 'instant' photograph of trends. These sources provide indications of popularity upon which to estimate the financial success of a production package.

2. Cristaldi pressed for the publication of the first statistical survey of Italian cinema. He astutely backed first features by directors, notably Rosi but more recently Tornatore and Carlei, but interspersed these with less problematic films. The same year that he produced Rosi's *Salvatore Giuliano* (1961), for example, he also produced Duccio Tessari's *Arrivano i titani* (*The Titans are Coming*), Giannelli's *Giorno per giorno disperatamente* (*Desperately Day By Day*), Germi's huge success, *Divorzio all'italiana* (*Divorce Italian Style*), and Petri's *L'assassino* (*The Assassin*) (Ferraù 1992: 8–9).

3. Interview with the author, 1 June 1987.

4. The situation led to the occasional nice irony, as when Gaumont proposed in the early 1970s to close its cinemas on Sunday evenings

because the 8.30 p.m. film emptied cinemas, although it was aware that the film programmed in that slot was, more often than not, a Gaumont product (Toscan du Plantier 1987: 14).

5. Interview with the author, 26 February 1987.

6. 'Cecchi Gori releases a film with 600 copies in his cinemas. Other films can't get exhibited because his films fill up cinemas.' Elda Ferri interviewed by the author, 23 October 1997.

Chapter 2 Popular Cinema and Box-office Hits

1. Margheriti and Bava also re-used the Anglo-Saxon names they had adopted when they made spaghetti westerns – Anthony M. Dawson and John M. Old respectively.

2. Veronica Lario later became Signora Berlusconi. According to Jean-Baptiste Thoret, her husband is reported to have excised her every scene when *Tenebre* was transmitted on his television channels. In another twist, the girl in the flashback is played by a transsexual actor, Eva Robbins-Roberto Coatti, a fact that would only be known from the secondary text of reviews and articles, and which adds another dimension to the interplay of desire and revulsion in the film (Thoret 2002: 153).

Chapter 3 The Epic and Historical Film

1. Engravings of famous history paintings of the nineteenth-century *bourgeois realism* genre epitomized by Lawrence Alma-Tadema and Jean-Léon Gérôme, were widely sold in the nineteenth century, some of them finding their way onto magic lantern slides and inspiring film sets. Blom has found paintings of gladiators surrounded by lions, for example, being used as source material for later films.

2. Guardian Interview, National Film Theatre, London, 23 August 1996.

Chapter 4 Realisms and Neorealisms in Italian Cinema

1. One of the popular categories of magic lantern show were slides of the eruption of volcanoes, in which fire and rocks were thrown into the air. Another category chose to illustrate a highly dramatic moment in (typically) major fires, and were accompanied by spoken narratives

giving 'all the details' of names of the gallant fire fighters, dates, times and places, who died and who survived. These early narrativizing techniques are the precursors of modern tabloid news items, with their concentration on the dramatic and emotional charge, but would have had a longer shelf life through the performance of itinerant lanternists.

2. The politician in charge of this legislation, Giulio Andreotti, used the occasion to censor neorealist films in particular. Andreotti went on to become six times Christian Democrat Prime Minister, and was tried in Palermo in 1993 for alleged collusion with the Mafia.

Chapter 5 *Auteur* Cinema

1. The well-known editor, Nino Baragli (who had also worked with Pasolini) on *La commare secca*; subsequently Roberto Perpignani edited the low-budget films up to *La strategia del ragno*. This latter film, produced by Bertolucci's brother, Giuseppe, and RAI television marked Bertolucci's collaboration with the internationally recognized cinematographer Vittorio Storaro. Other creative partnerships include the editor Franco (Kim) Arcalli from *The Conformist* to *1900*, and Gabriella Cristiani from *La luna* onwards. She is particularly interested in the possibilities of digital editing.

2. *ItaliaCinema* (2002) Interview with Bertolucci on the set of *The Dreamers*, 15 December. DVD produced by M. Canale, A. Morri, N. Vezzoli.

Chapter 6 Making Sense of Changing Reality

1. This trope of 'clean hands' was used to great effect in 1992–3 when investigating magistrates managed to bring many of those involved in the *tangentopoli* (financial kick-backs) scandals to justice.

2. Paolo Flores d'Arcais (2000: 15) is typical of the widespread coverage of the Cardinal in the Italian press, suggesting that his intervention was part of the conservative Right's struggle for power in the Vatican. Cardinal Biffi's views included the words, 'The criteria for admitting immigrants cannot be solely economic or charitable. We have to be concerned about saving the identity of the nation' (Owen 2000).

Chapter 8 Visual Style and the Use of Cinematic Space

1. Interview with the author, 28 July 1985.
2. Ibid.

Conclusion

1. When asked, Daniele Luchetti observed that his film, *Dillo con parole mie* (2003), had already covered its costs by television pre-sales. (Conversation with the author, Italian Film Festival, Riverside Studios London, 30 April 2004.)

Bibliography

Abercrombie, N., Lash, S. and Longhurst, B. (1992), 'Popular Representation: Recasting Realism' in S. Lash and J. Friedman (eds), *Modernity and Identity*, Oxford: Blackwell.

Accardo, A. (2001), *Age e Scarpelli: La storia si fa commedia*, Rome: ANNCI.

Addonizio, A., Carrara., G., Chiesi, R., De Simone, E., Lippi, R., Premuda, E., Roncaglia, G. (eds), *Loro di Napoli: Il nuovo cinema napoletano 1986–1997*, Palermo: Edizioni della Battaglia.

Aitken, S. C. and Zonn, L. E. (1994), 'Re-Presenting the Place Pastiche' in S. C. Aitken and L. E. Zonn (eds), *Place, Power, Situation and Spectacle: A Geography of Film*, Lanham MA. and London: Rowman & Littlefield, pp. 3–25.

Albano, V. (2003), *La mafia nel cinema siciliano da In nome della legge a Placido Rizzotto*, Manduria: Barbieri.

Allsop, D. (1989), 'The New Culture Club', *Options*, October, 22–6.

Amelio, G. (1994), *Amelio secondo il cinema: Conversazione con Goffredo Fofi*, Rome: Donzelli.

—— (1997), *Giuseppe Marotta: Al cinema non fa freddo*, Cava de' Tirreni: Avagliano.

Anderson, B. (1991), *Imagined Communities: Reflections on the Origin and Spread of Nationalism*, London: Verso, revised edition.

Angeli, O. (1979), 'Anatomia della crisi', *Cinema 60*, 125 (January/February): 7–8.

ANICA (2003), 'Il cinema italiano in numeri', *Cinema d'Oggi*, 1/2: 14.

Anon. (1950) 'Un referendum su la "Terra trema"', *Cinema*, 32 (15 February): 64.

Appadurai, A. (1990) 'Disjuncture and Difference in the Global World Economy' in M. Featherstone (ed.) *Global Culture: Nationalism, Globalization and Modernity*, London: Sage, pp. 295–310.

Aprà, A. (2000), 'Rossellini's Historical Encyclopedia' in D. Forgacs, S. Lutton and G. Nowell-Smith (eds), *Roberto Rossellini: Magician of the Real*, London: BFI.

Aprà, A. and Carabba, C. (1976), *Neorealismo d'appendice: Per un dibattito sul cinema popolare: il Caso Matarazzo*, Rimini-Florence: Guaraldi.

Aprà, A. and Pistagnesi, P. (eds) (1986), *Comedy, Italian Style 1950–1980*, Turin, ERI.

Argentieri, M. (1998), *Il cinema in guerra: Arte, comunicazione e propaganda in Italia 1940–1944*, Rome: Editori Riuniti.

Aristarco, G. (1977), *Sotto il segno dello scorpione: Il cinema dei Taviani*, Messina/Florence: D'Anna.

—— (1980), *Neorealismo e nuova critica cinematografica: cinematografia e vita nazionale negli anni quaranta e cinquanta: tra rotture e tradizioni*, Florence: Guaraldi.

Armes, R. (1971), *Patterns of Realism*, London: The Tantivy Press.

Atkinson, D. (2003), 'Geographical Knowledge and Scientific Survey in the Construction of Italian Libya', *Modern Italy*, 8(1): 9–29.

Bacon, H. (1998), *Visconti: Explorations of Beauty and Decay*, Cambridge: Cambridge University Press.

Barański, Z. G. (1999), *Pasolini Old and New: Surveys and Studies*, Dublin: Four Courts Press/Foundation for Italian Studies, University College Dublin.

Barański, Z. G. and West, R. J. (eds) (2001), *The Cambridge Companion to Modern Italian Culture*, Cambridge: Cambridge University Press.

Barile, P. and Rao, G. (1992), 'Trends in the Italian Mass Media and Media Law', *European Journal of Communication*, 7: 261–81.

Barlozzetti, G. (2004), 'La svolta della fiction televisiva italiana: Colloquio con Agostino Saccà, direttore di Rai Fiction', *Cinema d'Oggi*, 5/6 (19 March): 5.

Barthes, R. (1970), 'Le troisième sens', *Cahiers du Cinéma*, 222: 12–19.

Bartram, G. Slawinski, M. and Steel, D. (eds) (1996), *Reconstructing the Past: Representations of the Fascist Era in Post-War European Culture*, Keele: Keele University Press.

Baudrillard, J. (1990), *Seduction*, Basingstoke: Macmillan Education.

Bazin, A. (1967), *What is Cinema?* Vol. I, trans. H. Gray, Berkeley and Los Angeles: University of California Press.

—— (1971) *What is Cinema?* Vol. II, trans. H. Gray, Berkeley and Los Angeles: University of California Press.

Beck, U. (2000) *What is Globalization?* Cambridge: Polity Press.

Ben-Ghiat, R. (2003), 'The Italian Colonial Cinema: Agendas and Audiences', *Modern Italy*, 8(1), 49–63.

Bernardi, S. (2002), *Il paesaggio nel cinema italiano*, Venice: Marsilio.

Bernardini, A. (1982), *Cinema muto italiano*, Vol. III, *Arte, divismo e mercato 1910–1914*, Rome: Laterza.

Bertelli, P. (2001), *Pier Paolo Pasolini: Il cinema in corpo. Atti impuri di un eretico*, Rome: Libreria Croce.

Bertolotti, F. (1984), 'Rosi: la mia Carmen', *Avvenire*, 11 May.

Bertozzi, M. (2001), *Liimmaginario urbano nel cinema delle origini: La veduta Lumière*, Bologna: CLUEB.

Bizio, S. (2002), *Cinema Italian Style: Italians at the Academy Awards*, Rome: Gremese.

Bizzari, L. (1979, 'L'economia cinematografica' in M. Fasoli, G, Guastini, B. Retuccia and V. Rivosecchi (eds), *La città del cinema: Produzione e lavoro nel cinema italiano 1930–1970*, Rome: Roberto Napoleone.

Blom, I. (2001), 'Gérôme en Quo vadis? Picturale invloeden in de film', *Jong Holland*, 4: 19–28.

Bogani, G. (2003), 'Io, il porno e l'avventura del cinema italiano', http://www.kwcinema.kataweb.it/templates/kwc_popup_stampa/0,2670,123450.html. 13 May (accessed 29 July 2003).

Bolla, L. and Cardini, F. (1999), *Carne in scatola: La rappresentazione del corpo nella televisione italiana*, Rome: RAI-ERI VQPT 170.

Bondanella, P. (1983), *Italian Cinema from Neorealism to the Present*, New York: Ungar.

—— (2001), 'Italian Cinema' in Z. G. Barański and R. J. West (eds), *The Cambridge Companion to Modern Italian Culture*, Cambridge: Cambridge University Press, 215–42.

Boneschi, M. (1995), *Poveri ma belli: i nostri anni cinquanta*, Milan: Oscar Mondadori.

Bordwell, D. (1979) 'The Art Cinema as a Mode of Film Practice', *Film Criticism*, 4(1): 56–64.

Borgna, G. (1998), Preface to Ministero per i Beni Culturali e Ambientali, *Totò partenopeo e parte napoletano*, Venice: Marsilio, 12.

Bourdieu, P. (1993), *The Field of Cultural Production*, Cambridge: Polity Press.

Brooks, P. (1976), *The Melodramatic Imagination*, New Haven: Yale University Press.

—— (1994), 'Melodrama, Body, Revolution' in J. Bratton, J. Cook and C. Gledhill (eds), *Melodrama: Stage, Picture, Screen*, London: BFI, 11–24.

Brosio, G. and Santagata, W. (1992), 'Il film' in G. Brosio and W. Santagata (eds), *Rapporto sull'economia delle arti e dello spettacolo in Italia*, Turin: Edizioni della Fondazione Giovanni Agnelli, 321–47.

Brunetta, G. P. (1982), *Storia del cinema italiano dal 1945 agli anni ottanta*, Rome: Editori Riuniti.

—— (1986), 'L'évocation du passé: Les années d'or du film historique', in A. Bernardini and J. Gili (eds), *Le cinéma italien de La Prise de Rome (1905) à Rome, Ville Ouverte (1945)*, Paris, Centre Georges Pompidou, 55–60.

—— (1993a), *Storia del cinema italiano*. Vol. 1, *Il cinema muto 1895–1929*, Rome: Editori Riuniti, 2 edn.

—— (1993b), *Storia del cinema italiano*. Vol. IV, *Dal miracolo economico agli anni novanta 1960–1993*, Rome: Editori Riuniti, 2 edn.

—— (1999) 'Grammatica della visione popolare' in O. Caldiron and S. Della Casa (eds) *Appassionatamente: Il mélo nel cinema italiano*, Turin: Lindau.

Brunette, P. (1996), *Roberto Rossellini*, Berkeley and Los Angeles: University of California Press.

Bruno, G. (1993), *Streetwalking on a Ruined Map: Cultural Theory and the City Films of Elvira Notari*, Princeton: Princeton University Press.

—— (2002), *Atlas of Emotion: Journeys in Art, Architecture and Film*, New York: Verso.

Buci-Glucksmann, C. (1994), *Baroque Reason: The Aesthetics of Modernity*, trans. P. Camiller, London: Sage.

Buonanno, M. and Pellegrini, E. (1993), 'Mezzogiorno di fuoco. Come la fiction racconta il sud', in M Buonanno (ed.), *Non è la stessa storia: la fiction italiana. L'Italia nella fiction Anno 4*, Rome: RAI/VQPT 117.

Buscemi, F. (1996), *Invito al cinema di Liliana Cavani*, Milan: Mursia.

Calabrese, O. (1992), *Neo-Baroque: A Sign of the Times*, trans. C. Lambert, Princeton: Princeton University Press.

Caldiron, O. (1980), *Totò*, Rome, Gremese.

—— (1999), *Il paradosso dell'autore*, Rome: Bulzoni.

Caldiron, O. and Hochkofler, M. (eds) (1988), *Scrivere il cinema: Suso Cecchi d'Amico*, Bari: Dedalo.

Camerini, C. (1986), 'Les formes italiennes du "divismo": les années du muet' in A. Bernardini and J. Gili (eds), *Le cinéma italien de La Prise de Rome (1905) à Rome, Ville Ouverte (1945)*, Paris, Centre Georges Pompidou, pp. 61–8.

Campassi, O. (1949), 'Gli altri', *Sequenze*, 4: 35.

Canova, G. (1999), 'L'infiammazione della lacrima: il paradosso del mélo nel cinema italiano' in O. Caldiron and S. Della Casa (eds), *Appassionatamente: Il mélo nel cinema italiano*, Turin: Lindau.

—— (2000), *Giancarlo Basili: Spazio e architettura nel cinema italiano*, n.p.: Alexa Edizioni.

Capussotti, E. (2004), *Gioventù perduta: Gli anni Cinquanta dei giovani e del cinema in Italia*, Florence: Giunti.

Caputi, J. (1999), 'Small Ceremonies: Ritual in *Forrest Gump*, *Natural Born Killers*, *Seven*, and *Follow Me Home*' in C. Sharrett (ed.), *Mythologies of Violence in Postmodern Media*, Detroit: University of Michigan Press, 147–74.

Carabba, C. (1974), *Il cinema del ventennio nero*, Florence: Vallecchi.

Casetti, F, Mariotti, S. Pilati, A. Silva, F. (eds) (1998), *Cinema: secondo secolo terzo millennio*, Milan: BNL Edizioni/Guerini.

Casiraghi, U. (1954), 'Il festival di Cannes', *L'Eco del cinema e dello spettacolo*, 71 (30 April): 13.

Cecchi d'Amico, S. (1996), *Storie di cinema (e d'altro): L'Italia di scrittori, giornalisti, politici, registi, attori, musicisti dagli anni Trenta a oggi*, Rome: Garzanti.

Champenier, S. (1989), 'Quo vadis Cinecittà?', *La revue du Cinéma*, 451: 67.

Chapman, R. (1988), 'The Great Pretender: Variations on the New Man Theme', in R. Chapman and J. Rutherford (eds), *Male Order: Unwrapping Masculinity*, London: Lawrence and Wishart, 225–48.

Chiaretti, T. (1970), 'Allegretto con Pessimismo' introduction to M. Bellocchio, *China is Near: Writings on Film*, London: Calder & Boyars, 1–12.

Chow, R. (1998), 'Film and Cultural Identity' in J. Hill and P. Church Gibson (eds), *The Oxford Guide to Film Studies*, Oxford: Oxford University Press.

Cianfarani, C. (1984), 'Society, Market and Industry' in *Italian Cinema of the 80s*, Rome: EAGC, 13–14.

Ciment, M. (1976), *Le dossier Rosi*, Paris: Éditions Stock.

Clarke, D. B. (ed.), *The Cinematic City*, London and New York: Routledge.

Colarizi, S. (1996), *Storia D'Italia*, vol. 4, *La seconda guerra mondiale e la Repubblica*, Milan: TEA.

Colomini, B. (ed.), 1992), *Sexuality and Space*, Princeton: Princeton Papers on Architecture.

Consiglio, S. and Ferzetti, F. (1983) (eds), *La bottega della luce: I direttori della fotografia*, Milan: Ubulibri.

Cook, P. and Bernink, M. (1999), *The Cinema Book*, London: British Film Institute, 2 edn.

Corsi, B. (2001), *Con qualche dollaro di meno: Storia economica del cinema italiano*, Rome: Editori Riuniti.

Cosulich, C. (ed.) (1957), 'La battaglia delle cifre', *Cinema Nuovo*, 98, 15 January, in A. Aprà and C. Carabba (eds) (1976), *Neorealismo d'appendice: Per un dibattito sul cinema popolare: Il caso Matarazzo*, Rimini-Florence: Guaraldi, 84–9.

Cosulich, C. (1987), 'Cambia il ruolo del cinema non quello del produttore', *Cinema d'Oggi*, 17: 4.

D'Agostini, P. (2000) 'Un tè con Mussolini' in P. D'Agostini and S. Della Casa (eds) *Cinema Italiano annuario 1999–2000*, Milan: Il Castoro.

Dall'Asta, M. (1998), 'Donne avventurose del cinema Torinese' in P. Bertetto and G. Rondolino (eds), *Cabiria e il suo tempo*, Milan: Il Castoro, 354–64.

Dalle Vacche, A. (1992), *The Body in the Mirror: Shapes of History in Italian Cinema*, Princeton: Princeton University Press.

—— (1996), *Cinema and Painting: How Art is Used in Film*, London: Athlone Press.

D'Amico, M. (1985), *La commedia all'italiana: Il cinema comico in Italia dal 1945 al 1975*, Milan: Mondadori.

De Gaetano, R. (1999), *Il corpo e la maschera: Il grottesco nel cinema italiano*, Rome: Bulzoni.

—— (2000), *Tra emozione e ragione: Il cinema di Guido Chiesa*, Turin: Lindau.

—— (2002), *La sincope dell'identità: Il cinema di Nanni Moretti*, Turin: Lindau.

Deleuze, G. (1989), *Cinema 2: The Time-Image*, London: The Athlone Press, trans. H. Tomlinson and R. Galeta.

—— (1992), *Cinema 1: The Movement-Image*, London: The Athlone Press, trans. H. Tomlinson and B. Habberjam.

Della Casa, S. (1986), *Mario Monicelli*, Rome: Il Castoro/La Nuova Italia.

—— (2000), 'Cinema popolare italiano del dopoguerra' in Brunetta, G. P. (ed.), *Storia del cinema mondiale*, vol. III, *L'Europa: Le cinematografie nazionali*, tome I, Turin: Einaudi, 779–823.

Della Sala, E. (1988), 'La trasformazione del mercato: produzione, distribuzione ed esercizio dopo i network televisivi', *Cinemasessanta*, 6(184): 19.

De Masi, D. (1980), 'Nel mio film non c'è la parola FINE: è una storia di mandanti e sicari che dura ancora', interview with Francesco Rosi on the occasion of the anniversary of the death of Giuliano, *Paese Sera*, 5 July.

De Paoli, E. (1995), *Il cinema e la prima repubblica: Da "Roma città aperta" a "Il caso Moro"*, Barzago: Marna.

Domenico, R. P. (2002), *Remaking Italy in the Twentieth Century*, Lanham and Oxford: Bowman & Littlefield.

Duggan, C. and Wagstaff, C. (eds) (1995), *Italy in the Cold War: Politics, Culture and Society 1948–58*, Oxford and Washington DC: Berg.

Dyer, R. (1987), *Heavenly Bodies: Film Stars and Society*, Basingstoke and London: Macmillan Education/BFI.

—— (1991), 'Charisma' in C. Gledhill (ed.), *Stardom: Industry of Desire*, London and New York: Routledge, 57–9.

Dyer, R. and Vincendeau, G. (eds) (1992), *Popular European Cinema*, London, Routledge.

Eco, U. (1979), *The Role of the Reader: Explorations in the Semiotics of Texts*, London: Hutchinson Education.

Ellero, R. (2000), *Dove va il cinema? Critica e mercato nell'era dei multiplex*, Rome: Bulzoni.

Elley, D. (1984), *The Epic Film: Myth and History*, London: Routledge & Kegan Paul.

Elsaesser, T. (1996), 'Subject Positions, Speaking Positions: From *Holocaust*, *Our Hitler*, and *Heimat* to *Shoah* and *Schindler's List*', in V. Sobchack (ed.), *The Persistence of History: Cinema, Television, and the Modern Event*, London: Routledge, 145–83.

—— (2001), 'Postmodernism as Mourning Work', *Screen*, 42(2): 193–201.

European Audiovisual Observatory Statistical Yearbook 2002, Vol. 1 (2002), Strasbourg: European Audiovisual Observatory.

Fairclough, N. (1989), *Language and Power*, London: Longman.

Faldini, F. and Fofi, G. (1979), *L'avventurosa storia del cinema italiano raccontata dai suoi protagonisti 1935–1959*, Milan: Feltrinelli.

—— (1981), *L'avventurosa storia del cinema italiano raccontata dai suoi protagonisti 1960–1969*, Milan: Feltrinelli.

Fantoni Minella, M. (1998), *La legge del desiderio: Cinema erotico ed erotismo nel cinema*, Alessandria: Falsopiano.

Farassino, A. (1989), *Neorealismo. Cinema italiano 1945–1949*, Turin: E. D. T. Edizioni.

Featherstone, M. and Lash, S. (eds) (1999), *Spaces of Culture: City – Nation – World*, London: Sage.

Fellini, F. (1980), *Fare un film*, Turin: Einaudi.

—— (1981), *La dolce vita*, Milan: Garzanti.

Fenster, M. (1999), *Conspiracy Theories: Secrecy and Power in American Culture*, Minneapolis & London: University of Minneapolis Press.

Ferraù, A. (1949), 'Interview du producteur Dino De Laurentiis', *Il Giornale dello Spettacolo*, 2 (February): 7.

—— (1966), 'Lenta ma progressiva l'evoluzione dei gusti', *Giornale dello Spettacolo*, 7 (26 February): 4.

—— (1984), 'Vita breve per il film italiano', *Giornale dello Spettacolo*, 13: 14.

—— (1992), 'Il successo dei film di Franco Cristaldi', *Cinema d'Oggi*, 13 (23 July): 8–9.

F.F. (2002), 'Gli italiani all'estero troppo poco visibili', *Giornale dello Spettacolo*, 30: 4.

Flores D'Arcais, P. (2000), 'La doppia intolleranza che assedia l'Occidente', *La Repubblica*, (15 September): 15.

Fofi, G. (1972), *Totò*, Rome: Samonà & Savelli.

—— (1994), *Amelio secondo il cinema: Conversazione con Goffredo Fofi*, Rome: Donzelli.

—— (1997) 'Sacher Film 1987–1997: è stata davvero rivoluzione?' in P. D'Agostini and S. Della Casa (eds) *Cinema italiano annuario 1997*, Milan: Il Castoro.

—— (1997), 'Introduzione' in A. Addonizio, G. Carrara, R. Chiesi, E. De Simone, R. Lippi, E. Premuda, G. Roncaglia (eds), *Loro di Napoli: Il nuovo cinema napoletano 1986–1997*, Palermo: Edizioni della Battaglia, 3–8.

—— (1998), *Un secolo con Totò*, Naples: Dante & Descartes.

Foot, J. (2001), *Milan since the Miracle: City, Culture and Identity*, Oxford and New York: Berg.

—— (2003), *Modern Italy*, Basingstoke: Palgrave/Macmillan.

Forbes, J. (1997), *Les Enfants du paradis*, London: British Film Institute.

Forgacs. D. (1989) 'The Making and Unmaking of Neorealism in Post-war Italy' in N. Hewitt (ed.), *The Culture of Reconstruction*, Basingstoke: Macmillan.

—— (1990) 'The Italian Communist Party and Culture' in Barański. Z.G. and Lumley. R. (eds) *Culture and Conflict in Post-war Italy*, Basingstoke: Macmillan/University of Reading.

—— (1996), 'Post-War Italian Culture: Renewal or Legacy of the Past', in G. Bartram, M. Slawinski and D. Steel (eds), *Reconstructing the Past: Representations of the Fascist Era in Post-War European Culture*, Keele: Keele University Press, 49–63.

—— (2000), *L'industrializzazione della cultura italiana (1880–2000)*, Bologna: Il Mulino.

—— (2001), '*Nostra patria*: Rivisions of the Risorgimento in the Cinema, 1925–52' in A. Russell Ascoli and K. von Henneberg (eds), *Making and Remaking Italy: The Cultivation of National Identity around the Risorgimento*, Oxford and New York: Berg.

Forgacs, D. Lutton, S. and Nowell-Smith, G. (2000), *Roberto Rossellini: Magician of the Real*, London: BFI.

Foucault, M. (1977), *Discipline and Punish: The Birth of the Prison*, translation Alan Sheridan. London: Penguin Books. Trans. of *Surveiller et punir: Naissance de la prison*, Paris: Éditions Gallimard, 1975.

—— (1997), 'Of Other Spaces: Utopias and Heterotopias', in N. Leach (ed.), *Rethinking Architecture: A Reader in Cultural Theory*, London and New York: Routledge, 350–79.

Fragola, A. (1984), 'Il rapporto tra regista e produttore', *Cinema d'oggi*, 13 (11 July): 3.

Frayling, C. (1981), *Spaghetti Westerns: Cowboys and Europeans from Karl May to Sergio Leone*, London: Boston & Henley.

Galliano, G. (2003), 'Frutta: Metafore sociali', *Nocturno dossier*, 12: 44.

Gallo, M. (1986), 'Il modello produttivo europeo: il caso italiano' in Magrelli, E. (ed.) *Sull'industria cinematografica italiana*, Venice: Marsilio, 87–97.

Gelato, C. (2004), 'Creatori di luce: I direttori della fotografia deventano coautori del film', *Cinema d'oggi*, 5/6 (19 March): 20.

Ghezzi, E. (1998) 'Altrove (il disagio della regia)' in M. Martone, *Teatro di guerra: un diario*, Milan: Bompiani.

Giacovelli, E. (1999), *Non ci resta che ridere: Una storia del cinema comica italiana*, Turin: Lindau.

Gieri, M. (1995), *Contemporary Italian Film-making: Strategies of Subversion. Pirandello, Fellini, Scola, and the Directors of the New Generation*, Toronto: University of Toronto Press.

—— (1999), 'Landscapes of Oblivion and Historical Memory in the New Italian Cinema', *Annali d'Italianistica*, 17: 39–54.

Gili, J. (2000), 'La punta dell'iceberg: Il cinema italiano visto dalla Francia', in V. Zagarrio (ed.), *Il cinema della transizione: Scenari italiani degli anni Novanta*, Venice: Marsilio, 425–38.

Ginsborg, P. (1990), *A History of Contemporary Italy: Society and Politics 1943–1988*, London: Penguin Books.

—— (2001), *Italy and Its Discontents 1980–2001*, London: Allen Lane, The Penguin Press.

Giovannini, F. and Tentori, A. (2004), *Porn'Italia: Il cinema erotico italiano*, Viterbo: Nuovi Equilibri.

Gosetti, G. (2002), 'Le regole del noir' in M. Fabbri (ed.) *Noir in Festival 2002*, Rome: Noir in Festival.

Governi, G. (1998), 'Il cinema lo ha reso immortale' in Ministero per i Beni Culturali e Ambientali, *Totò partenopeo e parte napoletano*, Venice: Marsilio, 135–9.

Grainge, P. (ed.) (2003), *Memory and Popular Film*, Manchester: Manchester University Press.

Gramsci, A. (1975), *Letteratura e vita nazionale*, Rome: Editori Riuniti.

Grasso, A. (1992), *Storia della televisione italiana*, Milan: Garzanti.

Greene, N. (1990), *Pier Paolo Pasolini: Cinema as Heresy*, Princeton: Princeton University Press.

Guarini, A. (1953), 'Il neorealismo e l'industria', *Cinema*, 123: 320–3.

Guback, T. H. (1969), *The International Film Industry: Western Europe and America since 1945*, Bloomington: Indiana University Press.

Gubitosi, G. (1998), *Amedeo Nazzari*, Bologna: Il Mulino.

Hall, S. (1980), 'Encoding/decoding' in S. Hall, D. Hobson, A. Lowe and P. Willis (eds), *Culture, Media, Language: Working Papers in Cultural Studies, 1972–79*, London: Hutchinson/CCCS, University of Birmingham, 128–38.

Harvey, D. (1990) *The Condition of Postmodernity: An Enquiry into the Origins of Cultural Change*, Malden MA and Oxford: Blackwell.

Hay, J. (1987), *Popular Film Culture in Fascist Italy: The Passing of the Rex*, Bloomington and Indianapolis: Indiana University Press.

Heiney, D. (1964), *America in Modern Italian Literature*, New Brunswick: Rutgers University Press.

Henderson, B. (1976), 'The Long Take' in B. Nichols (ed.), *Movies and Methods: An Anthology*, Berkeley, Los Angeles and London: University of California Press, 314–24.

Hodgkin, K. and Radstone, S. (eds) (2003), *Contested Pasts*, London: Routledge.

Hughes, R. (1991), *The Shock of the New*, London: Thames & Hudson, 2 edn.

Hunt, L. (1993), 'What Are Big Boys Made Of? *Spartacus, El Cid* and the Male Epic' in Kirkham, P. and Thumim, J. (eds), *You Tarzan: Masculinity, Movies and Men*, London: Lawrence & Wishart.

Huyghe, R. (1961), 'Art Forms and Society' in R. Huyghe (ed.), *Larousse Encyclopedia of Renaissance and Baroque Art*, London: Paul Hamlyn, 329–32.

Ilott, T. (1996), *Budgets and Markets: A Study of the Budgeting of European Film*, London: Routledge.

Jameson, F. (1991), *Postmodernism or, The Cultural Logic of Late Capitalism*, London and New York: Verso.

—— (2000), 'Reification and Utopia in Mass Culture' (1992), in M. Hardt and K. Weeks (eds), *The Jameson Reader*, Oxford: Blackwell.

Jordanova, D. (2001), *Cinema of Flames: Balkan Film, Culture and the Media*, London: British Film Institute.

Kaplan, E. A. (2001), 'Melodrama, cinema and trauma', *Screen*, 42(2): 201–10.

Keith, M. and Pile, S. (eds) (1993), *Place and the Politics of Identity*, London and New York: Routledge.

Kezich, T. (1978), *Il dolce cinema: Fellini e altri (1960, 1962)*, Milan: Bompiani.

Konstantarakos, M. (2000), 'Is Pasolini an Urban Film-maker?' in M. Konstantarakos (ed.), *Spaces in European Cinema*, Exeter: Intellect, 112–23.

Koven, M. (2003), '*La dolce morta*: Space, Modernity and the *Giallo*', paper delivered at the European Cinema Research Forum conference, 'Reviewing Space: Space and Place in European Cinema'.

Labanyi, J. 'Feminizing the Nation: Women, Subordination and Subversion in Post-Civil War Spanish Cinema' in U. Sieglohr (ed.), *Heroines Without Heroes: Reconstructing Female and National Identities in European Cinema, 1945–51*, London: Cassell, 163–82.

Lagny, M. (1992), 'Popular taste: The peplum' in Dyer, R and Vincendeau, G. (eds), *Popular European Cinema*, London: Routledge, 163–80.

Landy, M. (1986), *Fascism in Film: The Italian Commercial Cinema, 1931–1943*, Princeton: Princeton University Press.

—— (1994), *Film, Politics and Gramsci*, Minneapolis: University of Minnesota Press.

—— (1996), *Cinematic Uses of the Past*, Minneapolis and London: University of Minnesota Press.

—— (1998), *The Folklore of Consensus: Theatricality in the Italian Cinema 1930–1943*, Albany: State University of New York Press.

—— (2000), *Italian Film*, Cambridge, Cambridge University Press.

Lapertosa, V. (2002), *Dalla fame all'abbondanza: Gli italiani e il cibo nel cinema italiano dal dopoguerra a oggi*, Turin: Lindau.

Laura, E. G. (2000), *Le stagioni dell'aquila: Storia dell'Istituto Luce*, Rome: Ente dello Spettacolo.

Lefebvre, H. (1991), *The Production of Space*, trans. D. Nicholson-Smith, Oxford: Blackwell.

Liehm, M. (1984), *Passion and Defiance: Film in Italy from 1942 to the Present*, Berkeley and Los Angeles: University of California Press.

Loschitzky, Y. (1995), *The Radical Faces of Godard and Bertolucci*, Detroit: Wayne State University Press.

Lucantonio, G. (ed.) (2001), *Il cinema horror in Italia: Dario Argento, Luigi Cozzi, Antonio Margheriti, Michele Soavi e altri*, Rome: Dino Audino.

Lumley, R. (1990), 'Challenging Tradition: Social Movements, Cultural Change and the Ecology Question' in Z. G. Barański and R. Lumley (eds), *Culture and Conflict in Post-war Italy*, Basingstoke and London: Macmillan.

Luperini, I. (1995), 'The Tavianis' "Tuscan Classicism": A Blend of Figurative Art and Cinema' in R. Ferrucci and P. Turini (eds), *Paolo and Vittorio Taviani: Poetry of the Italian Landscape*, Rome: Gremese, 26–34.

MacNab, G. (1997), 'Smilla's Feeling for Snow', *Sight and Sound*, (November): 52–3.

Magrelli, E. (2002), 'I salti nel vuoto di Marco Bellocchio', *Giornale dello Spettacolo*, 10 May: 3.

Maravall, J. A. (1975), *Culture of the Baroque: Analysis of a Historical Structure*, trans. T. Cochran, Manchester: Manchester University Press.

Marchelli, M. (1996), *Melodramma in cento film*, Recco-Genoa: Le Mani.

Marcotulli, A. (1993), 'Film in tv nel 1992: La carica degli undicimila', *Cinema d'oggi*, 5, 7.

Marcus, M. (1986), *Italian Film in the Light of Neorealism*, Princeton: Princeton University Press.

—— (2002), *After Fellini: National Cinema in the Postmodern Age*, Baltimore: Johns Hopkins Press.

Marrone, G. (2000), *The Gaze and the Labyrinth: The Cinema of Liliana Cavani*, Princeton: Princeton University Press.

Martinelli, V. (1998), 'Donne del cinema Torinese', in P. Bertetto and G. Rondolino (eds), *Cabiria e il suo tempo*, Milan: Il Castoro, 342–53.

Martini, G. (1992), 'Lo stato delle cose in cifre', *Cinema Nuovo*, 2(336): 23–34.

Masi, S. (1990), *Costumisti e scenografi del cinema italiano*, vol. 2, L'Aquila: Istituto Cinematografico dell'Aquila 'La Lanterna Magica'.

Massey, D. 1996), 'Masculinity, Dualisms and High Technology' in N. Duncan (ed.), *Bodyspace: Destabilizing Geographies of Gender and Sexuality*, London and New York: Routledge, 109–26.

Melanco, M. (1996), 'Il motivo del viaggio nel cinema italiano (1945–1965)' in G. P. Brunetta (ed.), *Identità italiana e identità europea nel cinema italiano dal 1945 al miracolo economico*, Turin: Fondazione Giovanni Agnelli, 217–308.

Meldini, P. (1989), 'L'abito e l'arredamento' in A. Farassino (ed.), *Neorealismo Cinema italiano 1945–1949*, Turin: EDT, 121–5.

Merkel, F. (n.d.) (ed.), *Gabriele Salvatores*, Rome: Dino Audino.

Miccichè, L. (ed.) (1975), *Il neorealismo cinematografico italiano: Atti del convegno della X Mostra Internazionale del Nuovo Cinema*, Venice: Marsilio, 2 edn.

—— (1988), 'Gli eredi del nulla: Per una critica del giovane cinema italiano' in F. Montini (ed.), *Una generazione in cinema: Esordi ed esordienti italiani 1975–1988*, Venice: Marsilio, 251–8.

—— (1990), *Visconti e il neorealismo: Ossessione, La terra trema, Bellissima*, Venice: Marsilio.

—— (ed.) (1992), *De Sica: Autore, regista, attore*, Venice: Marsilio.

—— (1995), *Cinema italiano: gli anni '60 e oltre*, Venice: Marsilio, fifth edition.

—— (ed.) (1997), *Cinema del riflusso: Film e cineasti italiani degli anni '70*, Venice: Marsilio.

Minnella, M. F. (1998), *La legge del desiderio: Cinema erotico ed erotismo nel cinema*, Alessandria: Falsopiano.

Miscuglio, A. (1988), 'An affectionate and irreverent account of eighty years of women's cinema in Italy', Trans. G. Ascelle and R. Howe, in G. Bruno and M. Nadotti, *Off-Screen: Women and Film in Italy*, London and New York: Routledge, 152–64.

Moe, N. (2001), 'This is Africa': Ruling and Representing Southern Italy, 1860–61', in A. R. Ascoli and K. von Henneberg (eds), *Making and Remaking Italy: The Cultivation of National Identity around the Risorgimento*, Oxford and New York: Berg.

Montini, F. and Spila, P. (1997), 'Mario Martone: la libertà e il rigore', *CineCritica*, 2(8): 12.

Morrione, R. (1978), *La Rai nel paese delle antenne*, Rome: Roberto Napoleone.

Mostra Internazionale del Nuovo Cinema (1985), *Cinecittà 1: Industria e mercato nel cinema italiano tra le due guerre*, Venice: Marsilio.

Mulvey, L. (1990), 'Visual Pleasure and Narrative Cinema' (1975), in P. Erens (ed.) *Issues in Feminist Film Criticism*, Bloomington and Indianapolis: Indiana University Press, 28–40.

Nast, H. J. and Pile, S. (eds) (1998), *Places through the body*, London and New York: Routledge.

Natta, E. (2002), 'Una crisi dei "generi"', *Filmcronache*, 2: 16–18.

Neale, S. (1980), *Genre*, London: BFI.

—— (1981), 'Art Cinema as Institution', *Screen*, 22(1): 11–39.

—— (1993), 'Masculinity as Spectacle: Reflections on men and mainstream cinema', in S. Cohan and I. R. Hark, *Screening the Male: Exploring Masculinities in Hollywood Cinema*, London: Routledge, 9–20.

—— (2000), 'Questions of Genre' in R. Stam and T. Miller (eds), *Film and Theory: An Anthology*, Oxford: Blackwell.

Nepoti, R. (1999), 'Deodato: diedi io il via al filone', *La Repubblica*, (5 August): 39.

Newitz, A. (1999), 'Serial Killers, True Crime, and Economic Performance Anxiety' in C. Sharrett (ed.), *Mythologies of Violence in Postmodern Media*, Detroit: Wayne State University Press, 65–83.

Nohrstedt, S. A., Kaitatzi-Whitlock, S. Ottosen, R. and Riegert, K. (2000), 'From the Persian Gulf to Kosovo – War Journalism and Propaganda', *European Journal of Communication*, 15(3): 383–404.

Nowell-Smith, G. (2003), *Luchino Visconti*, London: BFI, 3 edn.

O'Healy, Á. (1999), 'Revisiting the belly of Naples: the body and the city in the films of Mario Martone', *Screen*, 40(3): 239–56.

Olmoti, G. (1998), *Il boom 1954–1967*, Rome: Editori Riuniti.

Overbey, D. (1978) (ed.), *Springtime in Italy: A Reader on Neorealism*, London: Talisman Books.

Owen, R. (2000), *The Times*, 15 September.

Panero, A. (ed.) (1998), *Carlo Verdone: Un bel giorno mi imbarcai su un cargo battente bandiera liberiana…*, Rome: Gremese.

Parigi, S. (1988), *Roberto Benigni*, Naples: Edizioni Scientifiche Italiane.

Penz, F. and Thomas, M. (eds) (1997), *Cinema and Architecture: Méliès, Mallet-Stevens, Multimedia*, London: British Film Institute.

Perrella, G. (1981), *L'Economico e il semiotico del cinema italiano*, Rome: Theorema.

Picard, R. G. (1989), *Media Economics: Concepts and Issues*, London and New York: Sage.

Piesse, 'Abbasso la richezza!', Rivista del Cinematografo, 2, February 1947, 12–14.

Pile, S. (1996), The Body and the City: Psychoanalysis, Space and Subjectivity, London and New York: Routledge.

Pillitteri, P. (1992), Cinema come politica: Una commedia all'italiana, Milan: FrancoAngeli.

Pinkus, K. (2003), The Montesi Scandal: The Death of Wilma Montesi and the Birth of the Paparazzi in Fellini's Rome, Chicago and London: University of Chicago Press.

Pinna, G. P. (1997), 'Sound in Visconti's Bellissima', The Italianist, 17: 158–75.

Pinto, F. Barlozzetti, G. and Salizzato, G. (eds) (1988), La televisione presenta…: La produzione cinematografica della Rai 1965–1975, Venice: Marsilio.

Pintus, P. (1980), Storia e film: Trent'anni di cinema italiano (1945–1975), Rome: Bulzoni.

Placido, B. (1993), 'Adorabile bugiardo o istrione bambino', La Repubblica, (2 November): 29.

Pozzato, M. P. (ed.), Linea a Belgrado: La comunicazione giornalistica in tv durante la Guerra per il Kosovo, vol. 177, Rome: RAI-ERI, VQPT.

Pravadelli, V. (ed.) (2000), Il cinema di Luchino Visconti, Rome: Bianco e Nero.

—— (2000), Visconti a Volterra: La genesi di Vaghe stelle dell'orsa, Turin: Lindau.

Prolo, M. A. (1951), Storia del cinema muto italiano, Milan: Poligono.

Prudenzi, A. (1997), 'Il vizio di famiglia ovvero Gruppo di famiglia dal buco della serratura' in L. Miccichè (ed.), Il cinema del riflusso: Film e cineasti italiani degli anni '70, Venice: Marsilio, 334–40.

Pugliese, R. (1996), Dario Argento, Milan: Il Castoro.

Quaglietti, L. (1980), Storia economico-politica del cinema italiano 1945–1980, Rome: Editori Riuniti.

Radstone, S. (ed.) (2000), Memory and Methodology, Oxford and New York: Berg.

—— (2001), 'Trauma and Screen Studies: Opening the Debate', Screen, 42(2): 188–92.

Ranucci, G. and Ughi, S. (eds) (1996), Nanni Moretti, Rome: Dino Audino.

Ranvaud, D. and Ungari, E. (1987), Bertolucci by Bertolucci, Milan: Ubulibri

Reader, K. (2000), 'Subtext: Paris of Alexandre Trauner' in M. Konstantarakos (ed.), Spaces in European Cinema, Exeter: Intellect, 35–41.

Redi, R. (1999), Il cinema muto italiano (1896–1930), Rome: Bianco e Nero.

Repetto, M. and Tagliabue, C. (2000), 'Alla ricerca dello spettatore perduto' in La vita è bella?: Il cinema italiano alla fine degli anni Novanta e il suo pubblico, Milan: Il Castoro, 15–35.

Restivo, A. (2002), *The Cinema of Economic Miracles: Visuality and Modernization in the Italian Art Film*, Durham and London: Duke University Press.

Rhodes, J. D. (2000), 'Our Beautiful and Glorious Art Lives': The Rhetoric of Nationalism in Early Italian Film Periodicals', in G. Bertellini (ed.), *Film History*, 12(3): 308–21.

Rings, G. and Morgan-Tamosunas, R. (eds), *European Cinema: Inside Out. Images of the Self and the Other in Postcolonial European Film*, Heidelberg: Universitätsverlag Winter.

Rocca, C. (2003), *Le leggi del cinema: Il contesto italiano nelle politiche comunitarie*, Milan: Franco Angeli.

Roddick, N. (1990), 'New Worlds for Old', *The Listener*, (16 August): 37–8.

Rodier, M (2002a), 'Partnerships are Keys to Italian films', www.Screendaily.com, 5 November.

—— (2002b), '2002: the United States of Cinema', *Screen International*, 15 November, 1: 4.

Rombi, R. (1998), 'Parietti, Nudo Allo Yogurt: "Con L'Erotismo Cerco Emozioni Nuove Oltre la TV"', *La Repubblica*, (6 March): 44.

Rondolino, G. (1993), *I giorni di Cabiria*, Turin: Lindau.

Rosenstone, R. A. (ed.) (1995), *Revisioning History: Film and the Construction of a New Past*, Princeton: Princeton University Press.

Rosenthal, D. (2004), 'Repeat that in English', *The Times T2*, (19 March): 6.

Rosi, F. (1970), 'Colloquio con l'autore' in C. Cosulich (ed.), *Uomini contro di Francesco Rosi*, Bologna: Capelli, 53–60.

—— (1977), 'Introduzione' in L. Visconti, *La terra trema*, Bologna, Capelli.

—— (1996), 'L'avventura viscontiana di Aci Trezza' in L. Micchichè (ed.), *La terra trema di Luchino Visconti: Analisi di un capolavoro*, Turin, Associazione Philip Morris Progetto Cinema/Centro Sperimentale di Cinematografia – Cineteca Nazionale/Lindau, 3 edn, 21–6.

Rosi, F. and Scalfari, E. (1972), *Il caso Mattei: Un "corsaro" al servizio della Repubblica*, Bologna: Capelli.

Rossi, U. (1985), 'Arrivano i nostri: Cannon compra Gaumont Italia', *Cinema 60*, 1(161): 23–4.

—— (1988), 'Cinema: da fenomeno di massa a fattore *d'élite*', *Cinemasessanta*, 6(184): 3–8.

Rowlands, M. (1997), 'Memory, Sacrifice and the Nation', *New Formations*, 30: 8–17.

Ryan, M. and Kellner, D. (1988), *Camera Politica: The Politics and Ideology of Contemporary Hollywood Film*, Bloomington and Indianapolis: Indiana University Press.

Sabouraud, F. (1987), 'La génération perdue', *Cahiers du cinéma*, 395–6: 46.

Said, E. (1985), *Orientalism*, London and Harmondsworth: Peregrine Books.

Sassoon, D. (1986), *Contemporary Italy: Politics, Economy & Society since 1945*. London: Longman.

Scarfò, G. (1999), *Cinema e Mezzogiorno*, Cosenza: Periferia.

Schlesinger, P. (1982), 'Blow to the Heart: an Interview with Gianni Amelio', *Framework*, 22/23: 14–17.

Segal, L. (1990), *Slow Motion: Changing Masculinities, Changing Men*, New Brunswick: Rutgers University Press.

Sennett, R. (1994), *Flesh and Stone: The Body and the City in Western Civilization*, London: Faber & Faber.

Sesti, M. (1994), *Nuovo cinema italiano: Gli autori, i film, le idee*, Rome and Naples: Theoria.

Short, J. R. (1991), *Imagined Country: Society, Culture and Environment*, London and New York: Routledge.

SIAE (1976), *Lo Spettacolo in Italia*, Rome: SIAE.

Sieglohr, U. (ed.), *Heroines Without Heroes: Reconstructing Female and National Identities in European Cinema, 1945–51*, London: Cassell.

Silvestretti, E. (1988), 'L'anomalia necessaria e imperfetta dell'articolo 28', *Cinemasessanta* 6(184): 21–30.

Sitney, P. Adams (1995), *Vital Crises in Italian Cinema: Iconography, Stylistics, Politics*, Austin: University of Texas Press.

Soldini, S. and Leondeff, D. (2000), *Pane e tulipani*, Venice: Elleu Multimedia/Marsilio.

Sorlin, P. (1980), *The Film in History: Restaging the Past*, Oxford: Blackwell.

—— (1991), *European Cinemas, European Societies, 1939–1990*, London: Routledge.

—— (1996), *Italian National Cinema 1896–1996*, London: Routledge.

Spain, D. (1992), *Gendered Spaces*, Chapel Hill and London: University of North Carolina Press.

Spicer, A. (2001), *Typical Men: The Representation of Masculinity in Popular British Cinema*, London: I. B. Tauris.

Spinazzola, V. (1974), *Cinema e pubblico: Lo spettacolo filmico in Italia 1945–1965*, Milan: Bompiani.

—— (1990), 'Statistiche dell'industria cinematografica 1990', *Cinema d'oggi*, 1: 6.

Stella, G. A. (2002), *L'orda: quando gli albanesi eravamo noi*, Milan: Rizzoli.

Tambling, J. (1987), *Opera and Ideology*, Manchester: Manchester University Press.

Tassone, A. (1979), *Parla il cinema italiano*, vol. I, Milan: Il Formichiere.

Thompson, K. (1988), *Breaking the Glass Armor: Neoformalist Film Analyses*, Princeton: Princeton University Press.

Thoret, J.-B. (2002), *Dario Argento: Magicien de la peur*, Paris: Cahiers du Cinéma.

Thumim, J. (1992), *Celluloid Sisters*, London: Macmillan.

Todorov, T. (1993), *The Conquest of America: The Question of the Other*, trans. R. Howard, New York: Harper & Row, 1984, 143–5, quoted in M. Kinder, *Blood Cinema: The Reconstruction of National*

Identity in Spain, Berkeley, Los Angeles and London: University of California Press.

Toffetti, S. (1995) *Giuseppe Tornatore*. Turin: Lindau.

Torriglia, A. M. (2002), *Broken Time, Fragmented Space: A Cultural Map for Post-war Italy*, Toronto: University of Toronto Press.

Toscan du Plantier, D. (1987), 'La politique des producteurs, *Cahiers du cinéma*, 395–6: 14–18.

Turner, B. S. (1988), *Status*, Milton Keynes: Open University Press.

—— (1996), *The Body and Society: Explorations in Social Theory*, London: Sage, Second edition.

Ungari, E. with Ranvaud, D. (1987), *Bertolucci by Bertolucci*, London, Plexus.

Urry, J. (1995), *Consuming Places*, London and New York: Routledge.

Van Heer, N. (1998), *New Diasporas: The mass oxodus, dispersal and regouping of migant communities*, Seattle: University of Washington Press.

Veltroni, W. (1992), *I programmi che hanno cambiato l'Italia*, Milan: Feltrinelli.

Ventavoli, B. (2000), 'Ombre rosse: L'industria del cinema porno negli anni Novanta' in P. D'Agostino and S. Della Casa (eds), *Cinema italiano annuario 1999–2000*, Milan: Il Castoro, 147–157.

Viano, M. (1993), *A Certain Realism: Making Use of Pasolini's Film Theory and Practice*, Berkeley, Los Angeles and London: University of California Press.

—— (1999), '*Life is Beautiful*: Reception, Allegory and Holocaust Laughter', *Annali d'Italianistica*, 17: 155–72.

Viganò, A. (1995), *Commedia italiana in cento film*, Genoa: Le Mani.

Vincendeau, G. (2000), *Stars and Stardom in French Cinema*, London and New York: Continuum.

Visconti, L. (1978), 'Anthropomorphic Cinema' in D. Overbey (ed.), *Springtime in Italy: A Reader on Neorealism*, London: Talisman.

Wagstaff, C. (1989), 'The Place of Neorealism in Italian Cinema from 1945 to 1954' in N. Hewitt (ed.), *The Culture of Reconstruction*, Basingstoke: Macmillan.

—— (2000), 'L'assenza dell'oggi: Il cinema italiano in Gran Bretagna', in V. Zagarrio (ed.), *Il cinema della transizione: Scenari italiani degli anni Novanta*, Venice: Marsilio, 439–54.

White, H. (1973), *Metahistory: The Historical Imagination in Nineteenth-Century Europe*, Baltimore and London: The Johns Hopkins University Press.

—— (1996), 'The Modernist Event' in V. Sobchack (ed.), *The Persistance of History: Cinema, Television and the Modern Event*, London and New York: Routledge, 17–38.

White, J. (1987), *The Birth and Rebirth of Pictorial Space*, London: Faber & Faber, 3 edn.

Wood, M. P. (1994), 'Simple Stories: Adapting Sciascia for the Screen', *The Italianist*, 14: 286–304.

—— (1998) 'Francesco Rosi: Heightened Realism', in J. Boorman and W. Donohue (eds.), *Projections 8*, London: Faber and Faber, 272–95.

—— (2000a), 'Cultural Space as Political Metaphor: The Case of the European 'Quality' Film', www.mediasalles.it/crl_wood.htm.

—— (2000b), 'Representations of Rome in Italian Cinema: Space and Power', *Journal of the Institute of Romance Studies*, 8: 211–21.

—— (2002) 'Bertolucci' in Y. Tasker (ed.) *Fifty Contemporary Film-makers*. London: Routledge, 41–51.

—— (2004), 'The Dark Side of the Mediterranean: Italian *film noir*' in A. Spicer (ed.), *European Film Noir*, Manchester: Manchester University Press.

Wyke, M. (1997), *Projecting the Past: Ancient Rome, Cinema and History*, London: Routledge.

Zaccone Teodosi, A. (1986), 'Ipotesi di riscatto per una provincia dell'impero (audiovisivo): Per un'economia del cinema e della televisione in Italia, un progetto di ricerca' in E. Magrelli (ed.), *Sull'industria cinematografica italiana*, Venice: Marsilio, 29–72.

—— (1987), 'Il marketing del film "d'essai": Identikit dello spettacolo "specializzato" (il nuovo cinefilo)', *Cinema d'Oggi*, 14: 16–17.

Zagarrio, V. (1998), *Cinema italiano anni novanta*, Venice: Marsilio.

—— (2000) (ed.), *Il cinema della transizione: Scenari italiani degli anni Novanta*, Venice: Marsilio.

Zanchi, C. (1975), 'L'industria cinematografica italiana nel primo dopoguerra' in L. Micchichè (ed), *Il neorealismo cinematografico italiano*, Venice: Marsilio, 83–9.

Žižek, S. (1999), 'You May!', *London Review of Books*, 18 March.

—— (2000), 'Dove finiscono i Balcani?' in Grmek Germani, S. (ed.), *La meticcia di fuoco. Oltre il continente Balcani*, Turin: La Biennale di Venezia/Lindau, 29–30.

Index

Bold page number indicates image in text